Willard W. Waller

ON THE FAMILY, EDUCATION, AND WAR

Selected Writings

Edited and with an Introduction by

**WILLIAM J. GOODE,
FRANK F. FURSTENBERG, JR.,
and LARRY R. MITCHELL**

THE UNIVERSITY OF CHICAGO PRESS

CHICAGO AND LONDON

Standard Book Number: 226–87152–5
Library of Congress Catalog Card Number: 70–132287

THE UNIVERSITY OF CHICAGO PRESS, CHICAGO 60637
The University of Chicago Press, Ltd., London

Printed in the United States of America

Contents

Foreword

THE HERITAGE of sociology is more than the seminal contributions of that handful of major figures whose writings continue to dominate the discipline after decades of criticism and reevaluation. The heritage encompasses the solid achievements—the minor classics—of a cadre of craftsmen who have worked at the interface of theoretical constructs and empirical research. Their efforts have produced those enduring monographs without which the sociological endeavor would wither. Willard Waller is a splendid example of such a sociologist, who retired with only limited recognition.

I would judge Waller's *Sociology of Teaching* to be his central contribution. For many years this book was *the* volume in the field and it remains one of the leading references. But Willard Waller deserves inclusion in the *Heritage of Sociology* series because, as a craftsman sociologist, his interests ranged broadly. Thus, he left his indelible markings on the field of marriage and the family. These efforts have particular relevance in contributing to an interdisciplinary facet in sociology. His own personal style and his exposure to Ernest W. Burgess made him sympathetic to important elements of psychoanalytic theory.

The heritage of Willard Waller is more than the writings he produced. His life is a vivid account of the struggles and problems inherent in the emergence of sociology as a professional career. William J. Goode and his associates take the natural history approach in describing the career of Willard Waller, an approach Waller himself learned at the University of Chicago. Waller sought to become a university professor via sociology at a time when graduate training opportunities were few and informal, and the number of available academic appointments very limited. As a result, he had a hard time establishing himself.

He entered sociology from high school teaching, with a strong interest in the humanities and with his personal preferences and problems fully exposed. His graduate training was prolonged and interrupted and involved work at two university centers. This education took place in the 1920's. The extensive concern to reconstruct graduate training in sociology one half century later seeks to provide by conscious effort many of the experiences which Waller had to endure and which were then thought to be handicaps.

But this appraisal of Willard Waller by William J. Goode and his associates warrants inclusion in the *Heritage of Sociology* series for another set of reasons. Any exposition of the natural history of a career rests at the same time on a discussion of the institutional setting in which a personal career unfolds. The authors present important raw materials on how sociology operated at the lesser centers of university life at which Willard Waller first taught and at Columbia University where Waller prematurely ended his career. They have gone far in laying bare the details although the reader would prefer more explicit conclusions about the strengths and weaknesses of academic sociology at this time.

His appointment to Columbia University should have supplied him with the opportunity to complete an important academic career. However, it signaled the effective end of his intellectual career. Personal tensions and personal dissatisfactions that self analysis could not handle, plus a premature death, constitute part of the record. But Willard Waller also experienced a professional crisis which has become endemic in the sociology endeavor; namely, apparent chronic over-employment, or rather diffusion of effort. It was indeed unfortunate that Waller did not succeed in establishing at Columbia University his type of sociology—the so called Chicago empirical school—for to have done that would have speeded up the end of institutional parochialism in American sociology.

After his appointment to Columbia University he continued to publish, but the results were mediocre. He lost his scholarly autonomy. He became tied into the mass media and the public speaking circuit, and even to the consultantship, which was just beginning to develop. He partook of and oversubscribed to the variety of money making and prestige ventures which spelled in his case the death of the craftsman sociologist, and reflected the defects of the institutionalization of the sociological enterprise.

William J. Goode and his associates in this volume reveal how they became fascinated with Willard Waller. Perhaps they became too fascinated since they might have rendered him a greater service by eliminating more of his lesser materials. But only by presenting a complete overview could they effectively portray the decline of this man. They are to be congratulated for their efforts to be both sympathetic and detached. To write sociologically about one's own university is a hazardous assignment. Goode sees in Waller many of the conflicts and dilemmas found in contemporary sociology and in the immediate university environment.

The authors lay bare much of Waller's personal life including his publishing activities. The natural history of this volume, as a footnote to Waller's career, is equally in order. Goode and his associates undertook the volume, not as a part of the collective effort of the *Heritage of Sociology* series, but as an independent labor of love. They could not resist their sheer attraction to the man. However, for more than a brief moment, they came to believe that they were engaged in making up for the miserable career difficulties that Waller had when he first started to teach and write. They believed that they were bestowing on him honors that he justly deserved by introducing him to a new and vastly enlarged public. He was being presented not only to a new generation of sociologists, but also to the larger group of lay "intellectuals" who have come to consume sociology. But Waller's heritage really belongs to the academic sociologist. The manuscript was offered for publication to a commercial publishing house with personal ties to the Department of Sociology, Columbia University, which was believed appropriate for presenting Waller to the larger audiences to which Waller had become attracted when he joined Columbia University. However, it was rejected because of the usual commercial market considerations.

I welcome William J. Goode on Willard Waller into the *Heritage of Sociology* series, although he resisted all of my suggestions. I welcome his inclusion because Waller personifies the importance of detachment, objectivity, and self-scrutiny in intensive field work and institutional analysis. I welcome the volume because meaningful recognition of the craftsman sociologist comes first and fundamentally from the judgments of those who strive to be members of the sociological community.

Morris Janowitz

Preface

THE INTRODUCTORY CHAPTER of this book is, in large part, a biography of Willard Waller, but it differs from the usual academic biography, because we moved toward our task obliquely, having—to begin with—no intention of writing Willard Waller's biography. Initially, the two junior (in age) editors—convinced by reading Waller's works that he had been unjustly neglected—proposed merely to edit and republish some of his representative writings, together with a note on his life. But the senior editor, who shared the junior editors' opinion of Waller's intellectual worth, believed his life deserved more attention. The senior editor did not become a partner in this enterprise at first, but was willing to counsel and encourage the junior editors, and even to aid them by writing letters to some of his friends who had also been Waller's comrades. As the task grew, however, eventually an editorial troika of investigation and writing took shape, and the job expanded not only because of the difficulty of writing a laconic "biographical note," but also because the inquiry itself became more and more interesting. A terse note must be distilled from substantial knowledge, but none of us possessed it, and we could not abstract it from a standard biography. Thus, we continued to send off letters and general questionnaires, and to interview Waller's old friends, in order to write a slightly fuller introductory essay.

But even that modest change in intention became inadequate as we examined alternative biographical models. "Naked" biographies of literary figures are common, but accounts of professors' lives typically gloss over the intimate details of their personality, marriage, and conflicts—their private dramas. Perhaps it is assumed that people who live in ivory towers lead placid, uninteresting lives. (Of course, some details were deliberately omitted from our own account of Waller's life, because they might hurt the living.) More important may be the common belief that a professor's adventures in love or war are not the stuff from which his intellectual explorations grow and that the intimacies of his experiences do not illuminate his scientific work. Both of these beliefs are incorrect—and they conspicuously fail to hit the mark in Waller's life. More than most sociologists, he reworked his raw experiences to develop his ideas. A biography that seized only on the public events in his career would omit the larger part of the crude stuff from which his intellectual contributions were shaped. Consequently, we had to inquire into all the details of his life that could be found.

Doubtless, too, we were aroused by the challenge that has lured many previous biographers into tracking down wisps of evidence here and there: the aspiration of capturing the man whole, of painting a true likeness. Surely only few ever succeed, and we expect (with little serenity) that some of Willard Waller's friends will turn away from our portrait of him in puzzlement or annoyance, commenting, "No, that's not Pete at all." If a portrait is a painting in which there is "something wrong with the nose," doubtless a biography is a story in which the author distorts the hero unwittingly. Nevertheless, we found the man interesting as a person, and so kept on expanding our inquiry in order to analyze him more adequately.

We also explored further because investigating his life taught us about an era in the history of modern sociology. When Waller entered the field in the 1920's there were few sociologists. The discipline was vaguely defined, and its task unclear. The pioneers who explored it had been educated in other social sciences or had begun as newspaper reporters, ministers, or reformers. By the time Waller died in 1945, the métier of a sociologist had become distinct. What was it like to carve out a career during his time? What were the social forces that shaped the job movements of sociologists?

Waller encountered his world as an ambitious, small-town young man from the Midwest who, as a high school teacher of French, felt a vague stirring toward some unspecified larger stage. He did not begin with any intention of becoming a sociologist, but he watched himself (with a mingled pleasure and anxiety) grow in talent and achievement, and he perceived new opportunities, and rejoiced in greater recognition. He tried both to taste these experiences as a poet might and to analyze them rigorously as a scientist must. This complex interaction of a unique person with the academic social structure of his time is worthy of inquiry. If a biographical study helps us to understand Waller himself better, it also illuminates the growth of a field and thus contributes to the sociology of science.

We were always aware that we were engaged in a research task for which none of us had adequate training, that is, the writing of history, even though it was the history of a single man's life. Sociologists do not often try their hand at the historian's craft as contrasted with the mere embellishment of a sociological analysis with a few apposite historical illustrations, simply because archival research is hard, slogging work. Getting the data at all is difficult—and how can a few scraps of paper and a few anecdotes add up to a man's life? What do a few letters tell us about how young professors once evaluated job openings at a particular time? The bits and pieces are not ever a "representative sample," the gaps are immense, and the narrative must hew close to the facts.

Because we did not begin with grandiose notions of our own skills, however, we did not find the experience humbling. But we did enjoy the detective work, and the occasional breakthroughs in understanding, and we were confirmed in our prior respect for the achievements of the historian. On the other hand, we despair of reconstructing the whole truth, and we cherish still a suspicion that even the best historian may distort unwittingly.

For various reasons, most of which we discuss, the data on Waller's life are scanty. We are therefore especially grateful to the official agencies and private individuals who responded to our pleas for assistance with files and memories. Our chief debt is to the members of the Waller family, especially to Mrs. Josephine Bouchard, Waller's widow, who boxed up a bushel of miscellaneous records (Waller's files were destroyed shortly after his death), letters, manuscripts, and memoranda and shipped it to us for our use. This box of miscellany often yielded crucial information.

Howard Rowland of the University of Pittsburgh helped us by drawing Walleriana from his records on the social psychiatry movement, and by telling us which of the case studies in Waller's books referred to Waller himself, and we benefited greatly from the sensitive perceptions and tenacious memory of W. Wallace Weaver, who was a colleague of Waller's at the University of Pennsylvania in the 1920's.

We have been especially fortunate in having two fine editors read our manuscript. Both knew Waller well. We do not suppose that we could meet fully the severe standards of either Robert K. Merton or Stanley Burnshaw, but we are the wiser for having listened to their critiques.

Because much of the information we received from one person overlapped with that from another, it would be both unfair and difficult to single out or identify precisely who helped us at which points, though of course some of these sources are cited here and there in our manuscript. Perhaps it would be simpler merely to thank as many of our collaborators as we can now remember, and apologize to those whom we may inadvertently have overlooked. And so we thank Theodore Abel, Burt Aginsky, Ethel Aginsky, Donald Ambler, Nicholas Babchuk, Selden D. Bacon, Reed Bain, James Barnett, Herbert Blumer, W. Phillips Davison, Mrs. David Dudley, Cynthia Epstein, Sybil Golden, David D. Henry, Reuben Hill, Everett C. Hughes, Howard E. Jensen, Mirra Komarovsky, Clifford Kirkpatrick, Alfred McClung Lee, Robert M. MacIver, William G. Mather, Theodore M. Newcomb, Elizabeth K. Nottingham, Mr. and Mrs. Vance Packard, Charles H. Page, Natalie Rogoff Ramsøy, Stuart A. Rice, S. Stansfeld Sargent, Thorsten

Sellin, Peter Waller, Logan Wilson, C. S. Wyand, Donald R. Young, and Carle C. Zimmerman.

William J. Goode
Frank F. Furstenberg, Jr.
Larry R. Mitchell

Introduction

WILLARD W. WALLER: A PORTRAIT

I

WILLARD WALTER WALLER once told a colleague that he was unafraid of death, but hoped before he died to make a worthwhile contribution to sociology and, in addition, become a famous man. Cheated by an early death, he failed in his latter ambition, though by the time of his death he had made a substantial contribution to his field and to his generation.

Many factors conspire to enhance or diminish the magnitude of a scientist's reputation. For example, more than once it has been remarked how important to a man's reputation is simple longevity. At the same level of talent, the man who dies full of years and with his name on many books has a greater chance of being well-known, even beyond the confines of his own field, than a man who dies in his prime with many of his books as yet unwritten. The academic who seeks a place in history would then be wise to live a long time. Further, the academic who seeks a place in history is also wise to teach in the proper place at the proper time, surrounded by the proper people. He should, for example, teach in universities whose students are most likely to achieve high positions—Harvard, Columbia, Chicago. When these former students speak or write about him, others will remember him. A man who wants to become a famous professor should insist on having many graduate students, for they will cite his work often: it is the work they know best. A man bent on fame should also make sure that those men who are most productive and successful in his field respect (or at least know) his work, for these are the men who are writing the contemporary history of his field, and from them flow the footnotes and the gossipy references that establish who is in fashion and who is not. And just as it is useful to have many successful friends, it is equally useful to have the right enemies; both will make one's work known.

Waller was unfortunate in all of these matters. He died at age forty-six; he did not come from the right schools, nor did he ever become a member of a prestigious graduate school; he did not (until late in his life) have many successful, productive friends, and he never had successful, productive disciples. Although he was well known while he was alive, he was quickly forgotten once he was dead, for there were few to assert his importance and few to remind others of his work.

When all else fails, a man may achieve immortality by achieving a signal breakthrough in his field—a new departure in the form of the novel, a trailblazing scientific theory, or a startling, successful political idea. Unfortunately, however, most men who have aimed for the stars have learned, with some heartache, that this most effective path to fame is not open to them. Aspiring men cannot simply *choose* to achieve greatly. A painter once complained to Gertrude Stein that people spoke of the spiritual suffering that great artists experience in the act of creation, but in fact mediocre talents suffer just as much and never experience the exaltation of producing great paintings.

Here again Waller was unfortunate. He did not achieve a signal breakthrough in sociology—but then no such option was open to him. Neither he nor the other talented men working in his time created a revolution in sociology. In the era that ended with World War II, the field had moved well ahead of its European models by fundamentally improving its research skills, establishing its theoretical foundations, and applying its insights to a wide range of social behavior. It was a period of consolidation, and Waller was one of the finest at this kind of work, but consolidators are less revered and remembered than innovators. After World War II, and thus after Waller's death, sociology adopted a different intellectual orientation, one stemming mainly from the work of Talcott Parsons and others at Harvard. Waller was born too early to be of the generation that produced the new orientation, and died too soon to participate in it. The field moved quickly past him in the late forties and early fifties, and so again his reputation suffered.

But though such social factors largely determine how grand and how sturdy a man's reputation is, his books have a partly independent existence. Unlike conversational brilliance, or the concert pianist's greatest performances, or an actor's evocations of Hamlet, a man's writings remain after he is gone. Many students fail to read what their professor assigns, but (perhaps compensation) some will instead read what has not been assigned. Thus, each year some few young social scientists "discover" Willard Waller; and thus, though many accidents of his life conspired against a large fame, the insights in Waller's writings keep his name alive.

More important, in the past decade a new generation of sociologists has arisen to challenge their mentors, and to turn attention to Waller's kinds of problems. To be fair to the older generation, they *did* care about some of these problems—but they did not care very much. The new generation is much more intensely concerned with social change than the older. The attention of the present generation is focused much more on varying ways of playing out a given social role, than on the agreed-upon rights and obligations of a status; upon deviation from social prescriptions rather than upon conformity. In the new view, which was Waller's constant perspective, strain and tension are ubiquitous elements of any social system; conflict and collapse are expectable. Social action is fraught with uncertainty and instability, contingency and unpredictability. In the emerging view, order is a fragile state requiring a flow of commitment and work for its maintenance.

Waller shares still other concerns with the current generation of sociologists.[1] Both utilize social observation far more than the researchers of the generation just past, who developed the inter-

---

[1]   As the reader will recognize, part of Waller's perspectives and insights may be seen in the work of some modern ethnomethodologists. However, since those who call themselves ethnomethodologists are more cohesive in their rejection of mainstream sociology than in their doctrinal agreement, it is risky to assert those parallels without a lengthy excursus.

view and questionnaire survey to such a high degree of usefulness. Waller did not reject other sources of data, but he took most of his ideas and data from direct observation of social behavior.

Though all good social scientists will concede that beneath the supposed "message" one person gives to another, a different set of meanings may be found, Waller listened to these complexities more diligently than most scientists do, and at both psychological and sociological levels. The man who says, "I love you," but physically moves away from his wife when he says it, has contradicted his words. In the modern study of linguistic behavior, the observer may focus (as did Waller) as much on a speaker's gestures as on his words to learn what the speaker *intends,* as well as what he unconsciously *betrays* of his real feelings.

Waller, too, understood that a social interaction or process is *constructed,* as meanings are constructed; they are not simply a static structure, a set of preexisting pigeonholes into which people enter. The "deviant," such as a divorcée, a criminal, or a psychopath, is not simply a bundle of characteristics that others see or recognize (as one might recognize a wolf in the forest). A criminal is not simply one who has broken the law. The criminal role is *created* by a set of gradually or suddenly emerging responses of others, in interaction with those of the person defined as criminal.

In addition, Waller's own "method" of personal inquiry was often like the experimental inquiries of some ethnomethodologists. For example, he would begin with some doubt that a textbook description of behavior, attitudes, or values was correct, and then himself act so as to test that description. He sometimes angered or upset others by trying out a new role among old acquaintances or playing a role in a new situation, proposing extreme solutions to a problem, or pushing others to confess their underlying actions or motives; but by studying others' reactions in situations that he created, he had in effect tested or laid bare a wider range of behavior and attitudes, and could be more certain that his intuitions were correct.

Waller, then, worked brilliantly in what came to be viewed during his own time as an older tradition and with methods that were thought to be imprecise. He recognized that in our individual lives, *all* the forces of society are at work. Consequently, to understand social structure, he could use as data his own rich experience and the private experiences that others revealed so readily to him. He analyzed what he knew best—his own life and the lives of those he encountered in the widely diverse social circles he enthusiastically explored. This kind of introspective and personal sociology was mostly replaced in the forties and fifties by large-scale quantitative sociology. A new research technique became dominant and Waller's "method" went out of style.

In any event, however fashionable his method may once have been, it had one unfortunate characteristic—it was not transferable to others. Brilliant, probing intuitiveness cannot easily be handed over to students as a general technique. What Waller did, he did well, but others began doing other kinds of things, and so did not look to him as a model for their work.

Just as sociology was consolidating its intellectual heritage during Waller's career, it was also establishing its position as a distinct discipline within university life. Over the first half of this century, sociology was transformed from an undefined, unusual occupation pursued by, say, an apostate minister or a crusading reformer, and uneasily and precariously placed in a more secure department (social welfare, religion, economics), to a fairly clear position in the academic social structure. Waller participated in this emerging intellectual tradition and helped to establish sociology's place in the academic world. Consequently, an examination of his life not only yields the opportunity of knowing a unique sociologist and human being, but it also illuminates a historical phase of the science.

II

Waller obtained his most important social science training in the then dominant Department of Sociology at the University of Chicago, from which he went to obscure, second-rate schools and, finally, to an emerging major center—Columbia University. As a person, Waller lives on in numberless anecdotes of his contemporaries and elders. Some who came from more genteel social and intellectual backgrounds remember him as crude, brash, and undignified. Many others, including some whose backgrounds were impeccable, took delight in his iconoclasm, and to them Waller possessed the Midwestern virtues of being open, direct, and genuine.

He was born in Murphysboro, Illinois, on July 30, 1899, the elder son of a school superintendent, Elbert Waller, the son of a pioneer.[2] Because of a physical disability, Elbert Waller, the child of a second wife and a patriarchal, thrifty farmer, was allowed to escape the hard physical labor that was common in his family and region. Making decisions for him as he did for the rest of the family, Elbert's father took him to a nearby normal school, saw to the rental of his room and the purchase of books, paid the school fees, and left him with a minimum amount of money and food to carry him through the first steps of his training.

Elbert Waller followed a common American pattern for young teachers. He conducted school in the winter and went to school in the summer until his training was completed. After a few years of teaching experience, he became a principal. He was successful at the beginning of this job, as he was at almost every similar job he undertook in the course of a long and complex work history, and as one of the few professionals in town, he was one of the most desirable young men in the marriage market, so that when he fell in love with Willard's mother, he was able to persuade her to become his bride, even though their son came to feel that his mother had never been deeply in love with her husband.

Noted for his honesty and justice, Elbert's father gave his son a completely equipped farm as a marriage gift; this was his practice with all his sons. Teaching in the winter and farming in the summer, the young man expected his wife to assume without complaint the usual burdens of lonesomeness, isolation, hard work, and the crude life of a farmer's wife. Unfortunately, although his

[2]   Although we have checked the facts where possible, in this section we follow Waller's own account of his parents' marriage, "Forty Years of Marriage Conflict," in *The Family* (New York: Cordon Press, 1938), pp. 363–79.

wife was an orphan, she was the daughter of a physician and had lived a happy childhood with her aunt and three cousins, cultivating some of the social graces and enjoying the small-town pleasures of a genteel family. She expected, therefore, that her husband would be neat in dress and would bathe with some frequency; he was a bit lax on both counts. She also wanted response and gallantry from him, and enduring warmth from her friends, but in Elbert's hardmouthed family, such attentions would have been thought absurd, and his constant job changes disrupted whatever friendships his wife could make. Finally, she disliked sex relations, and he was a man of strong passions.

Willard Waller's home life was not, then, the idyllic domesticity supposedly typical of Midwestern rural life at the turn of the century. During forty years of unremitting marital conflict, his mother and father stormed at one another, adding up each other's sins of omission and commission, as well as errors of judgment, to make a formidable list of accusations and counter-charges. If Elbert had the advantage of being a male in a rural society, his wife "greatly exceeded him in sheer intelligence, and she was a better fighting machine."[3] Moreover, she was clever at dry, sarcastic wit, a type of edged humor that Willard himself cultivated with great success.

Waller's father did, indeed, make himself vulnerable in many ways. Anxious to be a hero, he enlisted when the Spanish-American War broke out, but had to come home after he had been exposed to measles; their only daughter died from the disease, and his wife never forgave him. Then he cosigned several notes for friends who failed to meet their obligations, and lost his farm.

His winning personality and energetic air always created immense support whenever he took a new job as superintendent of schools, but soon he would become embroiled in quarrels and have to seek a new job. This gave his wife added ammunition for their quarrels, since he was not providing her with what she considered to be a normal, respectable life. Even in dying she maintained her advantage. Not finding him at the bus station when she

3   *Ibid.*, p. 371.

arrived from a visit with her younger son, she began to walk home in a rage, suitcase in hand, although her heart was weak. Feeling an attack coming, she left the suitcase and returned back to the station. Her husband had meanwhile arrived, and was sitting comfortably in his car when he heard her call that she was dying. She lived long enough to place the blame where she thought it belonged.

Looking back at his home environment, Waller wrote, "A great deal of nonsense has been spoken and written about the relation of marriage discord to the personality adjustment of the children."[4] He always felt sympathy and affection for his father, and nostalgia rather than anguish for his childhood. In later years, this was expressed by a family joke that he never found strawberries that tasted as good as those of his Illinois childhood. He accepted his father's ideal of an intellectual occupation, and indeed some of his father's and grandfather's attitudes of domination over children. He and his brother directed their emotions into relations with childhood friends, and away from the turmoil between their parents.

Like other boys in rural America, at times he had to prove his masculinity by fistfighting. As an adult, he claimed a more than ordinary skill at boxing, and told his friends that he had developed this ability because as the superintendent's son he was always the target of attack from other boys until they learned that this was a costly way of expressing their hostility against the school's authority. Since Willard moved frequently, he got plenty of practice.[5]

During Waller's childhood, his father moved through at least half a dozen such jobs, and Waller later analyzed this high turnover as partly generated by the structural peculiarities of the occupation. He saw the superintendent as having a typical "life history" in the community. When he takes charge, he "has the support of nearly the entire community . . . the board is usually with him to a man." But this lasts only until a conflict occurs. This is a short

4   *Ibid.*, p. 375.
5   Much later, in an application to the Defense Department for a job in the Military Occupation of Italy—some have thought this was simply a way of *getting* to Europe, a recurrently frustrated dream of his life— he wrote, in answer to the question on "athletic skill": "Once a boxer, too old now."

honeymoon period indeed, because the superintendent has a job that requires him to mete out punishment, cooperate or not cooperate with groups, make policy, and so on. As Waller comments, perhaps in some sympathy with his father:

The essential weakness of his position is that it gives him an opportunity to make many more enemies than friends. Opportunities for becoming unpopular to the point, almost, of infamy are numerous, but opportunities for gaining friends are few.[6]

At the end of the first year, the superintendent has some enemies but most of the community still supports him. During the second year, his enemies become increasingly bitter, and he may engage in a feud with them. Moreover, by now some members of the school board itself may be his enemies. The central structural fact, as Waller saw it, is that the superintendent is in no position to restore the balance, and his chances of staying in the job—especially in a small town—past the third year may become very modest.

Waller states that his father was "never able to hold a teaching job for more than three years."[7] And in fact each of the few records available from his early schooling reveals a different geographical location. He was born in Murphysboro, Illinois, in 1899; his Certificate of Award for having been neither tardy nor absent during the first semester of 1905 was issued in Tamaroa, Illinois; by the time he was in the fifth grade, in 1908–9 (obviously he had advanced a year beyond his age peers) he was in Viola (and like other clever boys was maintaining his above-90 average); his still larger and more flamboyant Certificate of Award for being "wide-awake" and punctual for 160 days of attendance during 1911–12 was awarded in Jonesboro, while in the following year he was keeping up his high grades (again, as in the fifth grade, they are sometimes a bit below the line in deportment) in Cobden. When he finally graduated from high school in 1915 he was in Albion.

Elbert Waller's strong and persistent wish to reform the world

6   *The Sociology of Teaching* (New York: John Wiley, 1932; Science Ed., 1965), p. 100. This volume, chapter 15.
7   *The Sociology of Teaching.*

(he was an ardent prohibitionist and against cigarettes) was given a somewhat less costly mode of expression, and his marriage was granted a few years of slightly lessened tension, when he received a pension after the required twenty-five years of service. He was then able to use his wide acquaintanceship as a political base for election to the Illinois Legislature, and his wife could now at last settle in one community. She got additional pleasure from a small inherited estate, which permitted her a few personal indulgences.

By this time, of course, Willard Waller had gone on to college. He went first to McKendree College, a small, coeducational school in Lebanon, Illinois, and then to the University of Illinois. He entered McKendree in 1915, and there took his first course in sociology. He followed this, in his third year at Illinois, with courses in sociology under E. C. Hayes (1868–1928), who awakened his interest in the field. That Hayes was also a gymnast is not irrelevant to the awakening of Waller's interest in sociology, since Waller was attracted to men with athletic skills and tried always to keep himself in good physical condition. Hayes was attracted to Waller for the same reason; he professed to see a similarity between the young Waller and the image he had of himself as youthful and athletic. (A complement to his interest in athletics, Waller's compulsive work habits, also remained with him throughout his life, and is illustrated by one of the few stories he told about this period. He and his college friends made a pact to do as little work as possible. Waller could not, however, keep himself from working, and so at night he would pull down the shades in his room and study secretly.)

His college studies were interrupted by a brief tour of duty (August 13–September 30, 1918) in the Navy just as World War I ended.[8] For some unexplained reason, he did not return to school that fall, but since he attended summer school the following year and was given course credit for his military service, his graduation was delayed by only one semester, and the superintendent's son

8   The age on his discharge papers is given as twenty-three years, although he was nineteen.

managed to live up to his father's rigorous standards and get excellent grades.

Whatever secret aspirations Waller cherished at this time, his actual preparation for a job showed no high ambition, only a simple rural pragmatism. He had trained to be a French teacher. Since he graduated in the early spring of 1920, he could not begin teaching for some months, and with commendable energy he found a job with the *Evansville* (Indiana) *Courier*. Later, he described his duties on the *Courier* as "general reporting and editorial work." He must have shown the same skill in writing that appears in his sociological studies, since he received a five-dollar raise in that period of a few months. In view of his age, lack of experience, and the wage levels of the time, his final salary of twenty-five dollars weekly is rather impressive.

One event occurred in that summer that considerably enriched his understanding of human beings and of himself, and eventually formed part of the content of several of his publications: he met his future wife in Evansville. For the next two years, while teaching Latin and French at Morgan Park Military Academy, he returned whenever he could to Evansville to see her. Years later, he devoted many pages of published and unpublished pages to the analysis of his courtship, marriage, divorce, and later emotional adjustment.

In an unpublished document called "Case Number Twenty-Nine," excerpts from which appear here and there in the published version of his Ph.D. thesis, *The Old Love and the New*, Waller describes Thelma as being an "exquisite bit of feminity," attractively mysterious, a dainty brunette with deep, limpid grey eyes. She was the most popular girl in high school during her junior year, and from that time until Waller married her, three years later, she was surrounded by suitors. Talented both intellectually and musically, she was an excellent raconteur, and participated in all the student organizations of her school. The young reporter met her when she was a high school senior thriving on her success, and the young instructor of Latin and French pursued her not only at a distance, but in the face of considerable competition. Willard and Thelma were married on July 3, 1922, at the Hyde Park Presbyterian Church in Hyde Park, Illinois.[9]

Waller asserted that from the beginning he was closer to her emotionally than her other suitors, yet their courtship was tempestuous. He used to complain that her letters were too cool and infrequent. In the second year, their relations became more intimate, an intensity that is reflected in his pattern of attendance at the University of Chicago. In the first phases of his courtship (winter, spring, and summer quarters) after going to Morgan Park, he attended courses at the University (which was near the Academy), but as their relations became closer he stopped his classes. He did not attend again until the summer quarter of 1923, after his marriage.

How he got his job at Morgan Park Military Academy is not known, although his father's many contacts in educational circles undoubtedly played a part; nor has it been possible to learn why he chose to teach in a military academy. It is now even difficult to recapture his experience at Morgan Park, for this experience became thoroughly integrated into his broader sociological analysis of the high school teacher in the United States. While he was at the Academy, he held a commission as Captain in the Illinois National Guard. When he performed military and disciplinary duties, he wore a uniform. A pseudo-military atmosphere pervaded the place, and the teachers were (except for an occasional nonconformist) addressed as "Captain." Waller sketches, with some distaste, the attempts by a World War I veteran to force the lower school into a military mold. Waller describes this man as "more military than any *bona fide* officer . . . a perfect martinet." This man was vigilant, unremitting, and humorless. He succeeded in having the young children (down to a nominal ten years of age) clicking their heels in "a very acceptable small-boy imitation of the army." This episode came to an end, however, when the administrator's constant patriotic harangues and endless scolding undermined both the morale of the pupils and the support of his colleagues.[10]

9   The marriage certificate states that both were twenty-two when they were married. All the other evidence we have indicates that Thelma was several years Waller's junior.
10   *The Sociology of Teaching*, pp. 260–61.

At least later in his career, Waller was an exciting teacher. Drawn from introspection and omnivorous reading, his lectures ranged widely and brilliantly. He could rise to heights of formal eloquence or talk intimately to a class, analyze a situation with great detachment or shock his students with a scathing bit of iconoclasm. Whether he was so successful from the beginning of his career, we do not know. It should be kept in mind that the Latin teacher is somewhat handicapped compared to the sociologists. The sociologist talks about things that are immediate and interesting to the student; in Waller's time, the Latin teacher had only verbs to conjugate and nouns to decline. The sociologist can illuminate the student's past for him; in Waller's time, the Latin teacher could at best fill his pupils' minds with Caesar and Cicero. Yet in spite of these differences, there may be some factors in teaching success which remain constant. Waller wrote later, "The successful teacher is one who knows how to get on and off his high-horse rapidly."[11]

Waller worked as a high school teacher for six years, and later, when he came to write about it, revealed that he knew the role well. He comments that although the teacher role is inflexible in many ways, teacher and pupil can tolerate it because within the rigid framework a rapid alternation of supplementary or even contradictory role patterns can often take place. Thus the teacher can soften his authority by expressing personal interest or kindliness, or change from the amused adult to the stern father. He devotes several pages to these alternations in a case study of the life of a Latin teacher who attempts to expose the half-prepared, to excite the unmotivated, to praise sparingly the gifted, to flagellate the lazy and to devote extra attention to some incompetent when his parent visits the classroom with the principal.[12]

Waller loved to teach and was constantly rewarded for his teaching. Yet he was aware that

teaching makes the teacher. Teaching is a boomerang that never fails to come back to the hand that threw it. . . . Teaching does something to those who teach. Introspective teachers know of changes that have

---

11   *Ibid.*, p. 85.
12   *Ibid.*, pp. 326–32.

taken place in themselves. Objectively minded persons have observed the relentless march of growing teacherishness in others.[13]

As a good sociologist, he did not neglect the process of self-selection that singles out particular kinds of people as prospective teachers. Teaching's low pay and low social prestige, its function as an "insurance policy" for Midwestern students, its drudgery and restrictions that eliminate the virile and inspiring, its sheltered character that permits those who shrink from the battle of life to seek refuge in it, and its easy availability, all made teaching attractive to certain kinds of people. Yet Waller was equally concerned with the gradual shaping of the individual by the social forces impinging on the occupational role. He notes that "unfriendly commentators upon the manners of teachers are able to compile a long list of unpleasant qualities which, they say, are engendered in the teacher's personality by teaching experience." These include a mental inflexibility and a stiff and formal social manner—"into which the young teacher compresses himself every morning when he puts on his collar." This becomes "a plaster cast which at length he cannot loosen."[14] Others cannot penetrate his mask for he will seek to preserve his dignity at all costs.

The narrowness of the teacher's concern creates a man who, if he teaches long enough, "can wax unenthusiastic on any subject under the sun." He quotes Henry Adam's acerbic remark that no man can be a schoolmaster for ten years and remain fit for anything else. He is taught to fear the many possible threats to his position, not the least of them being his inability to control his classes. The teacher must be a hard master, either by duty or wish, and this "unfortunate role, that of Simon Legree, has corrupted the best of men."[15]

But perhaps the deadening of intellect was the most dismaying element in the occupational role of the teacher, for Waller was a hard taskmaster for himself. He denies that this occurs because of age; or, as he remarks caustically, "If all the deterioration in the

13   *Ibid.*, p. 375. This volume, chapter 17.
14   *Ibid.*, p. 381. This volume, chapter 17.
15   *Ibid.*, p. 383. This volume, chapter 17.

teacher is due to age, there must be a special type of short-blooming mind that is attracted to teaching."[16] Instead, Waller thinks that the causes can be found in the limited and unchanging world in which the teacher lives—the changeless rhythms of the day and year, the shallowness of the subject matter, the drilling of fundamentals without going beyond them, and the constant interaction with people living in a world of childish attitudes and values. He asserts that "the creative powers of teachers disappear because the teacher tends to lose the learner's attitude. . . . With this mental set, teachers cannot learn because so eager to teach; and nothing perhaps wearies them so much as to hear again what they think they already know."[17]

It is possible that all these factors led him, rather early in his career as a Latin and French teacher in a military academy, to consider alternative occupations. An expression of his rejection of a career in high school teaching can be found in his description of a French teacher who attends a convention of his colleagues in the discipline. Though teachers' conventions may strengthen a sagging morale, they may also crystallize a bitter rejection. As his "autobiographical document of a man teacher" expresses it,

. . . So I was always horribly shocked when I looked at a roomful of French teachers and realized that I was one of them, that the world classed me with them already, and that if I kept on in my profession I would be just like all the others. . . .

. . . These people are dead, I reflect. I wonder how long the body can live when the mind has died.

. . . I reflect that in another sense, too, this is a charnel house. This, I say, is really the house of the dead. It is the burying place of dead hopes. . . . The men, mingling with all these lost souls of women in this petty hell, what did they once hope? . . . There is defeat in the face of every person here.[18]

That some such attitude gradually took shape early may be inferred from his course work at the University of Chicago. In the winter, spring, and summer quarters of 1921–22 he was regis-

---

16   *Ibid.*, p. 391. This volume, chapter 17.
17   *Ibid.*, p. 394.
18   *Ibid.*, p. 423.

tered at the University. The content and result of those courses is revealing. In the winter quarter, his first, he took three courses in education. In one of these he did not take the examination, in another he failed to attend class, and in the third he made a "C." He tried again in the spring with two more courses in education. He managed to eke out a "B" in one and a "B–" in the other, hardly a distinguished record.

By the summer, he had apparently given up any interest in a lifetime career in high school teaching and administration, for he now took four basic courses in law: personal property, damages, criminal law, and remedies. His record here was not distinguished, either, for one so gifted: three "C's" and a "B." During the final period of his courtship and the beginning of his marriage, he took no courses at all. When he did return to Chicago, he began graduate work in sociology and his grades became excellent. He had at last found his métier.

Although the young teacher was finding his true vocation during this period, he was not succeeding, either by chance or wisdom, in creating a tolerable marriage. He was, however, later able to transform this painful experience into fruitful sociological insights. This was what happened to most of his experiences, especially the more painful ones. Intellectually understanding an experience is one thing, learning from experience is another. Writing to Thelma a decade after their divorce, Waller muses on what he learned from it all:

I have in mind nothing so vulgar as learning from experience, for I am not sure that I have learned anything very definite from the experience. Experience is a great teacher, or so I have sometimes heard, but it seems to me that he often mumbles his lectures and talks over the heads of his students and is generally unintelligible. Myself have studied in his school and got no wisdom—or none whose meaning is clear to me. I did not exactly *learn* from my experience with you, but I was sensitized and excited and thrown into a maelstrom from which I emerged as a different person.

For all the thousands of hours of thought that Waller devoted to his marriage, there is no evidence that he ever saw how similar were the relationship between his parents and the relationship between himself and Thelma. Both he and his father had courted women who were surrounded by many other ardent suitors. Both felt socially inferior to these women raised in well-to-do homes. Both felt awkward compared with wives who had cultivated the social graces, and even the latest modes, with such attention. Both were outsiders in the community. Both Waller's mother and his wife felt unwanted and unloved (though both were almost certainly wrong), and both had a deep emotional need for considerable response from others, though Thelma wanted response from other men, while Waller's mother did not. Both wanted to be surrounded by whatever glittering company their environments had to offer.

Waller felt, especially at the beginning of his relationship with Thelma, that his wife was less emotionally committed than he, just as his mother was less attached to his father. And, though his wife did generally enjoy sex relations with him, there were many periods—including the beginning of their marriage—when she refused any such intimacies. Waller thought of himself, and of his father, as men of "strong passions," but it ought not to be forgotten that a man who has missed many meals is likely to think of himself as having a good appetite. With reference to both the sex and love relationships of father and son, Waller observed the power advantage that not caring yields—he was later to call it the Principle of Least Interest;[19] that is, in any love relationship, the one who is less committed has a better chance of getting his way.

Both women were also somewhat more latitudinarian, more tolerant of the foibles of others, than were their moralistic mates. Though Waller was later to shock both students and colleagues by some of his iconoclastic views, the very violence of these views reveals his deep and continuing commitment to a strong moral position and his sense of injury when men could not or did not live up to high ideals.

[19]   Waller first mentions "The Principle of Least Interest" in print in *The Sociology of Teaching*, p. 240. But it is only mentioned in passing. He has an extended discussion of it in *The Family*, pp. 275–77.

Since both Willard and Thelma wrote pages of self-justification (though he published his, and thus had the last word), it is both unprofitable and impossible to make a judgment on their respective faults and virtues. This is especially so because the same trait was at one time a fault and at other times a virtue. Thelma was vivacious and often flirtatious, yet these were the very things which had attracted him. He was a bit self-righteous, and often withdrew into his work. Yet she depended on his moral strength and respected his dedication. Both were frustrated at Morgan Park. He was frustrated sexually and professionally—professionally because he thought his job did not challenge all his talents. She was sexually thwarted by her own occasional frigidity, and socially thwarted by an inability to recapture her position as the center of a loving and admiring group of men. Both, as Waller admitted, lived by their fictions, "the husband by fictions of what he would do and become, the wife by fictions which exaggerated her present importance."[20]

But as Waller has taught us so well, conflict is created not only by the husband and wife but also by those who form the social network of the couple. In the closed community of a military academy, every one of their acts was under constant scrutiny and judgment. The rhetoric of the other wives formulated Thelma's lapses as failing to care for her home properly, going to too many parties, and spending too much money on clothes. In such a small group, going to dinners or shows with other men was at least tolerated, but wives thought she took advantage of the privilege, and some men began to think she might be receptive to their attentions. Thelma did in fact adjust more to this restricted world than did her husband. Yet neither adjusted well, and the conflict between them increased. The gossip and criticism of others only polarized the conflict, which took the course that Waller analyzed in "The Process of Alienation" in *The Old Love and the New*.

When she finally left him in 1926, she went back to her parents' home. His "Case Number Seventeen," for the most part un-

<hr/>

[20]   *The Old Love and the New* (Philadelphia: Horace Liveright, 1930), p. 116.

published, describes in intimate and painful detail his anguished feelings of betrayal, his guilt at actually breaking up his marriage, his search for human and especially feminine solace, and the wild letters of attack and self-defense the two young people exchanged. In his bitterness, and contrary to his later analysis of how both husband and wife contribute to the alienation, he côuld write that he was "perfectly certain that it [his pain] was something which I in no way deserved."[21] He even thought of suicide, and in a burst of melodrama, he would "occasionally take my revolver, loaded, and point it at the spot in my temple where I thought a bullet might enter most easily."[22] During a Christmas visit to his wife, a visit she did not desire, he tried to get her to come back with him. While there, he "begged, pleaded, coaxed, cajoled, wooed, argued, debated, whined, wheedled, flattered, and commanded. I even feigned madness."[23] Even allowing for some permissible exaggeration in a man's own story-telling, clearly Waller did want his wife back at that time.

Waller believed that she continued to love him, and indeed there is some evidence that he was right. During the period of separation she wrote to him with affection, and with some fear that he would let another woman replace her without warning her. She also sent him some corrections of his "Case Number Twenty-Nine," adding:

You skipped over an important part, the part that might save someone else from the same fatal error. Be honest, dear, you have said things there about me I hate to admit as true. Your part in the story is necessary also, so admit the cruelty and selfishness of your final break with Nellie [Nellie is his fictional name for Thelma]. Tell why you did it and what it did to her.

When they separated, Waller left Morgan Park for the University of Pennsylvania to become a graduate student and instructor in sociology. Although he tried several times to renew

---

21 "Case Number Seventeen" (unpublished; courtesy of Howard Rowland), p. 8.
22 *Ibid.*, p. 15.
23 *Ibid.*, pp. 27–28.

the relation, he had entered a new life and so had new people creating new role definitions for him. During his years at Pennsylvania he did not forget Thelma and what they had been through. He brooded on the experience until he finally transformed it into sociology.

Three years after the divorce, his doctoral dissertaton was to focus on the processes of divorce and the adjustment to divorce. As to its effect on him personally, he was to write to her ten years after the divorce:

As for me, I am glad that we met and fell in step together for a while. I must add that I believe I am also glad that we parted. I needed to love you and to lose you and to realize that I could learn not to mind not having you.

III

If it was possible to receive good training in sociology during the 1920's, only the University of Chicago offered it. Waller could not have chosen a better place to study even if he had planned it carefully, and there is no indication that he planned it at all. Chicago was then the great center of sociology in the United States; nearly everyone who was important had been there, was there at the time, or would soon come there, either as a student or as a member of the faculty. Chicago was indeed the only intellectual center of American sociology. The social psychologist Ellsworth Faris (1874–1953), a powerful personality, presided over a department that contained such men as Albion Small (1854–1926), emeritus by the time Waller took his M.A. in 1925, who had been Giddings' (1855–1931) foremost opponent; Robert E. Park (1864–1944), who began sociological work on the city; Edward Sapir (1884–1939), whose perceptive analyses reoriented our understanding of the social aspects of language; Ernest W. Burgess (1886–1966), whose pioneer attempts at predicting parole success and marital adjustment laid the foundations for many types of index formation and prediction; and Floyd N. House (1893–   ), then considered a rising young theoretician of the field.

Besides these sociological stars, other luminaries were there during Waller's period of study. Louis Wirth (1897–1952), who contributed to our understanding of social life in the city, was a recent Ph.D., and Harvey Zorbaugh was another. Zorbaugh's later *Gold Coast and the Slums* startled readers with its contrast of riches and poverty in Chicago. Clifford Shaw (1896–1957), then an assistant in the department, was one of the first sociologists to use the new techniques of ecological analysis to study delinquent behavior. Another assistant, Ruth Shonle (1896–   ), later Cavan, in time became well known for her work on the family. Frederick F. Stephan (1903–   ), the statistician (retired from Princeton University) took his M.A. during this period, as did Nels Anderson (1889–   ), whose classic study, *The Hobo*, can still be read for pleasure and enlightenment. Everett C. Hughes (1897–   ), whose work on occupations and professions continues a great Chicago tradition, began his graduate work the same year as Waller.

Waller spent five quarters at Chicago during 1923–26 studying sociology. In the prestige rankings of graduate students (then and now) the sometimes large group of secondary school teachers ranks rather low. They have fewer close relations with the leading professors, are generally less talented, have less time to devote to study, exhibit a lesser intensity of dedication to the field, and of course enjoy fewer of the jobs or fellowships the department may offer. Waller belonged to this low-prestige group, yet the elite of his time did respect him. The elite then included L. Guy Brown the social psychologist, Herbert Blumer (1900–   ), Frederick Thrasher (1892–1962), Clifford Shaw and, after Waller's first year, Everett Hughes. Waller's articulateness in class brought him to others' attention. He also met Carle C. Zimmerman (1897–   ) in a seminar that Faris gave on theory and they quickly became friends. He met Blumer in another of Faris' classes and they became companions during workouts in the gymnasium and on the track. They talked frequently about athletics. Waller was fascinated by Blumer's stories about his professional football career, which he was pursuing while getting a Ph.D. at Chicago.

In 1925, a year before Waller left Morgan Park for the University of Pennsylvania, he received his M.A. for an essay titled,

"Fluctuations in the Severity of the Punishment of Criminals in England from the Eleventh to the Twentieth Centuries." Waller charts the changes over time in kinds of punishments prescribed for different types of crimes. His notion is that there is a connection between what a society values, the acts that it will punish, and the severity with which it will punish these acts. The idea can be found in Durkheim,[24] but there is no evidence that Waller was influenced by Durkheim in his own study. By the time he wrote his essay, he had studied its subject in courses on crime and punishment, social control, criminal law, and criminology, and he was to pursue these interests as a professor for the rest of his life. He did not, however, draw upon this potentially fruitful insight and historical material for any of his later publications in this area.

In the summer of 1926, Waller took more graduate courses at Chicago, and by this time he had completed his M.A. That summer, he met Wallace Weaver (1901–   ), an instructor at the University of Pennsylvania, who was also taking summer courses. Weaver, impressed by Waller, recommended him to Carl Kelsey (1870–1953), then head of the department at Pennsylvania. In September of 1926 Waller received an appointment at Pennsylvania and left the University of Chicago, his wife, and Morgan Park, in order to work for his Ph.D. in Philadelphia.

His old career as a high school teacher was now definitely finished and his marriage was over, even though the divorce had not yet taken place. If most people carry into their new lives the source of their old troubles—that is, themselves—Waller left at least part of his behind him. His painful experiences, his harsh self-analysis, and, perhaps, the attacks by his wife, may have saved him from a distressing kind of repetition. For with the move to Philadelphia, Waller's behavior and attitudes began to change. Doubtless, too, when a relatively new self is being created, people select companions to complement and sustain these changes, and the new environment at Pennsylvania provided many such companions.

[24]   Cf. *The Rules of Sociological Method* (Glencoe, Illinois: The Free Press, 1938).

While Waller was at Pennsylvania he submitted to amateur psychoanalysis, an experience certainly calculated to help a person create a new self or at least get the old one under control. As early as 1924, and possibly earlier, Waller had been interested in psychodynamics—once he had confounded the Colonel who was head of Morgan Park by characterizing a pupil as "anal erotic"—and Thelma herself had undergone a brief psychotherapy after their separation. At Pennsylvania, his roommate and best friend was James W. Woodard (1892–   ), a former Methodist minister, a daring aviator in World War I, and also recently divorced. Woodard, a sociologist and amateur lay therapist, was willing to apply his psychoanalytic knowledge to Waller's problems. (Lay therapy among friends was by no means uncommon then; it was a craze in the literary circles of New York and was seeping rapidly into the academy, thereby making it more and more respectable.) Waller was greatly influenced by Woodard's ideas about lay therapy and from this time on used psychoanalytic insights and techniques himself in giving therapy to others and in analyzing case studies.

One sidelight on the changes in his attitudes that were taking place as he moved from Morgan Park to Pennsylvania may be found in his official declarations about his religious preferences. His father, Elbert, was a Baptist, with a rock-ribbed antagonism to smoking, drinking, and other frivolities. His mother was a Catholic. We do not know what his childhood training was, but he may have followed the common American practice of attending a convenient and congenial congregation whose stress on doctrinal conformity was not great. In 1913, young Willard (then nearly fourteen years of age) was a regular attendant at the Presbyterian Sunday School in Cobden, Illinois. At Morgan Park, he became active in the Masonic Lodge, which indicates at least that he felt no conflict with any of his mother's Catholic background. When he first registered at the University of Chicago, in his first semesters of teaching at Morgan Park, he listed himself as "Methodist." But by the time he went to the University of Pennsylvania in 1926, he put down as his religious preference, "None."

His outspoken criticism of piety and religious conformity was evident to all who knew him after that. He made a strong effort to persuade his children to adopt anti-religious attitudes, and was to write to his second wife (when she spent a winter in Florida to improve the health of their eldest son) with some worry about the possible effect of parochial school on his children. When she reported Peter's statement that because of sin someone was going to hell, Waller answered (in part), "I do hope they [the children] don't go and get religious on us. I imagine it will be possible to talk Petie out of it after he gets back."

Many years later, one of his students at Columbia University encountered Waller one Sunday in the balcony of the First Presbyterian Church at Broadway and 114th Street. He went closer, not being sure that he had seen correctly. Waller turned to him and whispered fiercely, "I'm doing research!"

When he arrived in Philadelphia in the fall of 1926 he rented a single room. He felt deeply the humiliation of having fallen so far as to be forced to live in a furnished room, in someone else's house, and he also felt the isolation keenly. Weekends, when official duties were suspended, were the worst period for him, and he would consume part of them with long wanderings over the city. (He had always walked a great deal, and continued to throughout his life.) He was looking for women, for human companionship, even for friendship, but his own capacity for any of these was not great in this initial period; he was totally preoccupied with his own pain, and few people are entertaining in their misery.

At Pennsylvania, where few people knew him, he became, if not a totally new person, at least a different and more complex person. Someone who knew him in both Chicago and Philadelphia comments on this change. When he had first met Waller, he saw a young man who was "sensitive, insightful, composed, and certainly introverted. When I first saw him at Pennsylvania that September [1926], I was patently alarmed at his loud, aggressive, and sometimes quite belligerent behavior. Sensing it, perhaps, he explained to me that he was attempting, with hopeful success, to cultivate a more 'direct expression.' " Others, not aware of the contrast, added their own complexities. One of his fellow graduate stu-

dents remembers him as "a trifle aggressive, bitter, and cynical
. . . prone to challenge stuffed shirts in high places. With peers he
was a warm friend." Another friend asserted that Waller saw himself as a "disturber of the peace." From this point on, in fact, most
who knew him for any length of time could expect their peace to be
disturbed.

His own comments on these changes are illuminating. Writing
of his early days at the University of Pennsylvania, he notes, in a
way which reflects the bitterness caused by his separation and
divorce:

Bohemian attitudes became crystallized. I remember saying "Morality
is all right if you don't take it too seriously. As for me, I'm going to
be Bohemian from now on. I've tried the other and it didn't work."[25]

True enough, his "Bohemianism" was hardly spectacular, con-
stricted as it was by the harsh fundamentalism of Waller's male line
and limited by the occupational constraints of being a college
teacher in the Quaker city of Philadelphia. The libertines in the
Greenwich Village of the twenties would have given his efforts a
low rating for both imagination and daring. His Bohemianism
consisted mainly in drinking some bootleg liquor and helping
others to locate a bootlegger, taking part in drinking parties—
in one, his alcoholic exuberance was expressed in riding a bicycle
in the narrow hallway of Woodard's apartment—and a few half-
ashamed explorations of commercial sex.

But if this temporary "wild" behavior now seems modest
enough—more often taking the form of good-humored highjinks
—he was becoming and was to remain for the rest of his life a dedicated cynic, a man bent on stripping the mask from others and
exposing the false façade of social institutions. Waller had pene-
trated the surface, had seen the unpleasant truth, and now insisted
on loudly announcing it to others, whether or not they wanted to
hear it. The idealist who is driven by disillusionment after cutting
deeply to the truth rarely maintains any serene acceptance of other
men, if he ever possessed it. Waller's intellectual and emotional

[25]   "Case Number 17," p. 30.

rebellion took the form of harshly laying bare the inner structure of human beings and social organizations, and denying the myths by which people transform their acts from the reprehensible to the admirable.

Like his still more iconoclastic elder contemporary, Thorstein Veblen (1857–1929), he was always trying to force us to see that the "real" forces and processes that move men are not the ones we see most easily. Underneath the cool, perfumed beauty of the selfless young mother may lie the guts and drive of fighting, lusting animal, pushing for domination of her son and husband. Respectable people often let out yelps of indignation when Waller failed to pay the traditional respect to the sanctity of marriage, for the Nice-Nellyism of family sociology was nearly universal when his first writings appeared. In rereading his analyses of the family in this more jaded age, we are no longer shocked, but we are often forced to admit reluctantly that his portrait has caught our likeness, warts and all.

Although Waller was officially a part-time graduate student at Pennsylvania, his social position and self-conception were not those of a student. He had already been a successful teacher in a position of authority within the microcosm of a military academy, and he had been a household head for four years. He now entered a department where lines between hierarchical ranks were not sharply drawn, and his own talent gave him added prestige. From the time he entered Pennsylvania, he wrote, thought, and grew inwardly as a mature sociologist, writing scientific papers and taking an active part in professional conventions.

Early in his Philadelphia stay, Waller was identified as an exponent of the "Chicago School," which was respected but by no means dominant at his new university. It could be taken for granted that a young man who had spent all his graduate period at Chicago would have absorbed the "Chicago approach" and would be its natural champion, but true to his special intellectual style, Waller saw this identification as a process created by interaction with others, rather than one secured by his own acts alone. In an unfinished study of college teachers, that he started some years later, he describes this type of case:

When I was taking graduate work at Chicago ... I did not identify myself with the Chicago system of sociology or feel called upon to defend it. I accepted it and was trying to learn it. There was so much about the Chicago system of thought that I had not learned that I should not have dared either to defend it or criticize it when others were present who knew it better.

When I transferred to another graduate school, I met Mr. Y., who immediately began to attack the Chicago school of sociology and, as I thought, to ridicule me as a representative of it. He was joking, but he soon got me into a state of mind where I was not joking.

I regarded myself as the chosen defender of the Chicago system; I forgot that I did not know very much about the system of thought, I set out to prove its superiority to all other systems, and the superiority of systematic to unsystematic thought in general.[26]

Plunging headlong into teaching and taking further graduate courses—James P. Lichtenberger (1870–1953) on theory, Stuart A. Rice (1889–   ) on research methods, A. Irving Hallowell (1892–   ) on cultural dynamics—Waller became part of a rich life of work and companionship. Woodard, Clifford C. Kirkpatrick (1898–   ), and Waller became a fraternal enclave of young men who constantly argued about the problems of life and how to deal with them. During this period, Waller taught criminology with Thorsten Sellin (1896–   ), who was then editor of the *Journal of Criminal Law and Criminology*. In 1928, Waller wrote three book reviews for this journal; one was a French book, the other two, German. The talk in his young group, which included Weaver as well as Howard Becker (1899–1960), ranged from the sociology of Burgess, W. I. Thomas (1863–1947), and Faris, to the work of Georg Simmel (1858–1918) and Emile Durkheim (1858–1917). Waller was more likely to speak of German sociology than of French, since he was diligently studying the language at this time (as well as calculus). Others paid respect to his talents, and he was respectful of others' accomplishments. He was especially impressed—as who was not—by Howard

---

[26]   "Notes on the Transformation of the Teacher," this volume, chapter 12.

Becker's linguistic facility, especially in German, and by the vast range of his knowledge.

Gifted, colorful, and hard-working, Waller was soon asked by Rice to join him in a small research project. A full professor and a pioneer in the use of quantitative methods, Rice had come to Pennsylvania from Dartmouth when Waller came from Chicago, and he was later to occupy many important government posts. There was quick mutual identification between them, in part because they had both recently experienced serious marital difficulties which would end for each in divorce.

The research matured in the fall of 1927, but Rice was in ill health and could not attend the national sociological convention in Washington, D.C., to present their findings. As a consequence, the younger man presented his first paper, with Kimball Young (1893–   ) chairing the session. This was Waller's one foray into quantitative and statistical methods—a study of stereotypes. The experimenters had presented to their subjects photos from the *Boston Herald* which were to be identified by rankings of intelligence and craftiness. Subjects were told that the nine unlabeled pictures ranged from a premier (Herriot) and a senator (Pepper) to a bootlegger (Agel). After an interval of a week, the same subjects were given the correct identifications of each picture and again asked to rank the men by the same criteria, to obtain a comparison between their stereotypes and some cognitive knowledge of the men behind the pictures. The degree of concentration, the "bunching" of answers in the first step of the procedure was measured statistically, and was used to describe the extent of stereotyping. That is, after calculating the probabilities of chance identification, how much did the actual guesses depart from chance? In addition, indexes were made of the subjects' ratings of the specific men in the pictures. For example, those who guessed "senator" were likely also to guess that this person had a high intelligence, although the subjects generally failed to link the photo they identified as a senator correctly with the real Senator Pepper.[27]

[27]   Willard W. Waller and Stuart A. Rice, "Stereotypes," in *Personality and the Social Order*, Ernest W. Burgess, ed. (Chicago: University of Chicago Press, 1929), pp. 192–97.

IV

Graduate students were less affluent in Waller's time than now; they not only had less money, but they had to teach as well as work for their degrees. Waller received an instructorship in the department and was paid $1,800 a year. He was no stranger to teaching, but this was his first experience at teaching college students, and his very first experience teaching sociology. Looking back some years later at this period at Pennsylvania—in an article written for the *American Mercury* but turned down by its editor H. L. Mencken—Waller talks of these years:

My sojourn at Pennsylvania was entirely on account of my desire to understand life. . . . My conception of my role was a peculiar one. I regarded myself as a combination thinker and expounder on the subject of everything human . . . but soon found that there was considerable hindrance to my work in my capacity as thinker and that no one wanted to hear me expound. Few they were who heard me gladly. Not even my students cared to hear.[28]

The professor who has not perceived that students do not *care* to hear has been spared, perhaps even coddled, by fate. In this remembrance the idealist in Waller speaks again, once more hurt because the world differs from his hopes for it. If his first marriage left him with an unswerving insistence on describing the natural ugliness and savagery of marital life along with its beauty, his first college teaching experience (from the solo side of the lectern) was to alert him to many other elements in the university structure than the aspiration for intellectual achievement. The man who tries to teach the truth to the world—or even to students—will learn that people do not gladly give up their fictions.

Waller also comments, like thousands before and after him, on the Ph.D. assembly line:

I found that the routine of marking papers, especially those ten-minute quizzes that tradition requires at Pennsylvania, the routine of doing graduate work, the maddening business of acquiring the facts with

[28]   "I Was There: An Apology for Pennsylvania," unpublished manuscript, pp. 2–3.

which a Doctor of Philosophy is supposed to be equipped, interfered seriously with my main business of learning about human life and trying to understand it.[29]

This last was indeed his aim, and unlike countless others, he did not swerve from it. His choice of problems was always human beings in conflict and under tension—the human concerns of individuals; he hardly cared about abstract concepts and variables.

His conception of his "main business" becomes evident in the first piece of work he undertook on his own. In addition to his other activities, Waller was busily working on his thesis, a study of the adjustment to divorce. His motivation is obvious. It was an experience that intensely involved and totally preoccupied him. At any particular time, however, only certain subjects are proper for an academician to look into, and divorce as a topic was not then as acceptable as it is now. But Waller was fortunate. Stuart Rice provided him with the legitimation he needed to deal with this slightly unsavory and vaguely disreputable subject. In the 1920 elections, Rice had had a fling at reform politics in the Pacific Northwest, and had been badly mauled. After the campaign he told Franklin Giddings, under whom he was studying at Columbia, that he never wanted to hear of politics again. Giddings, however, urged him not to run away from the experience, but to integrate it into his life by *diagnosing* it, and out of this re-thinking came Rice's doctoral dissertation, *Farmers and Workers in American Politics* (1924). Rice offered Waller similar advice, though it should not be forgotten that Lichtenberger had written a thoughtful book on divorce some years earlier. Since Waller's dissertation, like his later books, was raw and bleeding, however, and even the title offended some men in his department, the existence of a respectable predecessor did not count for overmuch.

The Old Love and the New is remarkable in several ways, but as a piece of intellectual history it is striking in that it exhibits little, if any, influence of the Chicago school of sociology. Most of the analyses of interpersonal relations in it are psychodynamic; others are social psychological. Perhaps one might fairly charac-

[29]   *Ibid.*, p. 3.

terize them as literary and dramatic, rather than sociological. The material was collected in a consciously psychoanalytic way, within the limitations of Waller's skills at the time, and he defends both his technique and his use of psychoanalytic interpretations in his final chapter on the methodology of the study. In his Glossary, the only sociological terms explained are W. I. Thomas' "definition of the situation" and William Graham Sumner's "folkways and mores." He presents no ecological distributions, not even a city map with plottings of divorce by type of residence. In any event, his sample of thirty-three cases would not have permitted any serious statistical analysis. His aim was to describe the processes of alienation, divorce, trauma, and later adjustment.

He was, perhaps, at a deeper level, really following a Chicago model in his intellectual goal if not his techniques, since he was trying to create from his study of cases a "natural history of divorce." That is, he was not trying to ascertain the *"traits* of divorces and divorcees," but rather to describe the ebb and flow of hate and love; to capture the gradual development of particular forms of conflict from inchoate beginnings to the final divorce; and to illuminate the responses of persons when the social structure incorporating much of their emotions is torn apart and they must find places in new structures. All these processes seemed organic to him, and though they were structured by the usual elements of class, age, occupation, political and religious affiliation, or rural-urban origins, the processes not the structures seemed central to him. He dedicated his thesis to Ellsworth Faris, a sign that something did remain from his Chicago experience.

The doctoral degree is the journeyman's license in the academic world. After that, by social definition, he is his own man. As Waller moved toward this new academic status, he changed his marital status as well. In his last summer in Philadelphia, he married again.

During his second year at Pennsylvania he had met Josephine Wilkins, a popular secretary in the Merchandising Department at the Wharton School. (She immediately gave him the name of "Pete," asserting that he simply did not look like a "Willard," and over the years, an increasing number of his friends called him

"Pete" rather than "Bill.") With new social definitions given by others, the hurt spouse begins to define himself anew. And soon—in part because one's divorce is essentially a bore to those who did not take part in it—his new role became more important than the old. New wives-to-be are especially uninterested in discussing such matters, and perhaps this was an added motivation to complete the dissertation and so to forget his first wife.

With a degree nearly in hand and a wife about to be acquired, Waller received an offer to become an assistant professor at the University of Nebraska in Lincoln at what was for him the munificent salary of $3,000 a year. This was enough to allow him and Josephine to be married, which they did the summer before the Great Stock Market Crash.

In the present period of relative academic affluence, when many jobs are available, and when by the time a department has decided that a young candidate is really not talented enough the candidate writes that he has accepted a better job elsewhere, it is difficult to remember that job openings in sociology were scarce in the twenties, and nearly nonexistent in the thirties. Even talented protogés of powerful professors at major academic centers did not always find jobs immediately, and were kept on the departmental staff in a minor capacity until an appropriate opening occurred. Ambitious young men were alert to any new possibility, but often had to content themselves with posts at lesser colleges and universities.

Waller would probably have stayed on at Pennsylvania if anyone had asked him to do so, but no one did. He had some support among the senior men in the department, was popular among his peers, and was a brilliant teacher, yet he was not asked to remain. He was enough aware of this likelihood that at the end of his second year in Philadelphia he applied for an opening at Dartmouth. (Although Rice wisely and gently sent him the understated comment, "It would not suit you in the long run, I think," his support was actually given.)

Little can now be learned as to why Waller was not kept on at Pennsylvania, for old unrecorded controversies eventually become transformed and impenetrable. There may be no individual mystery at all. Each department has its own style of selection, and not all are wise. After all, during this period, the department had let other good men go as well—Becker, Woodard, and Kirkpatrick, for instance. From piecing together vague allusions and asides from our interviews, however, it seems possible that his divorce was held against him. It apparently seemed to a conservative administration that the Department of Sociology was experiencing an epidemic of divorces, and there was some pressure on the department to lift its moral tone by encouraging more respectable and conforming behavior. Waller compounded his deviation not merely by talking about his divorce, but by his frank revelations of the whole process in his dissertation. Perhaps the administration felt even surer of the wisdom of their decision when he refused to let his dissertation gather dust, but published it a year later. As if this were not enough, Waller and Woodard insulted the Chairman of the Department to his face and so assured themselves of having to look elsewhere for employment.

By the standards of the time, Waller's job at Nebraska was respectable. He had, after all, published only two articles, had no powerful sponsor, and did not come directly from Chicago, the only important center of sociology. He had revised his thesis and had found a publisher for it, but this accomplishment would not necessarily outweigh either the thinness of the job market or his failure to come through the standard graduate career. In any event, since a few major universities turn out most of the Ph.D.'s the majority of these new academics must teach at lesser schools. The University of Nebraska was a respectable school, but was not distinguished. Waller did not feel that he had been cast away by his former friends, but he knew what Nebraska was, and from the beginning of his brief stay there he engaged in the characteristic moves of the ambitious academic who is determined to get back into the big leagues—sending off manuscripts to publishers, talking with publishers about possible books, thinking up new projects, and reminding the urban centers that he existed.

Waller thought of Nebraska as a good place to be "for a while." Joyce O. Hertzler (1895–   ) was chairman of the Department, and the "powerhouse of the department" was Hattie Plum Williams who had studied with G. E. Howard (1849–1928). Howard had succeeded the great E. A. Ross (1866–1951) after Ross had left for Wisconsin. Waller developed a respect for Williams as well as for Duncan Strong, who came at the same time and who later became chairman of the Columbia University Anthropology Department.

Initially, social life in university towns is always pleasant. No one reveals his intransigence or his strong—and, since different from ours, wrong-headed—opinions until issues and interests arise. Waller found friendly people and, if he did not find close friends, that was satisfactory too, "because then I will get a lot more work done." He even liked his department head: ". . . I must say that Hertzler is just about the best possible boss—my Scotch grandfather, or somebody, makes me add, so far." The cautionary afterthought proved prophetic about a year later.

He had already begun negotiations with a publisher for his still unwritten *Sociology of Teaching*, and the following summer he introduced a sociology of education course. He also began that summer—and he was to continue this practice for years—to interview teachers about their occupations and lives. In many ways his analysis of education in school and university combines most happily his breadth of insight and his capacity for rigorous data analysis. By his second winter in Nebraska he had written a goodly part of his *Sociology of Teaching*, and he was to continue writing on this topic for the rest of his life.

Waller wanted to be successful and popular, but he also wanted the respect of his colleagues. He was aware that he had walked a thin line between drama and sociology in his book on divorce. Writing to Rice, a senior man who represented the then new and later dominant thrust of sociology toward exact quantitative methods, he expresses his ambivalent feelings: ". . . I had thought that the book might help to convince the members of a foundation that I had some research ability, as well as some skill in organizing my material and presenting it to the public." He disclaims responsibility for the title, *The Old Love and the New*, asserting that it had been chosen by the publisher. And by way of further disclaimer states (and surely inaccurately), "I am inclined to believe that it hindered rather than helped the sale of the book." He also expresses some embarrassment about the widespread publicity given the book (syndicated articles about it in newspapers reached millions of people), yet he could not avoid showing that he was pleased by all the notice, although disappointed that the widespread attention had not been translated into large sales.

From the Nebraska campus, Waller looked back with some nostalgia to his time at Pennsylvania. The mature phase of a graduate student's life, when most of his course work is over and others begin to treat him as a junior professional, is likely to be one of the more exciting periods in an intellectual's career—at least in retrospect. He is likely to be privy to some of the inside gossip about his seniors and to be a confidant of at least one of them. His younger friends and, still more, his quiz section students, see him as privileged and knowing. He can attack the dominant professors in the field, especially those at other competing universities, with snarling contempt, unburdened by the responsibility of meeting a counterattack in print. His dreams and projects are as yet unsullied by failure. As Waller himself noted, he can compare his own unwritten books with the written books of his predecessors much to the detriment of the latter. And finally, the duties of the successful academic—directing dissertations, committee meetings, clerical work for the university administration, chores for the professional association—have not yet begun to destroy the freedom and flexibility of his time budget; he is able at any time to explore ideas with his friends and professors.

In his first lengthy report to Rice from Nebraska, Waller expresses this feeling, but sees in the absence of his cronies a possible advantage for himself personally:

You and Woodie [Woodard] and Becker used to be great fellows with whom to discuss, debate, and argue, and I imagine that we were all somewhat sharpened by the rapid interchange and merciless criticism of ideas. That I most certainly miss, and I see no great prospect of anything else arising to take its place.

I must confess that this atmosphere of discussion was a heady draught for me, and I tended to live too much by it, and therefore got too little down on little pieces of paper.

Later, he often admonished students to write it, and not lose it by talking it out too much. At this time, he felt that the shutting off of discussion had driven him to write more, and envied both Rice and Becker, who seemed "unaffected by the draining out of your ideas in discussion." There is no evidence, really, that Waller's willingness to talk diminished his writing, but he believed in this zero-sum relationship and worried about it now and again. He talked easily and brilliantly, enjoying the wild play of ideas, however farfetched. His audience played an important role for him, forcing him to reexamine his more fantastic speculations, and stimulating him to attack problems anew. Although Waller was at his best with cronies who encouraged but also joined him in flights of imagination, acerb attacks on the verities, or pseudo-solemn examinations of problems not found in sociological textbooks (Is sex better with a wife or mistress?), he sometimes became restive even in good company, and wanted to be left alone for a while to write.

Waller's dissatisfaction with the intellectual life at Nebraska did impel him to work hard, if only to create for himself opportunities elsewhere. After one year, he had to admit that ". . . we do not like very many of the Nebraska people and we hate Lincoln." He had decided that going to Nebraska was a mistake. "The University is not even second rate, and the cultural isolation of the place is almost unbelievable."

One method long used by academics for escaping from intolerable situations is to obtain a grant to study something new and to study it in some new place. While he was at Nebraska, Waller became fascinated with Gestalt psychology. Although he had taken a course in Gestalt at Pennsylvania, he knew relatively little about it and decided that now was a good time to learn more. The logical place to learn more was, of course, Germany. In 1930 he therefore inquired of the Social Science Research Council whether they would be interested in financing such a venture. Unfortunately, they were not interested, which left Waller still at Nebraska.

The application to SSRC to learn more about Gestalt psychology embodied more than merely a desire to escape from Nebraska, however. During this period, there was raging a fierce debate among sociologists over the relative merits of qualitative versus quantitative methods in social research. Waller's first published work had been in quantification, but he quickly turned away from this kind of work, writing at the time to Rice, his collaborator in it, "My own work is apparently taking me further away from your main lines of investigation, but that should be an advantage rather than a handicap to our continued rapport, for we will be supplementing investigators rather than rivals." This remark expresses a position that he often took in this debate. He felt most comfortable using qualitative methods, yet with his usual tremendous industry he was continually gathering data, and he saw correctly that the debate was a false one. The two methods are necessary complements, and each is the poorer without the other. It was perhaps this belief in the complementarity of methods that made him study Gestalt psychology. For this competitor of mindless behaviorism (the rat in a maze or closed box *has* to solve the *experimenter's* problem, since it is not allowed to have problems of its own choosing; and *necessarily* by trial and error because it is allowed no useful information by which it could solve the problem in any other way) seemed to grant insight its due, while demanding rigorous experimentation. That Waller was looking for a bridge between the two modes of inquiry can be seen in his view that Gestalt psychology might be linked fruitfully with psychoanalytic theory. (It is also evident from his interests that Waller did not see himself as only a sociologist, or at least one with a narrow definition of boundaries. Rather, he was entirely willing to cross academic property lines into psychology if his search for answers led him there.)

Although the Social Science Research Council did not come to his aid, the University of Nebraska soon did. If he found Lincoln unsatisfying, certain people in it soon found him the same, and his sojourn there was abruptly cut short. In every university where Waller taught, his intimacy with students aroused criticism. In his talks with them, he was never content to ascertain that they had the proper number of credits in the stipulated courses, but quickly demanded—and gave—personal revelations. In many courses, he asked for detailed life histories from his students, a practice that was not uncommon during the thirties.

Further, he engaged in what was, essentially, lay therapy from time to time—not for a fee, but out of a compelling need both to understand and to be helpful. When Howard Rowland took social psychology from him at Nebraska, he and the other students in the class were required to read Freud, Jung, and Adler. Rowland, who as a sociologist was later to contribute to the development of social psychiatry, was asked by Waller to keep a pad by his bed so that when he awoke he could write out his dreams before they slipped away. Then he and Waller would analyze these dreams together.

Even when set against the standards of modern, more mechanized teaching approaches, when professors are expected to devote full time to scientific discovery and to serve as father-confessor-cum-teacher, Waller's approach to teaching seems both exhausting and admirable. Nevertheless, parents of his pupils sometimes became angry at being exposed in their children's term papers, and colleagues were envious of Waller's popularity, and concerned lest he overstep the formal boundaries between student and teacher. That he did so was inevitable, and in ways that would arouse criticism even today, for in a significant sense, Waller brought his students into his research work. They were not his equals, and he did not treat them as such, but they were his apprentices. At Nebraska, and indeed wherever he taught, he drove them to locate, analyze and articulate their own experiences. He never treated them as hired hands, and he was no armchair sociologist, spinning out his intuitions from the steady contemplation of his own navel. He sent out bands and platoons of students to gather data in addition to his own, to be studied, tested, and used—not only for Waller's own books, but for the students' enlightenment.

That some of these relations could lead to trouble is clear enough, and one of them finally led to Waller's being fired. Various versions of the story are extant, and the exact details can no longer be recaptured, but the official version is that he ". . . remained at the University of Nebraska from September, 1929 through June 30, 1931," with some hint that there was "some problem or issue" that "had some repercussion with a couple of parents in the community."

The essence of the story illustrates both Waller's style and that of the small university town in the thirties. One of the Wallers' babysitters had used their house, as babysitters more often do now, to entertain her boy friend. Unfortunately, they were careless, and scandal threatened when she became pregnant. Worse, both were children of university officials. Perhaps Waller would have been merely reprimanded because his house had been used, but the girl's parents found her diary, and from it learned that Waller, with his usual combination of compassion and need to know, had been counseling the girl about her difficult situation. In short, he was guilty of keeping secret what he had learned in the confessional.

Waller was fired in February, but the blow was softened by the payment of the rest of his year's salary. Waller was angry at the town's prudish response, and at its desire to protect authority instead of catering to human needs, but he was much more hurt by his department head's failure to come to his defense publicly.

A handful of academics have survived scandal and firing— one thinks immediately of such men as Bertrand Russell, Thorstein Veblen, and W. I. Thomas—and even more have survived scandal without being fired. Firing for Waller required him to bestir himself and set out his intellectual wares more attractively in order to demonstrate his essential worth, and he used his period of enforced leisure to great advantage. The Waller family (by this time a first son had been born) moved to Chicago, where they rented an apartment near the University. According to one informant, the University gave him a grant, which permitted him to continue work over part of the summer. He looked about for a job (but showed no great concern about the difficulty of finding one), and he completed *The Sociology of Teaching*.

The Sociology of Teaching is a mature sociological analysis, very different from his first book, and, of course, very different from his experimental study of stereotypes with Rice. The atmosphere of the book now seems a bit old-fashioned, in the same way that Dreiser or Sinclair Lewis now seem old-fashioned. Waller's own experiences as a teacher had been in a small military academy and his father's experiences had been in small town, Midwestern schools. Much of his case material for the book comes from his students at Nebraska who, of course, knew most about the small Midwestern towns of Sherwood Anderson, almost nothing about the big cities of Theodore Dreiser. This provinciality appears at its most striking in Waller's discussion of the moral regimentation that a town can impose upon its teachers, and anyone who still feels some nostalgia for the good old days might profitably read what Waller says about this. All schools do demand moral purity (or at least its semblance) from their teachers, but it is only in a small town that these demands can be rigidly enforced. In larger communities teachers can now escape the surveillance of the town and gown community by subway or automobile.

But if the type of community has changed, the sociological analysis is strikingly contemporary. Waller concentrates on presenting human beings in specified but changing role relationships within a carefully delineated social structure. The teacher is in constant face-to-face interaction with his pupils, but this interaction always takes place within a set of forces defined by the national society, the local community, the school board, the administrative staff, and colleagues. Waller analyzes what we would now call (following Robert K. Merton), the teacher's "role set,"[30] that is, the set of relationships with which the status of the teacher is linked: pupil, department head, principal, parents, and so on. Each of these individuals has a lesser degree of choice, and a more specified set of duties, because of the values and actions of all the rest. Each is moved by his own psychological needs, and Waller is perceptive in noting how these are expressed within the limits of the social structure. It is not the psychological, however, but the sociological processes that create the peculiarities of this social institution as distinguished from other types of organizations.

Finally, though this approach characterizes most of Waller's work, and so does not set this book apart from his others, he sees each of these relationships, and indeed the school itself, as a set of *tensions*. He does not view the social structure as adequately defined by its rules, or fixed by its regulations, nor the teacher's life

[30]   Robert K. Merton, *Social Theory and Social Structure* (New York: The Free Press of Glencoe, 1957) pp. 368–84.

as encompassed entirely within the rigid definitions of a status. Instead, he sees each of these social arrangements, indeed each daily interaction within a supposedly firm structure, as fraught with contingency, potential conflict, and even occasional chaos. In this view, again, he is fresh and contemporary. Although these role patterns and social institutions are "given"—they existed before any particular teacher entered them—he discusses at several points the adjustment to these "givens"; they are also continually being re-created by the renewed participation of each member.

The teacher must have enough authority over the children to be able to teach them; yet this authority is constantly threatened and could collapse at any moment. The social order, while it does persist, is continually being threatened with destruction. Conflict is endemic and inherent in the system. When people with different objectives, different backgrounds, and different personalities come together, order is not the most logical expectation. The system seems capable of falling apart at any moment, and Waller is intrigued by why it does not, by what keeps it going, what keeps conflict in bounds, what upholds the authority of the teachers, and what allows them to remain dominant. Waller is amazed that *anything* lasts for very long. He sees the pressures for disorder, change, disruption, chaos, everywhere, and yet empirically he knows that things do last and often for a very long time. This perspective leads him to be sensitive as well to those factors that support the persistence of a system.

Waller's first book, *The Old Love and the New*, hardly appears to have been written by a sociologist at all. By contrast, his second book could have been written by no one but a sociologist, and there is some evidence that Waller was self-conscious about making this book look more like the work of a professional sociologist. He tells the following story, surely about himself:

A young professor of sociology conceives of his science as an attempt to understand human life. He attempts to realize this broad conception of his task in his published work: he publishes a book in which he attempts to combine scientific writing and a proper appreciation of the tears of things. It probably is not a very good book. It fails to reach a wide section of the lay public because of its sociological stiffness, and it fails to impress the sociologists because of its popular looseness. The young sociologist is grieved that his literary career should begin so inauspiciously. He rebels for a time, and writes his next book for the academic audience.[31]

He was ambitious, and one way to get ahead was to work with the ideas of recent predecessors and within the bounds that they had set. Nearly everyone who was intellectually important at the time was given his due in Waller's second book. He discusses the four wishes of Thomas, and Faris' critique of them.[32] He uses Thomas's "definition of the situation,"[33] and Park and Burgess' classifications of types of interaction.[34] He refers throughout to Cooley and especially to such concepts as "primary" and "secondary" groups. Although he had obviously learned from these men, his use of their specific ideas often seems forced. He pays his respects, then quickly hurries on to analyze a case in his own brilliant way. He was never interested in abstract concepts and this is most clear when he brings them into the discussion. There is one idea, however, that he introduces here for the first time which he later uses in fruitful ways, the "Principle of Least Interest."[35]

The book finished, he obtained a new job. Through whose auspices he obtained his position at Pennsylvania State College (now University) we do not know, but by May of 1931 he had accepted an offer of an associate professorship there, heading a (nonexistent) Division of Sociology in the Department of Economics at a salary of $3,000 a year, moving up in rank, but not in salary. (After six years of successful teaching and writing at Pennsylvania State, and after becoming recognized as one of the leading intellectual figures on the campus, his salary had moved up to $3,250—meanwhile, all faculty members had taken a cut of 10 per cent on all salary above the first $1,000. Although he was

31   "Notes on the Transformation of the Teacher," unpublished manuscript, this volume, chapter 12.
32   *The Sociology of Teaching*, chap. 11.
33   *Ibid.*, chap. 18.
34   *Ibid.*, p. 15.
35   *Ibid.*, p. 240.

constantly short of money during this period, he was not resentful about his salary until his last year at Pennsylvania, when he learned how much other, and better, universities would pay him.) He expressed buoyant optimism about his new job, feeling that Pennsylvania State was an excellent place, the East was the region to be in, and that his period of isolation was ended. Over the ensuing years, however, he again came to feel dissatisfaction with the college as a source of mental stimulation, and with teaching as a satisfying activity. (Toward the end of his life this restlessness led him to engage in many activities outside the university setting.)

His initial optimism was hardly based on any realistic appraisal of the situation at Pennsylvania State. True enough, it was closer to the Atlantic Ocean than Nebraska, but it was none the less geographically and socially isolated. Not even the railroad tracks went through the little town of State College (though occasionally a train did arrive, stop, and back out again), and on the snowed-in roads of winter, even getting to the main railroad leading toward Philadelphia and New York could easily be a two-hour trip—if those cities were accessible at all.

Waller was not the first sociologist at Pennsylvania State but he was the only member in the department and remained the only member his first four years. Subsequently, his former student at Nebraska, Howard Rowland, became an instructor there, Ephriam Fischoff (later to join the New School for Social Research) was added as a lecturer, and in Waller's last year Seth Russell was made an assistant. The intellectual aspirations of Pennsylvania State students were rather modest, there was no stimulating group of graduate students in sociology, and the community itself did little to mitigate his intellectual isolation.

As usual, Waller poured much of his energy into teaching. He made an immediate reputation as a witty, iconoclastic, and highly literate instructor who could effectively use case material from a novel to illustrate a sociological principle. He was popular among the students in literature and writing, and especially among those who wrote for the campus newspaper and magazine. He continued to read widely—while writing *The Family*, for example, he read through the works of Edward Gibbon.

Waller enjoyed the sheer mischievousness of shocking his students, and students find endearing such attacks on conventional wisdom and entrenched authorities. Waller's talent for reaching students came fundamentally from his lack of dogmatism, his willingness to exchange ideas with his students, and his examination of both his own and his students' preconceptions. To shake them loose from their received wisdom, he would (as one of his Pennsylvania State colleagues put it) present "the other side" without bothering to counterbalance it first by stating the accepted, traditional position. He might, for example, devote an entire lecture to the positive contributions of crime, without once bothering to mention that crime might also be destructive.

Waller's courses, like those of most professors who can make their own choices, were a collection of past, present, and future research interests, with now and again a course that simply seemed to be necessary for students to take, however boring to the teacher. He did not specialize, but did concentrate on certain fields: at Pennsylvania State, his courses included the sociology of childhood, the family, social institutions, and social psychology—but also population problems.

The Pennsylvania State period for Waller was a transition between the obscurity he knew at Nebraska and the national recognition he was to achieve while at Columbia. He did considerable research and writing, but most of it was never published and much of it has been lost or destroyed. As at Nebraska, he pushed his students to gather data about themselves, about others, and about the college. When he arrived, Pennsylvania State had many local rituals, traditions, and customs, although many of these were to disappear as the College expanded far beyond its then 4,000 students. Waller began at once to chronicle these bits of folklore, and soon was able to give the origins of about fifty such customs. He had his students gather information about fraternities and sororities, which then and later dominated campus life.

Naturally enough, his data-gathering excited some criticism. He planted students in fraternities and faculty homes to do studies of student life and faculty wives and, of course, not all of these undergraduate researchers could be expected to excel in either technical skill or professional discretion. These were the first personal case studies on campus, and (as one informant put it) "were anything but anonymous." In some classes, the data-gathering was less threatening, but still hardly reassuring to parents. Virginia Matthews (along with Vance Packard, whom she later married) was a student of Waller's. When she took a course in anthropology from him, the entire class was assigned to do a sociological study of their home towns.

During his Pennsylvania State period Waller's interest in psychoanalysis had, if anything, increased. Howard Rowland recalls that with Seth Russell and William Henderson, one of their undergraduate students, the three younger men and Waller engaged in "almost continuous group analysis which we jokingly referred to as 'phyloanalysis.' " In a letter to his wife, Josephine, while she and their two children were in Florida for the winter, Waller reports

Bill [Henderson] and Howard [Rowland] and I had a long discussion in which we really took Bill apart and put him back together again. I think it was quite an experience for Bill, and there is no doubt that he will be a somewhat different person from now on. But that took us until very late at night, and I had to sleep until quite late today.

Perhaps goaded by memories of his father's attitudes, Waller thereupon resolved to keep more sensible hours and to drink less.

He did not confine his therapy to close friends. During this period, he sometimes gave (without fee) his professional services to people in the community. During the years following the publication of *The Old Love and the New,* he had received many letters from strangers who wanted advice on their marital problems. His responses were usually lengthy, but cautious, and it is evident that he enjoyed the role of adviser. His letters were always compassionate and he went to great trouble to think through others' problems. From some of these epistolary exchanges it is clear that he also gave elementary therapy to a few of these people in marital difficulties.

Though there were some raised eyebrows because of his unconventional teaching methods, Waller was promoted to full professor two years after he came to Pennsylvania, and in 1934 was asked to head the Division of Sociology (not a formal title, and still within the Economics Department). He had taken his hard and often cynical look at the high school; now he turned his attention to higher education, and it was during his years at Pennsylvania State that he began to collect materials for a large study. Fragments of this work still exist, but the entire work was never completed. In 1935 he published (with W. H. Cowley) a paper called "A Study of Student Life,"[36] and two years later published his frequently cited "The Rating and Dating Complex."[37] Both are small pieces of this much larger study.

The paper with Cowley is essentially a plea for help from his professional colleagues and an outline of a part of the projected study. The paper was originally read at the national meetings of the American Sociological Society. Waller notes that he is engaged in a national study of campus life and that "the interested and even enthusiastic response of three dozen sociologists over the country for co-operative assistance in the present exploration has been most gratifying."[38] He urges his listeners to help by acting as a campus representative in the collection of more data. Thirty-six colleges were not thought to be enough for the kind of work he wanted to do.

The main part of the paper reads like a research proposal, and like any modern research proposal it makes extravagant claims about the scientic reward. Student culture is depicted as a perfect place to study the invention and diffusion of culture, a problem that was occupying prominent anthropologists at the time. Waller saw clearly that with a large sample of schools one could determine how variables such as size, sex composition, and social affiliations could shape the culture of a school. The logic of contemporary comparative analysis was clearly the basis of this study.

[36]   W. H. Cowley and Willard Waller, "A Study of Student Life," *Journal of Higher Education*, 6, no. 3 (March 1935) : 132–42.
[37]   Willard Waller, "The Rating and Dating Complex," *American Sociological Review*, 2, no. 3 (October 1937) : 727–34; reprinted this volume, chapter 6.
[38]   "A Study of Student Life," p. 142.

But more was promised: A comparative study of colleges could elucidate how social control operated; it could help resolve the argument over whether the ability of an institution to control its members was the result of selection or socialization; and it could clarify what techniques of social control worked, when they worked, and why they worked. The college was not seen in isolation. How the larger society influenced it and what functions it served for that society were to be of central importance.

Waller did not deliver on all of these promises, but then if most of us were held accountable for promises made in research proposals, we would never publish our final reports. But Waller did begin, and his beginnings are fascinating.

In 1933 he published a note in *The Old Main Bell*, a pamphlet published by Pennsylvania State for the edification of the alumni. It was called "The Professor Looks at Students" and it dealt with one of Waller's recurring themes—posturing in interaction. The teacher can play his role in different ways. He can be stern and demanding or he can be prophetic and warm. Whatever mode he chooses, his students are bound to respond inappropriately. If he wants them to think, they will instead ask him what will be on the next examination. If he wants them to master facts, they will ask thoughtful questions. Both sides are trapped by images that never seem to fit together harmoniously, images which make honest contact impossible.

What remains of the education manuscript is probably a first or, at best, a second, draft. It shows clearly how Waller worked. He begins by analyzing his own experiences as a college teacher. His examples are nearly all either autobiographical or stories about his friends. They are used to make a general point, yet one has the feeling that the general point grows from the example rather than that the example is found to illustrate the general point.

Many of the themes that appeared in *The Sociology of Teaching* reappear here—the modes of interaction between student and teacher; the effects of the faculty culture on the personality of the teacher; the school's link to the stratification system of the larger society; the demands this society makes upon the college and the response the college makes to these demands.

Waller's own career to this point had sensitized him to see how the academic world as a whole was structured. He had been at a major center and he had been in the minor schools. He was acutely aware of what the academic class system looked like, and how professors moved up and down in it. Career management became an intellectual concern, probably because it was such a personal concern.

Waller knew that one managed one's career within a definite structure. One's place in the academic stratification system set limits, determined options, provided opportunities and forced compromises. Professors moved upward not only because their intellectual work was recognized and rewarded, but also because they made the correct strategic moves within the system.

Yet academic mobility is, to some extent, precisely a reward for intellectual work. This fact leads Waller to investigate a new problem, one that he had not previously considered. To move ahead, an academic must have ideas, if not original ones at least illuminating ones, for that is after all what the life of the mind is supposed to be about. The problem Waller seizes upon is one of the sociology of knowledge—how social arrangements affect the emergence and diffusion of new ideas. He knows that university centers, by definition, are places where new ideas are created, but he tries to determine how these centers can be creative and further how they can impose their newly created ideas on the rest of the system. Ideas do not arise randomly and they do not diffuse only because of their superiority over other ideas. Who knows whom, who has studied where and who reads what, these are all determinants of what the intellectual landscape will look like at any particular time. (Waller's years at Barnard would, no doubt, have enriched this analysis, for he was then in contact with a creative center. But he never returned to this project and now all but a few fragments have been lost.)

As always, Waller was acutely aware of what was happening to him and the effects his surroundings were having on him. During the six years that he spent at Pennsylvania State, he became increasingly dissatisfied with his position as "the big shot in such a small piddle." His unpublished writing about colleges and specifically about Pennsylvania State reveal his restlessness, his sense of confinement, and his need for a more challenging audience. Following his earlier portrait of the school teacher whose personality becomes distorted by his occupation, he notes how common is "schoolmasterishness" at second-rate colleges. We would now give the name of "locals"[39] to such "schoolmasters," that is, those whose concerns are with the committee work, the school dances and football games, the alumni, and teaching, rather than with the intellectual development of the field. Waller comments:

Schoolmasterishness is very easy to recognize and to identify, but somewhat difficult to define; it shows itself in the tendency of the mind of the person who teaches school to be mainly occupied with things that have to do with his job as a teacher. . . .

When I go to the University of Chicago I meet my friends and they ask me, "What are you writing, or what research are you doing?" I tell them and they are satisfied. When I visit the University of Pennsylvania the same question is asked. I start to tell what research I am doing and they interrupt, "Oh, no, I mean what courses are you teaching." They force me to tell the name and to define the content of every course that I am teaching, to tell what textbook I am using in every course, and to defend my choice.

Now, my friends at the University of Chicago know as well as these others that I make my living by teaching, but they prefer not to wound me by too obvious reference to this vulgar fact. Besides, they are not interested.[40]

The less demanding college impedes the talented and ambitious scholar in other ways. In the minor college, "The man of high ability is almost completely isolated. His colleagues are unable to criticize his ideas, and he soon falls out of the habit of discussing serious matters with them." Waller had few colleagues

---

[39]   Robert K. Merton, "Patterns of Influence: Local and Cosmopolitan Influentials," in *Social Theory and Social Structure* (Glencoe, Illinois: The Free Press, 1957). Alvin W. Gouldner has used this distinction in an analysis of college teachers. Cf. his "Cosmopolitans and Locals: Towards an Analysis of Latent Roles, I," *Administrative Science Quarterly* (December, 1957), pp. 281–306; "Cosmopolitans and Locals . . . , II," *Administrative Science Quarterly* (March, 1958), pp. 444–80.
[40]   "Notes on Higher Education."

to whom he could show his work, and from whom he could obtain critical comment. He felt that his flow of creativity was hampered because there were no colleagues to "relay to him, and digest for him, ideas which are floating around in the academic universe. . . ."[41]

Flattery and deference are enjoyable, but they may be bought at too high a price. Over time, the respect of lesser men becomes less valuable to the man who wants to whip himself forward. "The awe with which mediocre colleagues regard an able man is probably not a healthy environment for him."[42] With his inner press toward accomplishment, Waller felt that he was cheating himself at Pennsylvania State, that he was settling for less than he could do, and perhaps even seeking to escape reality. In two separate documents, Waller comments on different facets of this process. In one, he states: "College teaching furnishes a refuge for many persons who are not able to face reality."[43] The good teacher, Waller writes, is subject to pressures that keep him from developing into a scientist or scholar. In *The Sociology of Teaching*, he had analyzed why the high school teacher is likely to lose his zest for intellectual exploration. As to the excellent college teacher,

. . . the desire to hold the attention of his student woos him seductively to popularization. The popular teacher develops an unreal conception of himself and prostitutes himself to maintain his popularity. All the teacher's creative energies go into pleasing his students. . . . If it is an unfortunate thing to be a bad teacher, it is sometimes no less unfortunate to be a good one.[44]

Given these critical attitudes and his restlessness, it is not surprising that Waller was also aware of the restricted career opportunities of the man at the second-rate university, even if he is able. In his unpublished work on higher education, he asserts that a man in a first-rate university has, first of all, quick access to the newest ideas. More important, "When he publishes, the prestige of his university assures him a hearing. His work will be read and re-

41   *Ibid.*
42   This volume, chapter 19.
43   This volume, chapter 12.
44   This volume, chapter 12.

viewed by important people. And the people who review the books will be friends of the scholar."[45]

In spite of these handicaps, Waller did manage to publish several articles while he was at Pennsylvania. The two on education have been mentioned, and there were also two papers on the social reactions to deviant behavior. The first of these, in collaboration with the Pennsylvania State economist, Edward Russell Hawkins, is a limited attempt to assess accurately the costs of crime. As the authors point out, such estimates always include the losses of property or income, but do not take into account the economic *benefits* of crime. Viewed in strictly economic terms,

> The prostitute, the pimp, the peddler of dope, the operator of the gambling hall, the vendor of obscene pictures, the bootlegger, the abortionist, all are productive, all produce goods or services which people desire and for which they are willing to pay.
>
> It happens that society has put these goods and services under the ban, but people go on producing them and people go on consuming them, and an act of the legislature does not make them any less a part of the economic system.[46]

Fundamentally, the economic gain resulting from criminal activity must be *added to,* not subtracted from, the national income.

The authors pursue the argument further. *Because* criminal activities have beneficial consequences, the reformer's efforts to do away with these activities will be resisted by the "decent elements" in the community. Both the respectable and the criminal patterns have the same roots: these decent elements derive benefits from "the conditions that produce sordidness and crime, just as the druggist's wife puts in the collection plate on Sunday the quarter that bought the ginger ale for someone's Saturday night spree."[47] They hurl this challenge at those who preach against crime:

If it were somehow possible to eliminate all crime suddenly, the effect

---

45   This volume, chapter 19.
46   Edward Russell Hawkins and Willard Waller, "Critical Notes on the Cost of Crime," *Journal of Criminal Law and Criminology* 26 (January, 1936) : 684–85. This volume, chapter 5.
47   *Ibid.,* p. 693. This volume, chapter 5.

on our entire economic structure would be as disastrous as the collapse of any other industry of similar magnitude.[48]

It should be noted, however, that here as in much research, the authors spend most of their energy and argument in what we now see as a rather futile attempt to outline how correct figures on the cost of crime might be tallied.

A year later, Waller published perhaps his best known article, "Social Problems and the Mores."[49] In it he analyzes in more detail the thesis that social problems (in the thirties these included such phenomena as crime, prostitution, drug addiction, divorce, and juvenile delinquency) would not exist if they were not maintained and supported by "respectable" social institutions. Society will not tolerate solutions that infringe on the arrangements and advantages it has already come to approve. His comment on how society would react is also a comment on many of the contemporary "solutions" to the problem of poverty in the modern affluent society:

A simpleton would suggest that the remedy for poverty in the midst of plenty is to redistribute income. We reject this solution at once because it would interfere with the institution of private property, would destroy the incentive for thrift and hard work and disjoint the entire economic system. What is done to alleviate poverty must be done within the limits set by the organizational mores.[50]

The respectable people of the society, who base their enjoyable position on the advantages conferred on them by the organizational mores (as Waller calls the vested interests in existing institutions), limit the possible solutions to most social problems. The humanitarian who fails to take these interests into account will be constantly thwarted in his attempt to remedy social ills. Waller does not analyze this idea further, but does make use of it almost a decade later in describing the social adjustment of veterans.

In one other major article of the Pennsylvania State period,

[48]   *Ibid.*
[49]   Willard Waller, "Social Problems and the Mores," *American Sociological Review* 1 (December, 1936) : 922–33. This volume, chapter 6.
[50]   *Ibid.*

"Insight and Scientific Method,"[51] Waller took part in the bitter polemic of the thirties that swirled about the issue of quantitative methods in sociology. As noted earlier, he had written from Nebraska to Stuart A. Rice to tell him that he was departing from the type of analysis that Rice favored—"departing," since he had collaborated with Rice on the quantitative investigation of stereotypes, and had studied calculus at the University of Pennsylvania. He had also directed a further quantitative study of stereotypes while at Nebraska (but was even then beginning a new, phase of more sophisticated structural analysis in *The Sociology of Teaching*).

Contemporaneous with this type of thinking, and occupying far more of his attention, was his focus on case histories and introspective inquiry. At the risk of some oversimplification, it may be asserted that Waller felt freer than many of his contemporaries to use whatever methods worked, though he himself felt most comfortable in intuitive analyses drawn from huge quantities of data. His own press toward a deeper understanding of how things worked led him away from the analysis of *individuals* to the analysis of *people-in-institutions*.

In this context, then, and remembering the fierce debates of this period about whether sociology could, or should, become "scientific" by taking over the research methods of the established sciences, Waller's methodological position becomes clearer as well as more sophisticated. Many students who have read Waller casually, and enjoyed his perceptive but compassionate dissections of individuals, have placed Waller in the anti-statistical, anti-quantitative camp. He does not belong there.

On the other hand, he does insist on the central importance of the fruitful idea, the seminal configuration:

The essence of scientific method, quite simply, is to try to see how data arrange themselves into causal configurations. Scientific problems are solved by collecting data and by "thinking about them all the time." We need to look at strange things until, by the appearance

---

[51] Willard Waller, "Insight and Scientific Method," *American Journal of Sociology*, 40 (November, 1943) : 285–97. This volume, chapter 2.

of known configurations, they seem familiar, and to look at familiar things until we see novel configurations which make them appear strange.[52]

He goes on to say, "Quantification is not the touchstone of scientific method. Insight is the touchstone."[53] As to the use of statistics, he asserts that the statistical method

. . . is successful as a means of discovering truth when it is used to subserve insight, and . . . not if it is used without insight or in such a manner as to obstruct insight.[54]

He objected to the blind faith that some sociologists had in statistics. George A. Lundberg attacked Waller's paper "Insight and Scientific Method" at the 1935 meetings of the American Sociological Society. In a peroration calling for a new methodology to replace "the shackles of Aristotelian verbalisms, logic, and laws of thought," Lundberg derided the older sociology for following outmoded methods of inquiry:

We cannot deal with the physical world with the tools of 1935 and at the same time confront social problems with the tools of the Middle Ages, or of 5000 B.C., without the most serious schizophrenic consequences to social behavior.[55]

In his "Discussion" of this attack, Waller conceded the importance of operationalism, which Lundberg was espousing, but denied that it excluded all other procedures. His response is a thoughtful but severe critique of rigid quantification in social scientific research, in a mechanical imitation of the physical sciences.

No one questions that physical science methods can be employed in social science to a certain extent, but it is also clear that literalism in the application of physical science rules can lead only to a parody of science.[56]

[52]   *Ibid.* This volume, chapter 2.
[53]   *Ibid.*
[54]   *Ibid.*
[55]   George A. Lundberg, "Quantitative Methods in Social Psychology," *American Sociological Review*, 1 (February, 1936) : 54
[56]   Willard Waller, "Discussion," *American Sociological Review* (February, 1936) : 55.

Waller then returns to his own view of how human behavior should be studied:

The view which I should like to see established is that artistic and quantitative methods are interlinked in such a way that progress in the one necessarily involves corresponding progress in the other. There is no conflict, but an inter-dependence between these methods.[57]

In a letter to Waller five years earlier, commenting on an early draft of the "Insight and Scientific Method" paper, Rice had correctly seen Waller's position as agreeing in many ways with his own, even though others, as Rice said incorrectly believed him to be in ". . . opposition to anything that was not strictly quantitative." Rice adds,

. . . You have taken issue not so much with statistical method, to which you allow a very wide field of importance, but rather with the disassociation of "science" and "insight" which was attempted recently, for example, by Ogburn.

Waller was, of course, aware of the criticisms against his style of investigation, and of the "dangers and imperfections of my method of work . . . [it] depends almost altogether upon the concurrence of qualified observers for verification."[58] He goes on to explain, "I try to skirt some of the dangers by sticking to fairly obvious and well established points, by finding many statements of the same principle in different universes of discourse, and by paying attention to the comments which others make upon my work."

It was not possible in the period just before World War II to avoid this methodological debate, or to avoid being placed at one extreme position or the other. When Waller came to Columbia University in 1937 the department was sharply divided by this conflict. The arguments between Robert S. Lynd and Robert M. McIver went on throughout all the years Waller was at Columbia, although the issues were not always methodological.

[57]   *Ibid.*, p. 58.
[58]   Letter to Robert K. Merton from Brunswick, Maine, August 1, 1938.

Waller continued the debate in a sharp letter to Read Bain (1892–   ) in 1940, when Bain was editor of the official journal of the American Sociological Society, the *American Sociological Review*, protesting that Bain had rejected papers from young sociologists because they were supported by Waller, or thought to be. The occasion was Bain's rejection of Arnold Green's article, "The Cult of Personality and Sexual Relations," which was an account of courtship practices among lower-class Poles, and which later received considerable attention when it was published.[59] In his letter, Waller reminds Bain that he had previously urged him to shed his dogmatism concerning methodology, and to make the *Review* representative of the best sociological thought of all schools. Waller had even become a subeditor, partly "to prevent you from inundating us with articles in which your own or some other methodology was expounded."

Waller was not, in his letter of protest, arguing that his own kind of sociology should be dominant, but that the *Review*

. . . should publish principally articles reporting the results of some kind of investigation, thinking, or research. By so doing, we will convince youngsters in the field that there is a market for such researches . . . and concrete studies will increase in number and improve in quality.

He expressed his view that Bain had followed a program in stark contrast to his recommended encouragement of *research:*

The evidence of your entire life is to the effect that you believe that the way to get research is to publish articles in praise of research, to split hairs concerning what is and what is not scientific, to indulge in medieval disputations concerning points which can never be proved or disproved. [Thereby] . . . you create a market for methodological disputations, and you get more methodological disputations, and that is all you do get.

Taking the battle to his opponent's camp, he argued that the editor does not have the right to impose his own methodology on potential contributors, since the *Review* belongs to the entire society of sociologists. Before going on to point out rejections which he thought had been based on Bain's belief that the writers had been somehow associated with Waller, he makes a final saber slash that must have cut deeply:

I am also going to be mean enough to point out that you have not so far made any discoveries within the framework of your own method, although some of your work done outside your method is quite creditable.

In answer to Waller's angry attack, Read Bain—no mean opponent with the saber himself—did not respond in kind, but gave a detailed, reasonable explanation for having rejected the various articles Waller thought should be published. He expressed his personal warmth for his friend again, and even his belief that it was therapeutic to let off steam. In turn, Waller apologized for his violence, but once more iterated his "inextinguishable horror" of young people being caught up in the struggles of their elders, and thus failing to get their work published.

Amusingly enough, after typing his more resonable letter, Waller adds in longhand with somewhat more emotion,

Upon thinking it over, I still think there is too much methodology in the Review!! I have almost reached the point where I should consider it desirable, in order to encourage concrete researches, to publish a poor research paper rather than a good paper on methodology.[60]

In this instance the debate had two main issues: (1) whether or not so many articles on methodology should take up space in the *Review*, and (2) whether or not the scientific methodology Waller (along with Becker and Woodard) believed Bain was promulgated would be fruitful. An accurate historical perspective on this latter debate, which has lost none of its pungency or relevance in the modern period, must emphasize that this was not a conflict between generations, not a conflict between the young, fact-hungry Turks and the older humanists who scorned science. True enough, the younger men coming to the fore in the 1930's,

[60]   Letter dated February 20, 1940, from the Read Bain Files, Michigan Historical Collections.

such as Lynd (1892–   ), Bain, Lundberg (1895–1966), and Stouffer (1900–60), were urging the necessity of empirical research and statistical data, but their age peers—Blumer, Znaniecki (1882–1958), Abel (1896–   ), and Hughes—were their strongest opponents. MacIver (1882–   ) was slightly older, but so was Stuart Rice who represented (in the eyes of most sociologists) the new "statistical approach."

In fact, the debate is many generations old, and may be really an argument between two different temperaments. Every field embraces both. In physics, the stereotype of the experimental physicist is very different from that of the theoretical physicist. Darwin was willing to count earthworms, but many of his contemporaries in biology were not. John Howard (1729?–90) insisted on empirical studies of prisons and quarantine *lazarettis,* but most of his peers in the eighteenth century were little attracted by such inquiries. In every age, some men are more comfortable intuiting, observing, and thinking without a formal study design, while others work best only when they have gathered a mass of data themselves within a rigorous research plan.

Waller continued to work on these problems after he had left Pennsylvania State for Columbia. Indeed, the publication of *The Family* in 1938 intensified his interest in methodological issues. In a letter to Merton (then at Harvard) in that year, he confesses, ". . . the publication of the family book left me with a considerable feeling of insecurity." Thus, as earlier, he was acutely conscious of the limitations and defects of his method, "not the least of which is that the method depends almost altogether upon the concurrence of qualified observers for verification."

His doubts, and his interest, were also intensified by his experiences at Columbia, where Lynd and MacIver were constantly engaged in arguing about these matters, both in committee meetings and in print. (Lynd later opposed Waller's candidacy to a post in the graduate department because he preferred a colleague with a greater dedication to quantitative sociological studies. In that discussion, one colleague reported, ". . . as usual, Lynd got routed, but he nevertheless insisted that such a man would enhance Columbia's reputation.")

Perhaps as a consequence of these debates, and undoubtedly as a result of his continuing interest in methodology, Waller appears to have embarked on a project to examine these issues more closely. Whether he planned a series of short papers like his earlier "Insight and Scientific Method," or a major critique of social science methodology, cannot now be judged, since only several drafts on related topics remain. In one of these, Waller collaborated with a graduate student, Saul Levine. How much is Waller's work is not clear. The style is Waller's, but the content often branches into technical epistemological areas that he did not ordinarily deal with in his publications. Most of these essays contain no date, and no author is noted. The references all suggest that they were written while Waller was at Columbia. The titles are: "On the Nature of Concepts," "The Implications of a Logical Concept of Scientific Progress," "The Quantitative Application of Sociological Categories," and "A Textbook of Operationally Defined Concepts."

As the titles suggest, his early methodological concerns were broadening into a more general interest in the philosophy of science and scientific method. Little of his originality or grace is to be found in these essays, though of course they are no more than drafts. In the best of them, "On the Nature of Concepts," he examines the problem of the development of sociological concepts, arguing that often our concepts have no empirical referent at all, and that their meanings may shift easily because of their vagueness:

A writer gets to playing with definitions, and presently he arrives at combinations of words for which he has no attendant patterns of perception. . . . An attempt is made to communicate a conceptual system, and what is communicated is only a set of words. . . . The literature of sociology gives abundant testimony that this defect in one's equipment does not always prevent him from contributing books and articles to the field. He knows the words, but does not know what they refer to; does not know, indeed, that there is a "what" to which they sometimes refer.[61]

This "vice of verbalism" can best be counteracted, Waller

[61]   "On the Nature of Concepts," unpublished manuscript, p. 9.

urges with his characteristic affection for literature, by a literary approach that uses rich and well-chosen descriptive material to evoke and convey the central meaning of the sociological concept:

... the communication of perceptual patterns must remain an essentially literary task, and the good sociologist must therefore be a master of the arts of language.[62]

It is not surprising that Waller, like others who took part in this conflict, concludes by justifying the kind of sociology he does best:

Methodological discussions on the abstract level cannot accomplish much; even the critique of concepts is less a matter of pure logic than of research. If one determinedly and intelligently attacks reality, he will, almost of necessity, improve his concepts, i.e., his methodology.[63]

That is, we sharpen our concepts by the research experience itself.

Unfortunately, and ironically, the other methodological papers support by example his accusation that such discussions "cannot accomplish much." They achieve little more than a review of the methodological foundations of his own inquiries.

That the "artistic-insight method" can be a source of ideas is clear, but how can its findings be verified? Waller states one criterion: "... if the artistic insight school is to contribute at all ... then the validity of perceptions (insights nonrepeatable, by definition) must depend on properties of consistency uniquely defined for the system."[64] He then goes on to lament, as many with his leaning have complained before and since, "Frequently it is the very profundity of an insight which makes it difficult to [repeat]."[65] Certainly none of the papers provides an answer to the problem. Perhaps the very arduousness of the task led him to delay the preparation of a final, publishable draft.

Nevertheless, Waller remained optimistic that "social scientists [would develop] a more exact and adaptable means for determining the truth values of their observations."[66] Until a "great

[62]   *Ibid.*, pp. 10–11.
[63]   *Ibid.*, p. 15.
[64]   "The Implication of a Logical Concept of Scientific Progress," unpublished manuscript, p. 13.
[65]   *Ibid.*
[66]   August 1, 1938, letter to Merton.

modern revolution of scientific thought" occurs, he would solve the problem of validity in his own research by "sticking to fairly obvious and well established points, by finding many statements of the same principle in different universes of discourse, and by paying attention to the comments which others make upon my work."[67]

The many reservations this practitioner of the "artistic insight" method felt about his own research techniques are omitted from his introduction to Edward C. Jandy's biography of Charles Horton Cooley.[68] Here especially it is clear that Waller looked to Cooley as a legitimation for his own research methods. His portrait of Cooley could easily be an idealized self-portrait:

He was a seer. He was a man who used his own mind as a broad highway into the mind of the human race, and a man who loved to express his thoughts well. He became a sociologist because the developing science of sociology gave him free scope for the kind of thing he wanted to do.[69]

Waller does, however, give some recognition to the inherent difficulties of the method in the hands of lesser men: "The trouble is that when most people try to use Cooley's methods the results are not very gratifying." His "solution" is really a hope rather than a procedure, but perhaps Waller had a potential candidate in mind when he prophesies:

Let them try, and let them come to their foreordained failure. Or let them try some other useful but easier sort of social investigation. Make scholars of them and let them pile up facts. Some day another Cooley will come, perhaps a tougher-minded one who knows more of the world, and he will take up where the original Cooley left off.[70]

V

In the winter of 1936–37, Josephine was pregnant again, her health was poor, and the oldest of their two boys had a mastoid

[67]   *Ibid.*
[68]   "Introduction," in *Charles Horton Cooley* (New York: Dryden, 1940), pp. 1–6. This volume, chapter 1.
[69]   *Ibid.*
[70]   *Ibid.*

condition. The Florida sun seemed to offer a healthful alternative to the bitter winter of Centre County, and so Josephine took the two boys south for several months, while Waller and Rowland shared the house in Boalsburg. From December, 1936, to March, 1937, we have an almost daily chronicle of Waller's life, for his letters to Josephine have been preserved. Interspersed among the frequent reports of crises with the furnace (no trivial concern in a region where the temperature may drop to 25° below zero) and the nocturnal escapades of their young cat, are descriptions of departmental affairs, personal comments, and reports of his work.

The winter of 1936–37 contains the key to much that happened to Waller later in New York City. During these few months, he was hard at work on *The Family* manuscript, Harvard recognized him by an offer of a summer appointment, and he accepted the chairmanship of the department at Wayne State University, only to turn it down in favor of an offer from Barnard College at Columbia University. The events of that winter altered Waller's conception of himself in relation both to the field of sociology and to his own position at Pennsylvania State. As job offers signaled his recognition, he indulged in some euphoria, along with some feelings of resentment that he had been slighted for so long. In the long run, as we shall see later, the expansion of opportunities that continued from this point until the end of his life seemed to be as professionally destructive as it was personally rewarding, but at this early stage Waller could, of course, only be pleased that others were beginning to recognize his worth.

In a fundamental way, this change in his external position was a vindication of his inner dreams, his stubborn sense that he would some day create and achieve. In looking back on his initial marital failure, he had clearly seen that just as Thelma had lived by her fictions about her importance within her social circle, so he had lived by his fictions. To experience the first stages of a vindication of one's fictions is heady indeed.

By 1936, as noted earlier, he had become dissatisfied with his position at Pennsylvania State. Not only did he feel it was a second-rate school, but he also felt that it was going downhill. (Here, he was wrong. Kingsley Davis replaced him and taught there for several years; Robert K. Merton taught there in the summer of 1938; and both Wilbert E. Moore and George Eaton Simpson added to the luster of the sociology department for some years. In the psychology department, several talented men were to come, including the scholar C. Ray Carpenter, whose field studies in the social psychology of primates were not to be equaled in the subsequent two decades.) Waller saw opportunity as partly dependent upon a man's university and department, and he was an ambitious man.[71]

"The Wayne situation," which Waller mentions in his first letter to Josephine in Florida, was created by his friend Jack Richards, who had been Assistant Dean at Pennsylvania State but who had recently joined David Henry's administration at Wayne University in Detroit. Richards had taken a Ph. D. in English at Pennsylvania State, and had known Waller before the Wayne offer came. The Wayne Department then had no chairman; such contingencies facilitate the recognition and upward mobility of even the most talented men. Usually, the men whom those contingencies favor believe they are worthy of the job and, usually, the men who offer the jobs believe they have given the inside track to the best man.

It may slightly surprise those younger men of talent now at major universities who are considering which of many offers may be worthy of them that Waller would be flattered by an offer from Wayne, but it should not be forgotten that even creative men did not easily find posts at the great university centers in Waller's time. Robert K. Merton was moving up the academic ladder at Tulane University, but in 1940 left a full professorship there to accept an assistant professorship at Columbia. Paul F. Lazarsfeld, almost Waller's age, was eking out a marginal existence at Princeton. And Talcott Parsons at Harvard, only three years younger than Waller, did not rise above an assistant professorship until 1936, when he was elevated to the dignity of an associate professor-

---

[71]   For a study of the relationship of prestige of school and recognition, see Stephen Cole and Jonathan R. Cole, "Visibility and the Structural Basis of Awareness of Scientific Research," *American Sociological Review* 33 (June 1968) : 397–413.

ship just before the publication of *The Structure of Social Action.*

In his letters Waller expressed to his wife his usual optimistic miscalculation of the opportunities the new job seemed to offer. After a visit to Wayne in December, where he was met formally at the train and had talks with the administration and the sociology staff, he became aware of his increased stature. He thought Wayne was a "coming institution," and that the faculty had "a sense of going places and doing things." He reviewed imaginatively the problems of being chairman: "I feel I could certainly handle them. I must have learned a good deal more in the past few years than I had ever realized, because they seemed very much like simple souls. . . . I would have no difficulty in ultimately being their boss." Seeing his greater stature in others' eyes, he came to believe in it himself.

On the same day that he learned by the grapevine that the Wayne chairmanship would be his, Pitirim Sorokin asked him to teach in the summer school at Harvard University. (Sorokin was aware of his work, and in 1932 had written a complimentary letter to the publisher of *The Sociology of Teaching.*) Waller wrote, ". . . I was completely flabbergasted . . . I wired my reply . . . and went around the rest of the day in a daze." A few days later, the Wayne post was offered officially, with a salary of $5,000 and automatic increments for a few years, an increase of more than fifty per cent over his Pennsylvania State salary.

Waller then went to the December meetings of the American Sociological Society in Chicago with a new sense of his own importance, and so did his colleagues. He held the key to one chair, at Pennsylvania State, and as the new chairman at Wayne, the power to appoint men to new jobs. Whatever prior evaluations people hold, official recognition validates some and questions others. After the fact, many men can announce, in all honesty if minimum correctness, that they "had always expected" acclaim would be given to the newly appointed man. The chairman-to-be of Wayne was aware of all this, and was not entirely pleased. He wrote Josephine:

The news . . . had apparently already changed my status in the sociological universe. That really irks me no end, because I was just as good a man two years ago as I am now. . . . Why should people who had no time for me then have so much time now?

In Chicago, he and MacIver had a long talk in which the elder man praised his work at length and mentioned that a position might be opening up at Barnard College of Columbia University in a year or so. Waller reflected on this—almost too naively, one suspects—"I wonder why he told me all that." He learned from Howard Becker that there might be a chance to go to Harvard permanently, since Becker seemed then to be out of the running. In mock simplicity Waller comments, "It is a little bewildering to poor old pop, who was ready to retire to the farm some three months ago.

He now became aware that he might actually realize some of his fantasies and dreams, and become important in sociology. And all this after some years of work and struggle where the outcome had not been evident: "I have a feeling of going through an immensely difficult period of my life, of undergoing hardships which I hope will soon pass away." As he wrote his wife in this period, "I have been using myself very hard and hoping that I survive both mentally and physically."

At the convention, he found he had become a "sociometric star," in the jargon of the postwar period. His work had, perhaps, reached a critical mass, and people had begun to identify him with positions, issues, styles, and particular research studies. He was also perceptive enough to turn his new status around, and look at it coolly from the other side. The convention was "one grand, confused blur" but he began quickly to sort it all out. People who wanted to come to Pennsylvania State or Wayne sought him out. He began to see for the first time that there were burdens that accompanied the privileges of power

. . . every time I appeared in the lobby there seemed to be ten or fifteen people waiting to catch hold of me . . . several times . . . I would be talking to someone, and then someone else would come up . . . and I would go away to talk to him for a minute, and someone else would come up and pull the same stunt.

Well, I am getting a lot of insight into the whole thing now. I see how hard it must be for the really big shots in the society to get anything done at all.

And I understand now why I was never able to meet them as easily as I wished . . . they were all closeted with persons whom they wanted to know, just as I was at [this] meeting.

Though he rejoiced in the opening of these doors, an inner tension remained. (While at Pennsylvania State he had begun to be plagued with migraine headaches, and these continued for the rest of his life. He learned to anticipate when they were coming, and to lessen their impact by taking long walks or by hard physical exertion, but he was never able to escape them altogether.)

MacIver's attempt to feel out his availability for a Columbia position linked with several other small events, which soon crystallized in a definite offer from Columbia. Theodore Abel was then at Columbia, and had been favorably impressed with Waller through conversations at meetings and reading his work. Knowing of the Barnard job, Abel brought Waller to MacIver's attention. Doubtless, too, Waller himself was a more impressive figure in his intellectual exchange with MacIver because of his greater confidence after the Wayne offer. The social validation of the Wayne job led others to pay Waller more respect, which would have made his candidacy more persuasive to the Columbia men. Finally, it is likely that the small accident of his work on the manuscript of MacIver's book *Society* gave further evidence of his abilities.

In the fall of 1936, Farrar and Rinehart had asked Waller to write a criticism of MacIver's manuscript. Almost all academic manuscripts are sent to younger men (because they are most willing to accept the task, being perpetually short of funds) to be examined for factual or theoretical errors, omissions, and plain foolishness. To some men, the task is pleasant enough, because one can attack and dissect without fear of reprisal: the author does not know his critic. This aspect of book writing is less savage than it might be, because most men will not invest much intellectual energy in the job; a high percentage of manuscripts are too boring to be read carefully, and only rarely does the anonymous critic encounter the happy situation in which the manuscript is fun to read and contains enough complex problems to excite him to detailed argument and comment.

Waller found himself in just such an exciting situation. MacIver's book was excellent enough to become for some years a widely respected statement of sociological principles. MacIver had done, and done very well indeed, the kind of sociological work that Waller most respected; the kind of work that Waller, at that time, was trying to do with his family book. Waller wrote to the publishers that "the book is as original as Sumner's *Folkways,* and as thoughtful and beautifully expressed as anything of Cooley's." If someone had wanted to please Waller by praise this is exactly the praise that would have pleased him the most; original insight expressed in great prose was what he wanted from himself and what the men he most respected had accomplished. "The fact-grubbing pedants," as he called his scholarly colleagues, might accomplish something, but not anything that he would greatly respect.

His comments on MacIver's manuscript were detailed and apparently helpful. Aside from his excitement over the work itself, he labored over the manuscript, for he hoped that if his critique was first-rate, his fee from the publishers would be more substantial. (Nor was he disappointed. In January, 1937, he wrote to Josephine, "After the lecture, I went to the office and found the long and ardently awaited letter from Farrar and Rinehart. And a check for thirty-five dollars. I think I can meet all the bills. . . .")

Authors do not usually learn—for publishers do not want to create dissension among colleagues—who writes such critiques, but they can sometimes find out if they tell their publisher they judge the critique to be excellent. It is possible that MacIver did not know at just this time that Waller had written the laudatory critique, but he found out at some point, since he later expressed his gratitude for Waller's suggestions. It would have been, in any case, only one of the several minor events that interlinked to create the job offer.

Feeling free to reveal his secret dreams, Waller wrote to his first wife after the convention (he and Rowland had visited her and her second husband briefly), "It begins to seem not wholly unreasonable to believe that I have some chance of being one of the important persons of my generation." Looking back at this crucial period, a Pennsylvania State friend wrote that the school was a sort of "launching site" for Waller. Perhaps, as Waller himself thought, Pennsylvania State had held him back from rising in the profession even earlier. Unfortunately, as we look more closely at his work during the Columbia period, we may also conclude that it was good that Waller had not been launched earlier.

When MacIver's formal letter of inquiry came in mid-February, Waller sensed correctly the appropriate style to follow in responding to Columbia. The letter asked whether he was irrevocably committed to Wayne. His response was restained, emphasizing the excellent terms Wayne had offered, and his moral obligation to go to Wayne unless the school was entirely willing to release him—but cautiously predicting that the Wayne people would surely not wish to stand in the way of such a challenging opportunity as a position at Columbia. To Josephine, however, his emotions were less inhibited:

> I opened the envelope all unsuspecting and read the . . . startling words. . . . A new job prospect beyond all my immediate dreams. . . .
> . . . If I am considered at Columbia and do not get it, that is all right. I can take it, and I will still be glad to be at Wayne. But if I am not considered, I would always have the thought in the back of my head that I have messed up the only good chance that ever came my way.

A few days later, having wallowed for a while in the delight of rising expectations, he wrote again to his wife:

> Absolutely no news on the job front today. Nothing from Harvard yet and nothing from Chicago. . . . I have decided that if Columbia will give me fifteen thousand I will go. And maybe I will go for less than that, but not for a cent less than five thousand.

The swirl of excitement distracted him from working, however, and he remarked wryly, "Funny how the price for my services has been going up. I have an awfully uneasy feeling . . . but the good old ego is a great help." At a deeper level, he saw the possibility of failure. Up to this time, he had not faced any challenges that he could not master, and secretly he had envisioned himself on a still greater stage. But what if he overshot, or what if he donned the new robes only to trip over them? What if his writing did not meet Columbia's standards? Writing of these thoughts to his wife, he muses:

> . . . imagining what it would be like to be a big shot at the top of the field and drawing a top-flight salary—thinking about living in New York City—all these things don't help the work very much.
>
> There is also the fact that I want everything to be perfect if it has to be issued from Columbia—if I go there.

Over a mid-winter period of a few weeks, his prospects had so radically changed that he lost his solid base of prosaic self-evaluation. At one moment he resents the neglect he had suffered at Pennsylvania State and is excited at the idea of how important he can and should be: at another, he is anxious that he cannot meet Columbia's standards. One day he leaves the Wayne staff sure he can "handle" them; on another day he takes a second and sobering look at his Pennsylvania State colleagues, a group for whom he had previously had little respect, and expresses a different view, understanding simultaneously that what had happened to them might have happened to himself, if Columbia had not come forward:

> The meeting of the division heads left me with really mixed emotions. They are stuffy fellows and haven't got much on the ball, as anyone can see. But at the same time, they do look and act somewhat impressively when they get together.
>
> At one moment I am glad that I am getting away from them and at another doubtful of my ability to come out in any very much faster company. I guess the point is that they are really persons of some ability, but so tied down with their job and with the schoolmasterishness that goes with it, that they will never amount to any more than they do now. Whereas, I keep hoping that I can go on learning.

As in Cooley's "looking glass self." Waller say in others' eyes a different, bigger man reflected, and had to believe that some of what he saw mirrowed reality. On the other hand, he had devoted a lifetime to doubting the validity of the judgments made by the official world.

In mid-March he went for an interview at Barnard. In order to be better able to handle the intellectual exchange that he imagined would occur, he read all of MacIver's work. He thought that preparations had been made for an interview with Virginia Gildersleeve, then Dean of Barnard College, and believed that her father was the great classicist Basil Gildersleeve. His strategy for this interview was more oblique:

I got out my Cicero this morning and have been re-reading him. It is surprising how quickly it all comes back. I shall plan to read a little every day, and mow Miss G down by a few nicely rounded periodic sentences.

Actually, as so often happened at Columbia then and later, no preparations had been made for an interview—which may have been fortunate, since Basil Gildersleeve was not, as it turned out, Dean Gildersleeve's father.

Waller believed himself to be qualified, but was not so confident as to suppose that others would surely recognize his merit. After talking with MacIver at Columbia his self-confidence returned, though he was not certain about the job. Writing of his disappointment that adequate preparation had not been made for his two main appointments, he adds, ". . . what an anticlimax Columbia has been so far. . . . After looking over Columbia, I am not so terribly impressed."

On a later visit after this fiasco, however, he did talk with the appropriate Columbia people, received an offer, and was released by Wayne University from his obligation to accept the chairmanship there. After his summer classes at Harvard University in 1937 he joined the Barnard staff—salary, $5500 a year.

New York City and Columbia University offered all that Waller anticipated, but contained much that he had not anticipated. Although his *Sociology of Higher Education* takes full cognizance of the material and intellectual advantages a first-rate academic center offers to the ambitious young man, it neglects both its dangers and the "adult socialization" necessary to guard against these dangers. A talented young man who is "reared" at, say, Harvard University is guided and encouraged not only in his scientific growth, but also in his evaluations of the widening opportunities that the world offers him. His mentors discourage him gently from taking seriously, say, a chairmanship at high pay in a lesser school, because, as they point out, the facilities for research are meager. If he is in financial difficulties it is permissible to give a popular lecture or a series of lectures to an adult night school, but it is understood clearly that this is not an appropriate activity and is an unwise allocation of limited energies. Prematurely accepting a teaching post, while a man is still working on his graduate degrees, is judged to be not merely foolish, but possible evidence that the man has wrong values. Intellectual growth is much more important than getting started on the job ladder: after all, *that* kind of success can be taken for granted if one is talented and hard-working (and is backed by such sponsors).

It is erroneous to claim, as do some critics of the academic establishment, that the young professor loses standing by writing for popular journals, or roving the lecture circuit, but (unlike the evaluations at lesser colleges) whatever success he has in these spheres gives him absolutely no standing whatsoever in the eyes of his colleagues. They may envy his success or deplore it, but when they come to judge him professionally his excellence in such areas helps him not at all. They will take seriously only the core, his scientific work. If that is first-rate, his importance in other spheres will not harm him. On the other hand, if it is not, they may well ask whether he has in fact allocated enough energy and talent to his main job, which is to move beyond the frontiers of knowledge.

Such a socialization is likely to begin in a man's undergraduate days, when he first starts to think seriously of dedicating himself to research and scholarship. Waller's undergraduate period, by contrast, was spent at colleges where this mandarin pattern was uncommon, and it must be kept in mind that his goal at that time was to become a high school language teacher.

At the University of Chicago, he was a part-time student, living at Morgan Park and still not a protegé or apprentice to one of the great professors. He was a graduate student in the center of things at the University of Pennsylvania, but by that time he was already a college teacher, embarked on his career.

The recurring pressures of social control are as important as the socialization process in shaping behavior. The young academic learns from such influences not only that it is *wrong* to succumb to nonacademic opportunities, but that it is unnecessary and unprofitable. In general, academic virtue actually pays off. Never having had a sponsor who saw to it that academic opportunities would appear at the appropriate times, Waller had learned merely that opportunities were rare. Having lived through a depression, he was hungry for a wide variety of new experiences and fields for exploration, although the professor for whom the system of social control has worked will know that these experiences will come along anyway, and can be enjoyed without neglecting a life of scholarship.

Even at Columbia, he was not invited by the insiders to join them, so that when alternatives to a dedicated academic life appeared, they seemed especially attractive. By contrast with the apparently low payoffs (rank and security) to be encountered in a career devoted only to social science at a major university, Waller could perceive innumerable interesting and profitable alternative roads to pursue once he had settled in New York.

Perhaps equally important in determining his behavior for the few remaining years of his life was another factor, a strength of his that concealed a weakness: the virtue of many young academics, like that of many young women, is saved by never being tempted. The academic who naturally appeals to laymen must be more wary than others if he wishes to hold fast to his main goal of intellectual creation. Otherwise, he will be seduced away from that austere aim. But Waller appealed to people of high and low rank, to intellectuals and to lowbrows, and even had a talent for business (as well as a keen interest in it.) Many of his intellectual concerns were the concerns of most human beings, and so his rising popularity could have been predicted.

With perhaps pardonable exaggeration, one can speak of his intellectual "suicide" in New York City. In one of the few classics of sociology, *Suicide*, Emile Durkheim argues from an analysis of the economic cycle that though the suicide rate rises when an economic depression occurs, it will also go up when a sharp burst of prosperity occurs. In simple terms, those who experience sudden good fortune—what Morris Zelditch once called the "sociological bends"—lose the possibility of satisfaction, because satisfaction can only arise from a close correlation between hopes or expectations, and reality. When the reality expands beyond the standards by which we measure how well we are doing, the standards lose their sway, aspirations soar still higher, and soon nothing is adequate. Doubtless the anomie of failure is more destructive than the anomie of success (it is certainly more frequent), but both occur, and Waller exhibits richly the difficulties of holding to a straight course when opportunities are offered from all directions. Like a hungry small boy at a great feast, he grabbed with both hands, but in the process he forgot that he was merely hungry. The result was disastrous for his academic work. A wiser perspective that specifies the catastrophe, however, will also limit its dimensions, and remove from it the taint of cliché. The mere failure of a man to reach his highest creative potential is unfortunate but can hardly be classed as a disaster, for it is as nearly the common lot of men as disease, or death.

Can we delineate the character of Waller's defeat? In the forced absence of the data, we can only wrestle with the tantalizing question of what Waller would have explored had he been granted enough time to transmute his new experiences into new ideas; or indeed whether he would have dedicated himself once again to creative sociological analyses. Because of Waller's style of work, it seems fair to argue that his particular defeat was narrowly intellectual, and perhaps only temporary. Had he lived even a decade longer, he might once again have drawn rich insights from his life. It is even possible to sketch the general directions those new explorations might have taken.

It is equally possible, however—and we believe this is the more likely guess—that had a really exciting position or opportunity presented itself outside of academic social science, he would have accepted it. At the deepest levels he was an intellectual and ambitious, but he did not have the same dedication to a professorial life that he had to the intellectual life, or to life generally. He would not have been seduced easily by money alone, but he could have been diverted from academic sociology by a challenging task beyond the academy. But the years left to him were few, and no exciting job away from the university was offered to him.

In the narrowest sense of intellectual output, Waller published little creative sociology after *The Family* in 1938. In the period 1937–39, he published only two articles of note, one of them his perceptive analysis of rating and dating and the other an application of sociology to the problems of education.[72] The former was written before he came to New York.

In the period 1940–45 (when few creative men were doing work outside the war effort), his only professional article of consequence is an analysis of Charles Horton Cooley, written as the introduction to a biography of that master of intuitive observation.[73] But during that same five-year period (and aside from his two books on war and the veteran) he published at least twelve popular articles, and in the last eighteen months of his life, we have a record of about forty-five speeches, radio appearances, conferences, or talks of a formal type, together with invitations to contribute short articles to special-interest publications such as *Future* (Junior Chamber of Commerce), *The Record* (New York Veteran's Service Agency), and the *Chicago Defender*. From the correspondence, it may also be deduced that he rarely refused these invitations. (Almost all of this activity had to do with the returning veteran.)

Waller wrote and spoke with facility, and tried to prepare new ideas or perspectives for these appearances. The speeches (we have a few outlines) and articles are adequate as journalism, but hardly add to our fund of sociological knowledge. At best, we are underestimating his allocations of time and energy to essentially jour-

[72]   "The Rating and Dating Complex," *American Sociological Review*, 2 (October, 1937): 727–34, this volume, chapter 6; "Contributions to Education of Scientific Knowledge About the Organization of Society and Social Pathology," National Society for the Study of Education *37th Year Book*, pt. 2, 1938, pp. 445–60.
[73]   Edward C. Jandy, *Charles Horton Cooley* (New York: Dryden Press, 1942), pp. 1–6; reprinted this volume, chapter 1.

nalistic activities, for while we have a complete record of his sociological writings, only scanty remnants of correspondence remain from which to total his journalistic writings and public speeches. Moreover, we are leaving aside for later comment his other nonscholarly activities, which doubtless bulked large in his total time budget.

In the lives of some men, these bare figures would have a self-evident meaning: the scholar, scientist, or artist has gradually abandoned his metiér and sought the easier, immediate rewards of public success. Clichés abound to describe this process; We say that the novelist has been corrupted by success, or has abandoned his high aspirations in order to court applause. The talented actor goes to Hollywood and accepts typecast roles so that he can pay for his expensive ménage. An F. Scott Fitzgerald compromises his art because his tastes are expensive. The painter is seduced by the plaudits of suburban clubwomen and postures as an esthete rather than confronting a continuing artistic challenge. The social scientist becomes a prophet because that is easier than seeking order amid the bewildering surface phenomena of human behavior.

But we are not entirely certain that we can apply these clichés to Willard Waller, however diffuse and intellectually superficial many of his activities in this last period may seem. First, and perhaps most important, Waller wanted both to learn and to teach, but it was his view that these tasks ought not to be confined to the university. To leave the university, then, would not have been the same self-betrayal for Waller that it might have been for a man whose inquiries and reports to others would cease when he left academic life.

Second, few men ever change their *styles* of work, and Waller's remained constant: to work hard, and to draw upon his life for his sociological formulations. He drank deeply of the intoxicating brew that is New York City and the higher levels of academic life. As always in the past, he "tried on" new roles and assimilated them into his thinking. Everything was grist for his sociological mill. He had utilized the roles of date, bridegroom, husband, divorcé, graduate student, high school teacher, professor, military man, and veteran, and now he entered new ones: editor, business man, and investor; power manipulator and consultant; research director and sponsor; public figure and advocate for veterans; administrator (chairman of the department, school board member); and journalist and public speaker.

He may have *seemed* to be neglecting his work for such activities, and certainly he delighted in them for their own sake, reporting to friends his new observations about these fascinating worlds. He felt that he was moving behind the scenes into relationships that he had previously only read about. However, his style was to probe them intellectually, to try out his analyses in the classroom, and eventually to integrate them into a sociological framework. This period might have been, then, not the corruption of the small-town boy by the big city, but a phase of field work, of gathering data, during which it is only natural to forego publication.

Of course, all sociologists use their personal experience when they engage in research. Even the most slavish devotee of survey research does this. Most do not, however, report their personal lives so openly as did Waller. The more theoretically oriented try to move outside their personal experiences, while being motivated or sensitized to important relationships because of these human adventures. Some sociologists treat such events as clinical cases; others use them to formulate new and interesting problems; still others suppose their own experiences, though forming a sample of only one case, can be viewed as an adequate sample of the universe without need of correction, and as a result some odd biases may result.

Waller's analyses remain closer to his raw experience than is common in contemporary sociology, but they are saved from personal bias by three factors—which also might have prevented him from being really corrupted by the many temptations to abandon scientific work that this last period offered. First, he did not give complete allegiance to any of these roles or personal experiences, since he was pulled away by still other possible experiences and people. He always observed; he did not merely participate. Second, he retained intact a core of derisiveness, an insistence that the façades and symbols, the pomp of authority (even his own) have a certain hollowness at their core. He could laugh at his own personal dramas. Third, and methodologically of greater consequence, in such private happenings Waller was a precursor (as noted earlier) of those contemporary sociologists who demand more rigorous proof that social reality is as the textbooks describe it. When Harold Garfinkel suggests that we test whether a supposed norm does exist by watching what happens when we violate it— for example, ascertaining whether the "fixed price" *is* a norm, by haggling over the price of an emerald at Tiffany's or a sofa at Macy's—he is stating formally what Waller was often doing in his idiosyncratic explorations of his new roles. Waller was capable of making outrageous suggestions, or of offering offbeat interpretations, as a way of testing social limits, of ascertaining the real dimensions and forces in social interaction. He would enter much further into a new relationship, without being committed to it, than most sociologists would, because he wanted to "see what would happen."

These three factors, then, forced a continuing confrontation between his individual guesses or hypotheses and external reality. Thus, many potential biases from personal experience were corrected. At the same time, those same factors made it somewhat less likely that any group or set of roles would have been able to capture him entirely, or deflect him from his dedication to scientific work—except, possibly, a highly exciting practical challenge that would have put his sociology to work.

In these terms, then, the catastrophe of his last period was limited, and might have endured for only a short time. Waller did almost cease to publish sociologically important work in his appetite for exploring alternative areas of possible success, but he died before he could weave these new observations into a still more creative design, if indeed he was heading in that direction.

To recreate the last period of Waller's life is peculiarly difficult. Ironically, he begins to "disappear" from our records precisely when he becomes an important figure on the national stage—called to Washington to consult, invited to lecture before university and popular audiences, asked to contribute articles to mass-circulation magazines, introduced to other distinguished men—but though this is ironic, it exemplifies several changes in the life style and status of professors in our time. Now as in the past, of course, if a man achieves success early and lives a long time he is likely to acquire both the motivation and the facilities for organizing and maintaining his files. Others suggest this pattern to him, and sometimes even a biographer may appear to affirm this procedure. Unfortunately, Waller did not reach eminence early, and his files were not kept for the biographer.

However, the altered status of the professor has also changed the kinds of records available to us. Most striking is perhaps the disappearance of letters. This is partly an age difference: Fewer of the younger scholars now write at length or keep letters. However, it is also a generational *change*, one that was beginning when Waller came to Columbia. Coping with the modern flood of communication at all is a problem for many, and as people become successful the flood increases. Fewer professors now try to compose real letters than did a generation ago. Correspondingly, since a higher percentage of letters are either trivial, or merely formal notices that are important for only a brief time, still fewer professors bother to maintain their personal files.

In addition, the modern, itinerant academic is more likely to cull his old files, since he moves more often. As a consequence, far fewer of those letters which permit the biographer to locate events, emotions, or relationships in time and place are now available. Not only were Waller's own files destroyed shortly after his death, but many of his friends' files have been destroyed or discarded since that time.

Another change occurred to Waller that he shares with the modern professor: His social network expanded greatly. Waller's social network encompassed capitalists and laborers, students and professors, veterans' organizations, and governmental agencies. The change may make the biographer's task more difficult. His network was, in the technical sense, "loose"; that is, many people saw him, but only a few of those people saw one another. Thus, locating one group or set does not inevitably lead to knowing about others.

In addition, in such a loose, large network, each person knew *less* about him than his old friends had—and even his friends could not keep track of this wider social pattern. People who knew him may remember a brilliant conversation (whose content is now lost), but they did not see enough of his daily life over time to describe more than an encounter. As so many essayists have remarked about these processes, life in a large city is likely to be compartmentalized, and interaction superficial. Thus, our interviews with the many people who knew Waller in his later years often give us less added understanding about the man than a long perusal of a dead document, such as a transcript of courses taken in graduate school.

These processes have become part of the life style and status of modern professors, and they are intensified by still another factor. Academic people are the keepers of records, as they are the authors of histories, but they have not expended much energy on records of nonscholarly acts. Much of Waller's later life took place in nonscholarly circles—popular audiences, patients in a naval hospital, a radio forum, a business luncheon—and records of such events have a short life. Perhaps this growing involvement of professors with the nonacademic community was exhibited first among physical scientists, in the early 1940's, and gradually spread to other fields.

The relatively successful sociologist of the late 1930's took two major trips each year, one to the meetings of the American Sociological Association (then Society), and the other to teach summer school when, through adroit log-rolling, a friend arranged that welcome addition to his income. His contemporary peer must, by contrast, watch cautiously to avoid overextending himself in too many conferences. Sociologists still wrote lengthy letters in the early 1940's, offering their new hypotheses and interpretations of social events, or a brief review of a book just read. The modern social scientist picks up the telephone to report, or ask, what is going on. He "sees" his colleagues more often, by jet or telephone, and indeed often wishes that he could sit undisturbed in his study, as his academic ancestors did. Whatever the cost, the result is a slimmer body of useful archives for biographers. Among moderns, perhaps only the very successful political figures as a class are likely to be surrounded by staff and apparatus enough to bring together all their materials for later historians and biographers.

The modern sociologist has far more voice in national affairs, more opportunities to be heard by popular audiences, a larger income from both salary and other sources, and more research grants, but he has paid for it all at a rather high cost: He is devoured by his very opportunities. Waller seemed to be, too, in the last years of his life, but there is no evidence that he lamented. He had long wanted all these experiences. Moreover, though the sociologist now judges that such activities take him away from his real work—social research—for Waller they were the essence of his data-gathering.

During his tenure at Columbia, the center of power was located in the professorial staff in the Graduate Faculty of Political Science: Robert MacIver, Robert S. Lynd, Theodore Abel, the statistician Robert Chaddock (1879–1940), Paul F. Lazarsfeld, and Robert K. Merton. In 1937 Lazarfeld had brought the Office of Radio Research, later transformed into the Bureau of Applied Social Research, to Columbia. In 1940, he became a member of the department. In 1941 Merton left his chairmanship and full professorship at Tulane to join the staff as an assistant professor. During Waller's tenure at Columbia, only the University of Chicago had a stronger department of sociology. MacIver had been engaged for some time in the task of strengthening sociology at Columbia, and though not all was harmony during his leadership, without question Columbia was in the forefront of sociological research when he retired.

Waller was on friendly terms with all of these men, but they were not the center of his social network, and he was very much on the periphery of theirs. Since a new man typically enters a department with the advantage that his colleagues know little of his bad qualities, it was not the occasional abrasiveness of his personality that placed him somewhat on the outside. At that time, and during the ensuing two decades, a sharp structural division separated the subdepartments of Columbia University. Both Teachers College and Barnard were on separate budgets, but any significant appointment at Barnard was unlikely without the approval of the Graduate Department. Until recently, only Edmund DeS. Brunner (1889–   ), the distinguished rural sociologist, had a joint appointment in both Teachers College and the Graduate Department. Bernhard J. Stern (1894–1956), whose Marxian sociology illuminated many areas of American life, taught some courses in Columbia College, but worked mainly in what later became the School of General Studies. William Casey, who published little but who was for years the most popular sociology teacher in Columbia College, occasionally taught a graduate course, but was not a member of "the" Department and indeed was not promoted to a full professorship until his retirement. "Outsiders" like Alexander von Schelting and Thorsten Sellin came from time to time to offer courses in one or another of these divisions, but they did not become part of the inner group.

Thus in Waller's time, as well as later, there were in effect five relatively independent sociology departments at Columbia, and their formal arrangements required only minimal interaction. As persons, men could freely choose their friends or intellectual companions. The effect of such formal separations, however, the immensely greater power and prestige of the Graduate Department, and the physical separation of offices is obvious: by and large, men within any subdepartment saw more of one another than of men in any of the other subdepartments; and the focus of attention was on the graduate professors.

Since this is not the usual departmental structure in other universities, perhaps an additional comment is warranted. As noted earlier, Merton had been a full professor and chairman at Tulane, and joined Columbia in 1941 as an assistant professor. In academia, as elsewhere, brilliant young men are willing to go at some cost to where the action is. Merton was *not*, however, a member of the Graduate Department at first, and neither was Lazarsfeld when he was first appointed. At Columbia, this full acceptance was denied, in sociology as in other fields, to many men who seemed equal in merit to those on the inside. It is fair to say, however, that on the average the achievements of men in the graduate departments were greater than those in the other subdepartments. In any event, men in the graduate departments were the senators. Their decisions determined events in the other divisions of sociology; academic social structures have generally supported free speech, but not equal suffrage.

It is unfortunate that Waller was not brought into this circle of mandarins, for he might have made insightful (and doubtless acerb) analyses of its structure. He might also have observed one of its peculiarities, one which affected his own position. Although MacIver was easily the dominant figure, all the members of the department were strong, brilliant, and competent. No one could ignore the opinion of another. One result of this was that a vote was rarely taken. In the face of sharply divided opinion, the issue —or a candidate—was dropped. When Lynd strongly opposed inviting Waller to "cross the street" (as MacIver had done) and become a member of the Graduate Department, Waller's candidacy was dropped. Instead of Waller, Lynd suggested they invite Louis Wirth, Leonard S. Cottrell (1899–   ), or Samuel Stouffer. These men represented "quantitative sociology," while in Lynd's view Waller lacked any interest in quantification. Lynd failed to convince his opponents of the need for quantifiers in the Department. The others challenged him to name the "quantification" monographs that could stand comparison with *The Polish Peasant*, his own *Middletown*, or *The Negro Family in the United States* by E. Franklin Frazier (1894–1962). Lynd could not, but senatorial courtesy prevailed and Waller was never asked to join.

Waller felt that his work was not receiving adequate recognition, and he was, in fact, never promoted to full professor. Now, two and a half decades after his death, it is not possible to ascertain whether this represented a strong negative judgment. Such matters are often lost historically, and indeed are sometimes not easy to pin down while they are happening. A nonpromotion may not have been an explicit decision. A younger man is delayed because "he is not ready," though just what being "ready" means is not clarified. An older man's possible promotion may be left undiscussed because it might be a problem, or because it is viewed as an issue of low priority. In any event, it must be remembered that Waller had been a full professor and chairman and had stepped down in rank in order to accept the Columbia offer.

In the early 1940's, as MacIver has remarked, promotion was relatively slow. There was no shortage of college professors, and universities had curtailed many of their operations because of the war. Further promotion at Columbia was not solely a departmental matter, but was decided by a committee made up of one member from each of the five departments in the Graduate Faculty of Political Science. If a man's work was not well known to men outside his department, his chances were lowered. Moreover, MacIver was trying to build the department, which meant that any available money was more likely to be used to hire new people than to promote those already there. Under such possibly ambiguous circumstances, a man is more likely to feel at worst a vague resentment rather than an active hostility toward his colleagues. In fact, though Waller never hesitated to criticize his fellow sociologists severely, he liked them.

But though he remained an associate professor as well as an outsider, Waller's position should not be dramatized or romanticized. He was not a loner, and he was certainly not snubbed. He did not participate in the regular poker games that included mainly the members of the Graduate Department, but poker was not his idea of fun. The maverick is typically outside in part by choice. Other things interest him more than being inside, and he judges the cost of entrance to be overly expensive. His colleagues liked Waller and respected his work, and though some of his fellow professors outside sociology thought his work was not scholarly enough, his fellow sociologists did not share this opinion, and did not think his work was falling off in quality in the period before his death.

He would not have felt, or behaved, like a senator, however, even had he been brought into the inner circle. At Barnard, he was willing to violate the unspoken rule (observed generally in university life) that colleagues are not to mention publicly that a man is engaged in empire building, or that he wishes to add a course or change the curriculum for his own advantage. He did not hold back his opinions in order to maintain the pleasant fiction of harmonious colleagueship. Charming as he was in conversation with his fellow professors, Waller was intense, almost fierce, in his challenge of accepted beliefs, so that interaction with him was not easy or smooth. His office mate, Mirra Komarovsky (1905–   ), remarks that it was difficult to get work done when he was there. He was too stimulating, too full of ideas, too ready to drop the pedestrian, necessary tasks in order to probe yet another social phenomenon.

His cynicism, too, made some colleagues uneasy, for he forced them to inquire into deeper motives for their or others' actions. This social trait is unsettling to others, though its utility for a social analyst is clear. In commenting on Waller's "sardonic detachment," Everett C. Hughes (who had been a classmate at the University of Chicago) writes:

Some people mistake this for an utter cynicism or for a misanthropic attitude. That is entirely wrong. This detachment which sounds a little bit cynical is found at its best among people whose attachment to the human race is very deep. Their attachment is not to one race or breed, but to the whole species.[74]

As more than one philosopher has remarked, a fierce cynicism is often the hurt reaction of the idealist to the failure of people to meet the highest standards. Consequently, though Waller came to Columbia with the same optimism he brought to every previous job, and a small-town boy's heel-clicking pleasure at his public success, it was inevitable that he would eventually decide that his colleagues were not so meritorious as he had hoped. And, no matter how cordial such a man may be, those about him soon correctly sense that they have been found a bit wanting.

But though such challenges and unmaskings make collegial interaction occasionally uneasy, they are an essential part of the professor-student relationship. Even when the student is outraged or troubled by such behavior, he is more likely to seek it and be exhilarated by it—perhaps because, unlike the mature professor, he can still do something about his own ignorance and failings. At Columbia, as at other universities, students felt that Waller's courses were a necessary part of their education: he changed his students, made them more aware and perceptive, and stretched their minds. Some (like his adult acquaintances) resented this assault, but most remembered the experience as rewarding.

[74]   Personal correspondence.

His lectures were not systematic, and had the defects and virtues of a personal interpretation. He often failed to present a sober "survey of the field," or a "balanced" statement of the facts on both sides. He would offer a plausible hypothesis with the same spellbinding enthusiasm that a fully tested one might deserve. His own aliveness and joy in examining a curious specimen of social behavior imbued his lectures with excitement.

Yet he was no narcissistic orator, content to hear his own voice. He tried to draw out, in class or in his office, the most timid student, and criticized those who would not step outside their assigned roles in order to examine them critically. In a student profile written in 1940, a student reported his opinion:

One of the main faults of Barnard students, [a cultural trait that persisted for years] is not speaking their own minds often enough. Professor Waller thinks . . . they ought to take more chances sticking out their necks. He believes they have some of a critical sense and an analytical one, too, under their silent exteriors.[75]

It is not surprising then that students took his courses in order to experience his mind, rather than because they were interested in the field of sociology. He was always free to talk with students, and had no large-scale research projects to make him regret the time he spent with them. He was not so much bringing them a message as engaging them in a common search for truth.

His influence was not confined to Barnard, but extended to graduate students at Teachers College and Columbia. For example, he lectured at Teachers College to majors in student personnel administration in the winter and spring of 1943–44, and to students in counseling during the following summer.[76] Through Burt Aginsky, the anthropologist, Waller met Abram Kardiner and began to participtate in some of the work he was doing at the Col-

[75]   Marjorie Davis, "Tough Guy," *Barnard Quarterly*, 1940, pp. 16–17. This issue also contains Waller's article, "Women and War," pp. 18–22.

[76]   In her letter to Waller of May 23, 1944, outlining the course arrangements, Esther Lloyd-Jones wrote that for the final meeting of her department, "you are the person whom we would most like to invite to be our guest speaker."

lege of Physicians and Surgeons with anthropological data.[77] This collaboration lasted only a short time for Waller thought Kardiner was simply "picking his brains," since Kardiner seldom said anything and Waller, as usual, talked all the time.

Although social relations in graduate sociology at Columbia University have a well-deserved reputation as being somewhat less than warm and intimate, whether among the staff or between staff and students; and the hierarchical distance from professors down to students has been described as too great to allow for adequate visibility, Waller *did* see graduate students both in and out of class. Unlikely as such an event may appear to alienated post-World War II sociology students who complain of being treated like unscanned IBM cards, their predecessors would frequently drop by Waller's house in Radburn, New Jersey, for an evening of drinking and lively talk, and from time to time, professors and students gave parties together. At one of these, which took place at the Vanguard in 1939, they put on a show, and later a group of students went with Abel, MacIver, Waller, and Kimball Young to Milla A. Alihan's (1908–   ) house, where Waller held the center of the stage with his witty stories. Waller also gave advice on research projects, and began his extended collaboration on the methodology of the social sciences with one of his Columbia students.

He was not, however, simply permissive, supportive, and tolerant with his students. He wanted to lay bare their postures and pretensions, to require of them the same detached analysis he sought, the same harsh probing of self and others. He had little admiration for mass education, and could be warm and close only with those who were willing to work hard.

VI

Waller's book, *The Family*, was completed before he came to Columbia University. Its publication in 1938 added greatly to

[77]   Kardiner had used his psychodynamic insights to analyze the anthropological data of Ralph Linton. Linton and Kardiner eventually published a book together: Abram Kardiner, *The Individual and His Society: The Psychodynamics of Primitive Social Organization*, with a Foreword and Two Ethnological Reports by Ralph Linton (New York: Columbia University Press, 1939).

his scholarly reputation and fame among laymen. It is an example of that increasingly rare phenomenon in sociology, a textbook that is a statement of basic principles and a contribution to the field. Just when he began to work on it is not clear, but certainly from his graduate period at the University of Chicago (presumably with Ernest W. Burgess) he had been studying the field, and he had taught the course for years. He knew that he would offend some by his approach:

. . . the sociologist must sometimes begin by making people unhappy; before he can construct he must destroy certain illusions. In the long run these illusions are harmful although they are often pleasant . . . there is no half-way house.[78]

After a period of initial worry about its reception, Waller was pleased to find that his text was widely used. After his death, it was revised by Reuben Hill (1951), and even now enjoys a steady sale, three decades after its first edition.

Since he wanted to lay a firm social psychological foundation for his analysis, almost a fourth of the text was devoted to a statement of an interactionist framework. It is, in fact, a short textbook on the social psychology of interaction, drawing on the work of Cooley, George Herbert Mead, Freud, James, Piaget, and Dewey in order to explain the development of the social self. He gave special attention to the notion of "habits" that had been utilized by Dewey in *Human Nature and Conduct*. These behavior patterns cannot be explained except through the habits of *others:*

We must therefore . . . show how the habits of the individual grew in the soil of the society which was there before he was. This is the essential conservative factor in society, and it is also the reason for the peculiar importance of the family, for the child forms more of his habits in the family environment than in any other.[79]

The term "habits" permits him to consider under the same rubric the development of isolated attitudes, behavior patterns, and social roles. His focus constantly sweeps from the individual to the social patterns that shape the person. For Waller, socialization

---

[78]   Willard Waller, *The Family* (The Cordon Company, 1938), p. 14.
[79]   *Ibid.*, p. 69.

is fraught with tensions and contingencies. Habits demand expression, but cannot always be gratified. The adult must abandon some habits that were originally imposed on him as a child. Habits increasingly make the growing human being less receptive to new experiences, more fettered by old ones. This is especially illustrated by the child-rearing patterns that are transmitted from parent to child:

Many persons would like to believe that they are very different from their parents . . . but in fact resemble their parents closely. . . . Rebellion against the parent does not make one different from him, for the parent may have rebelled in his day, and it may happen that the rebellious child shares with the hated parent the very characteristics which he finds most odious in him.[80]

Into a general theory of habit formation, Waller wove case material, hypothetical examples, and witty asides. At the end of each chapter, he suggests student projects. Some are fanciful, but they do illustrate his sociological style and imagination. Here are a few:

Take notes on the conversation of a group of students in a "bull session," and classify the speech according to Piaget's categories.

Study the behavior of a person addicted to smoking. Induce him to quit smoking and to describe his experiences to you.

If habits are constantly formed and re-formed, what is the sense of the statement that character is established by the fifth year?

Analyze Mother Goose rhymes in order to see what effect these may have upon the child.

Make case studies of William and Henry James. What were their similarities and their differences and how do you account for them?[81]

Waller's analysis of courtship and marriage in *The Family* is less easily read than his discussion of how people acquire their social patterns. The latter is solid and wise though not especially original. By contrast, the former is illuminating, and leads the reader to observe these processes as he has not done before. Once he has been guided by Waller, the reader cannot go back to his

80   *Ibid.*, p. 120.
81   *Ibid.*, chaps. 2, 3, 4.

ordinary perceptions. He does make good his earlier promise to destroy the "irrational sanctity of the home." He makes insiders of us, and we then see we have been insiders all along.

It is, in any event, Waller who is most pained at shattering the fictions about the family. He delights in pulling off the masks, but he is also disillusioned. He is a moralist, outraged to find that the world is not what it pretends to be.

He views courtships as governed, like all other social relations, by an exchange between two parties. It is a process of trial and error, of complex bargaining. If the terms are acceptable, the couple move gradually toward marriage. If not, "the tendency to love is [not] released. "Love can occur only under certain conditions.

> . . . the young man of a good family may be greatly attracted to the chorus girl and may consider marrying her, but in another part of his larynx are other and different sub-vocal responses and it usually does turn out otherwise.[82]

He considers it perfectly normal that class attitudes shape love attitudes. Love does not undermine a system of "like marries like," but operates within it.

In speaking of courtship without mental and social conflict, he comments wryly:

> We can attain to such an ideal conception of the love-life of our time only by considerable reworking of the empirical realities, by cutting the pieces of the picture apart and pasting them together again in a more pleasing pattern.[83]

The romantic love pattern obscures the exchange process, since a person begins to idealize another, and replaces the other person with "a creature of his own imagination." But, as a consequence, he displays only an ideal part of himself to his beloved; and his beloved reciprocates by presenting a similarly false self to him. Of course, either may feel an impulse toward getting something for nothing, so that bargaining may move into exploitation. This move-

[82]   *Ibid.*, p. 242. This volume, chapter 7.
[83]   *Ibid.*, p. 214.

ment does not ordinarily go very far because the terms are not set by the interacting parties alone, but by the community. When these controls break down, then, unfair bargains are often made. Both may only be seeking thrills, or one may pretend emotional involvement in order to exploit the other.

Waller had caused some controversy at Pennsylvania State when it was learned that he had planted some of his students as observers in campus fraternities and sororities. He used some of this material in his observations on courtship. In college dating, the fraternity replaces the boys' and girls' home community by regulating who may date whom. Fraternities and sororities, like social circles in the home town, enunciate what are the appropriate standards of behavior and rate each individual on the basis of desirability—a "smooth line," the ability to dance, handsomeness, etc. Those who rate highly will date others who rate highly, or suffer the penalty of dropping in the social ratings. He was describing, then, the pattern of courtship not merely at a college, but in any group. He also notes that the interaction between any boy and girl is controlled by the Principle of Least Interest, that is, that person dominates who has the lesser stake in continuing the relationship.[84] Waller's conclusion is that courtship trains one less for marriage than for courtship.

If courtship fosters idealization, marriage destroys it:

Before marriage we have our phantasies . . . after marriage we have the person, which brings with it its own delights, but the phantasy is usually nobler and more kind.[85]

Some readers and reviewers have felt, after studying Waller's analyses, that successful marital adjustment is a rare event. He does emphasize marital tensions (though not alone unhappiness), refusing to say

. . . the ivy-covered institution is really right and that the things which seem to be wrong with it are really all right too if we can just understand them.[86]

[84] He notes that this principle is not new and cites E. A. Ross as one of his own sources.
[85] *The Family*, p. 312.
[86] *Ibid.*, p. 313.

Moreover, in his treatment of conflict he contends (following Simmel) that it may be therapeutic, and is sometimes the "... only means by which unworkable schemes can be shuffled off and new ones formulated."[87] Similarly, far from merely deploring divorce and postdivorce adjustment, he notes that divorce may be salutary for both parties.

With this book, Waller made an impact on the field as he had with his earlier *Sociology of Teaching,* and for much the same reason. He moved from the hortatory and didactic, the namby-pamby and idealistic, to a clear-eyed (if sometimes pained) view of the sociological realities. He applied sociological principles to areas in which common sense, with its typical avoidance of inner processes, had formerly seemed to be adequate. He probed the intimacies of personal interaction, and he persuaded his reader to laugh with him as they explored together.

VII

In the fall of 1938, Waller was given further recognition by his colleagues, though it was not fully public in nature. In that year, he and Talcott Parsons were elected to the Sociological Research Association. This organization, founded to promote empirical research within sociology, was limited to a membership of one hundred sociologists, presumably distinguished for their achievements in the field. It may have begun as a clique, but by the time of Waller's election it encompassed all the schisms within the field. Clearly it did not exclude men who had no great enthusiasm for quantification, since neither of these new members nor MacIver who was president that year could be so classified. The organization has held its formal dinner annually during the meetings of the American Sociological Association, though it is not part of that society and most of the society's members do not know that the Sociological Research Association exists. The year of Waller's first meeting, the formal discussion focused on the problem of prediction in sociology, and specifically on the new marital prediction research then being completed by Ernest W. Burgess and Leon-

[87]   *Ibid.,* p. 314.

ard S. Cottrell. Perhaps the little group hoped to convert its two junior but illustrious members to the creed of quantification, but it is more likely that their election was a simple recognition of their merit as sociologists.

Not long after he had settled down at Columbia, Waller was given further professional recognition by his election to the presidency of the Eastern Sociological Society. His presidental speech, "War and Social Institutions," was given in the spring of 1940 at Asbury Park, New Jersey. He had not reached, at the time of his death, the age at which men usually attain the presidency of the national society, and the significance of this regional recognition is not trivial.

The presidency of a learned society is a peculiar position. It yields no salary, and controls almost no power. The constitution permits the president to have a hand in arranging the annual program of learned articles, but bars him from harming the organization by imposing many of his biases on it. Neither grant money nor promotions flow from the post. To accept it is to take on a considerable burden in correspondence, committee meetings, decisions, and interactions with hotels, local host colleges, employment bureaus, publishers, and caterers. It is a burden with few rewards, even in prestige, since election to the post is a recognition rather than a conferral of prestige.

Indeed, one could argue that the presidency itself is a payoff *from* the professorial constituency, a recognition that they have received prestige as a member of the president's group because of his achievements. He in turn revalidates their right to share in his prestige by accepting the post and serving the organization.

The presidency of the Eastern Sociological Society has been occupied by a long line of distinguished sociologists.[88] Politicking for the post is forbidden, and would very likely guarantee defeat in the election. Two factors are preponderant in the choice of a president: scholarly achievement and service to the guild. A lower rating on the second of these factors, service to the guild, has in

[88]   Among them, Robert M. MacIver, Talcott Parsons, Robert S. Lynd, E. Franklin Frazier, Thorsten Sellin, Wilbert E. Moore, George Homans, Robin M. Williams, Jr., to select only a few from an eminent list.

some cases delayed the granting of the presidency to a man whose intellectual contribution to the field was substantial. Perhaps "interest in the guild" or "recognition of the guild" is a better description of this factor. Some men demonstrate this by serving on the many committees of a learned society, but this alone is not enough. It is essential to participate actively in the annual meetings by giving papers, talking sociology with students and peers, taking part in drinking sessions, attending business meetings, or conferring and corresponding in advance about the issues facing the profession or who should be elected to office. Waller enjoyed these activities and had been attending the Eastern meetings from the early 1930's, when he first went to Pennsylvania State. (He had been attending the national meetings since the late 1920's, and doubtless had also gone to the regional meetings as well in that period.)

Waller's tenure as president gave him a special delight which he experienced several times in his life: to be genuinely at the center as well as behind the scenes, so that he could both play the role he had dissected from the *outside,* but still mock it from the *inside.* As befitted his dignity, the hotel management put him in the bridal suite, along with Paul F. Cressey, then secretary-treasurer. This gave rise to a series of sardonic wisecracks about both his dignity and the suite, and stimulated a bibulous gathering of friends to meditate (amid much joshing) on his new, complex role adventures.

His presidential speech, given on the eve of the war, was deadly serious, however. It expressed his deep Midwestern isolation and his hatred of war. An expanded version of it appeared that same year as a major essay in his book, W*ar in the Twentieth Century.*[89] It heralds his continuous concern with war and its aftermath for the rest of his life. It is also his first attempt to apply his sociological knowledge to a total society. In his previous work, his broadest canvas was a single institution, such as education, and he never strayed far from describing how people interact in concrete situa-

[89]   *War in the Twentieth Century* (New York: Dryden Press, 1940), pp. 478–532. Partially reprinted in this volume, chapter 20.

tions. Here, though hampered by the theoretical deficiencies that characterized sociology generally, he traces out the impact of war on all the major institutions of a society.

His analysis emphasizes society as a structure of values, of moral commitments, and the complex ways by which the concentration of moral energy on war undermines the ordinary business of a nation. As he puts it, ". . . war changes the *mores* of a people" because:

These moral commitments are no longer adapted to the new situation;
Adults and children are removed from family controls;
Group structures alter, permitting individuals to escape from group controls;
War ruins some people, who then lose their stake in the moral order;
People migrate, so that culture conflict is created;
Wartime propaganda, emphasizing some social habits and attacking others, disturbs the *balance* or integration of the *mores*;
The increased importance of the soldier's moral system, with its emphasis on short-term hedonism, affects the rest of the nation; and
Centralized authority takes over, undermining the individual's feeling of moral responsibility.[90]

He then considers in more detail the alterations war makes on the family, the educational process, the church, and community organization. Although he does take note of the humanitarian spirit, the pressure toward sacrifice in the interest of the collective aim, most of his evidence constitutes an indictment of war, a detailed tracing out of the complex processes by which this new goal perverts all others.

In his comments on the special area of social problems and welfare, he notes how war changes the balance of moral impulses. All reform movements cease, except those identified with war aims. Women, the underprivileged, and minority groups make some temporary social gains, because the war machine needs their help. In speculating about the further consequences of war, he wonders whether the Prohibition movement might not have been a consequence of the Civil War, since Carrie Nation's husband died from

[90]   This volume, chapter 20.

excessive drinking after he returned, a vice he acquired as a soldier: "that bride, cheated of her husband by the demon rum, became the Carrie Nation who at the turn of the century terrorized saloon-keepers with her hatchet."[91]

His trenchant description of military life itself emphasizes its ritualization, its caste patterns, its reduction of men to delimited role obligations, the development of a group orientation that neglects both patriotism and individual responsibility, the weakening of taboos against petty theft, drinking, or sex, and even its compensations (such as social security and tribal solidarity). "If anyone doubts that army life has its compensations, let him attend a convention of the American Legion. It is perfectly clear that for many of the veterans, their war experiences mean about the same thing as his college does to the old grad at the reunion."[92]

He concludes with a brief sketch of the processes by which war leads to revolution. He notes the special case of dictatorships: "A dictator-ridden country is like a boiler with suspected weaknesses and without either a safety-valve or a pressure gauge. There is no way of letting off steam or even of knowing how great the pressure is. The first intimation of trouble is an explosion."[93] Finally, he points to a possibility which in fact did not become important in the United States, but which concerned him greatly in the last years of his life, the revolutionary potential of the bitter soldier.

Although Waller talked constantly about political men and events, he was a moralist rather than a political thinker. He espoused no systematic ideology, and had little of that assiduous concern with political ideas and the structures of political groups that marks the enthusiastically political intellectual. He was more inclined to take positions against or for concrete actions and decisions, rather than to espouse a political philosophy. He saw himself as a tough-minded realist, unencumbered by ideological baggage.

By contrast, most of his friends *were* political, and political

---

91   *Ibid.*, p. 524. This volume, chapter 21.
92   *Ibid.*, p. 524. This volume, chapter 21.
93   *War in the Twentieth Century*, chapter on "War and Social Institutions."

in a special way. Not only were they concerned about Hitlerism and the political structure of Europe, but they had for years lived in that peculiarly intense New York political battleground where most people of consequence were identified by their former and present allegiances—which ones had denounced which friends for heresy, their position on Trotsky or Jay Lovestone, whether they had contributed to the *New Masses,* or had tried to "bore from within" by accepting a reform job under Roosevelt. Whether Communists or merely liberal, Waller's friends viewed him as at best apolitical and at worst silly or wrong. Unlike many of them, he did not join groups, organize political rallies, seek contributions for a cause, or view himself as a member of an embattled group. Neither did he accept the idea that we were fighting for democracy and freedom against the barbarians. Politics dealt with power and not ideals. Those who would not recognize this were, according to Waller, soft-headed. He was the realist; others were deluded. But to men as politically sophisticated as Abel, MacIver, or Stanley Burnshaw the poet, editor of Dryden Press and former editor of the *New Masses,* Waller had political attitudes rather than political ideas.

The beginning of the War in Europe and America's later involvement forced Waller to enunciate his opinions, find out where he stood on issues, and decide what action he would take. Waller began with a Midwestern isolationist position. He was anti-Hitler but anti-England as well. As the war progressed his position changed. In a letter to Read Bain in 1942 he outlines where he stood by this time.

I thought the sociologists lost their heads by going all out for war much too soon. They utterly refused to consider the consequences of war. The sociologists, who should have been the last to develop war fever, were in fact among the first. I watched the whole thing with great disgust. My own system of belief, which was at least integrated and consistent, was to the effect that we could have stayed out. I believe that if Hitler had Europe on a silver platter tomorrow, he could not keep it, and he could not successfully exploit it. Slavery disappeared from West European culture partly because it was uneconomic. The Nazis have not invented a new technique for exploiting and utilizing slave labor.

Remember also that the interventionist propaganda began before Russia entered the war. If we had gone in when only England was our ally, our chances of winning would have been slight. Now that Russia is in, there is a good chance to win; in fact, I am sure we will win. When Russia went in, I became less violently isolationist, because the odds were different (you see I am not wholly non-quantitative in my thought).[94]

Several of Waller's friends remember disturbing political discussions with him. In one of these, shortly before the United States entered the war, he argued against intervention. He contended that instead of becoming involved in European affairs we ought to become an imperial power and colonize Latin America. Needless to say, neither of these views was acceptable to his friends.

As the war progressed, Waller became more and more concerned with what would happen to this country after the war. In the same letter to Bain quoted above, Waller goes on to predict what the future would be.

I think we agree as to the certain results of the war on American society. We will come out of the war with what amounts to a domestic version of Fascism. I hope, but am not sure of it, that our version will be mild, and that it may disappear in a generation. I agree wholeheartedly with your analysis of the elements brought to the top by war, also with the probability of a drive on all liberal elements.

In fact, I go further. The balance of forces being what it is, we cannot hope to win the war without tyranny. So let it come. . . .

Anyhow, I have been through a long period of depression and emerged. I feel that American democracy as we once knew it is gone for the foreseeable future. I predict a great rightist swing, and even welcome part of it. If the sonsofbitches must come to power to fight the war, then the sooner the quicker. I therefore welcomed the defeat of the New Deal in the last elections. And if liberals of the old sort were so soft-headed as to get us into war, then I shall be glad to see that kind of liberalism disappear. I assure you that arriving at this conclusion cost me a great deal of mental anguish.

Waller predicted a fast move toward totalitarianism after the war, a rise of anti-Semitism, the passage of anti-Negro legislation,

[94]   November 16, 1942, from the Read Bain Collection, Michigan Historical Collection.

the abolition of trade unions, the suppression of free speech, the emergence of a one-party system with power concentrated in Washington, and the takeover of leadership by the military. He was not suspicious of a military conspiracy, but rather he believed that the wartime undermining of the social structure would simply allow power to fall completely into their hands. Although he presented himself as a realist and so accepted the inevitable, he certainly did not welcome the part he believed the military and the veterans' movement would play in American politics. He warned repeatedly that the turn toward Fascism which the war had begun would be intensified by the return of resentful veterans.

But though he sometimes spoke of the potential political power of the veterans, and perhaps wanted to be involved, his speeches indicate no real bent for power, or any specific program for gaining it. More harmonious with his general behavior is the interpretation that he saw the veterans as an army waiting for a leader, a potentially organizable group for whom some kind of leadership would arise; and if he could be a successful representative of their views, he might experience the excitement of being at the center of the turmoil.

Further evidence that he had no specific plans but rather an eagerness to be in the thick of things may be drawn from his continued effort to obtain some sort of policy or administrative job. As the country moved toward war, the movement of talent to Washington was accentuated, while he was stuck in New York. The time was fraught with *possibility*. He wanted in, when the war finally came. He thought that Ruth Benedict and Gene Weltfish were wrong to use their scientific names for political purposes, but he wanted to serve in some capacity. One of his friends asserted that he expected to be called up for war service, though we have no evidence of his trying to enlist. Certainly he was excited by the many war stories he heard from his brother, from Seth Russell (who served as a chaplain on the *Santa Fe*), and from his former student, Bill Henderson (who had done a study of the Warwick reformatory under his stimulus), and other friends.

In addition, he applied in 1942 to the War Department for a job in military government, military intelligence, or the care of war prisoners. According to his widow, he tried to obtain a position in the wartime administration of Italy, but was turned down because he failed the physical examination. He then went through other further examinations to ascertain what the War Department physicians had found out, but failed. A short time before his death, he told Burnshaw that he had actually been accepted for service by the Navy, and (ironically, we now see) slapped his stomach to show how fit he was.

From the early part of 1942 he was a consultant to the Office of Price Administration, a job requiring occasional trips to Washington. He contributed an editorial for the War Production Board to be distributed to newspapers. He spoke to governmental agencies on the policies they should pursue in helping veterans adjust to civilian life. He outlined an extensive program for the administration of Germany after the war, and an earlier policy statement focused on the uses of propaganda to keep up civilian morale during the war. He tried, in short, to participate wherever possible in the political activities of the war period.

Whatever the original motivations that pressed him into a great concern with war and its aftermath—perhaps originally his simple hatred of war—from 1940 until his death almost everything he wrote dealt with some aspect of war. He published three books on the topic, at least twelve popular articles, and three professional articles. A preoccupation quickly became an occupation.

The first of these books, *War in the Twentieth Century*, is a collection of essays of which Waller contributed two. In the first of these, he begins with a review of different theories of why wars start. He suggests some ideas of his own, after pointing out that prior speculations seem inadequate and banal, but his own turn out to be equally inadequate and banal. Perhaps he sensed this, for he quickly changes the subject to the natural history of war, a description of its phases. This subject is glossed over quickly and he concludes the essay with the assertion that "war does not settle anything." Approaching the phenomenon with the assumption that people are rational, he is incredulous that wars still exist; the incredulity impairs his ability to analyze.

The second essay, "War and Social Institutions," is an extended version of his presidential address before the Eastern Sociological Society. By specifying the broad range of social structures that are undermined by war, he describes how war accelerates social change and frequently generates revolutionary processes as well. To accompany *War in the Twentieth Century*, he published a small paperback, *War and the Family*, which merits the neglect it has received.

As usual, Waller was not pleased with the sale of his book. Like most authors, including those who claim to be writing for only a select few, he felt hurt when people did not rush to buy his work. He expressed his sentiment to Merton: "The war book has come out, and has sold about a thousand copies the first month in the text edition. The trade edition is in the doldrums, but I attribute that to the fact that [the] publishers are keeping the existence of the book a carefully guarded secret."

In 1943 Waller began to realize an old ambition, to publish in the popular press. As far back as the early 1930's in his Nebraska days (and perhaps still earlier, since one of his first jobs was on a newspaper) he had been writing articles meant for a larger audience than sociologists, but no one would publish them. "Revolt in the Classroom,"[95] published in the *Saturday Review of Literature*, was his first appearance before a national audience. The article calls attention to the disappearance of male teachers from the classroom during wartime. Males are the centers of control and when they disappear discipline breaks down. He goes on to excoriate the school systems for allowing this to happen. They impose rigid moral standards on teachers, and allow a bunch of "nitwits, nincompoops and crackpots, hypocrites and timeservers" to hold positions of power, thus driving men away. Judging from the teachers' letters which flowed in, he touched a sensitive spot and was applauded for his stand.

One popular article does not make a journalist. Other people must begin to request, if not press, for more articles. No one asked Waller to be a spokesman for anything. But when he published *The Veteran Comes Back*[96] the following year he immediately became a journalist. When he was editing *War in the Twentieth*

95   *Saturday Review of Literature*, 26 (September, 1943) : 4–6.
96   *The Veteran Comes Back* (New York: The Dryden Press, 1944).

Century, his editor, Stanley Burnshaw, had insisted that there must be a successor dealing with the returning soldier. This latter book was widely publicized and became successful. By the end of 1944 it had gone through three printings, and Waller was nationally known. Requests poured in for articles and speeches, sometimes from specialized groups such as a naval hospital and sometimes from organizations wanting popular lectures. In one form or another, his message appeared on radio networks, and in *This Week, Colliers, The New York Times, Science Digest,* and other publications. His work may be the only sociology book ever to be turned into a radio play (over WGN in Chicago).

Waller meant to reach a large audience with this book and he did. He wanted to affect public opinion and policy. Consequently, his idea system in *The Veteran Comes Homes* is a simple one. His assertions are repeated until even the dimmest reader can grasp them. The subtle distinctions, the playfulness and tentativeness so much appreciated by his colleagues, are absent.

The main argument is as follows. The goal of an army is different from the goals of a society, and its value system is so structured as to motivate men to throw their energies toward that goal. To achieve this, they must be socialized; and thus must be cut off from the ordinary society that had trained them differently. They acquire a new code of ethics, attitudes, relationships, and skills, but the skills are either irrelevant or harmful to the larger civil society. When this changed man returns, he has lost his economic position and his close ties with family and wife. His army values of group loyalty, valor, hardness, and fitness are useless. He has been through a frightening experience, and will be bitter when he understands that others do not sympathize with him or comprehend what he has undergone. He will be difficult to rechange into a civilian, will be loyal to his fellow veterans, and will demand political action in his favor. The veteran will, in short, be unfit to live in civil society and will use his power to transform the society for his own benefit.

To avoid this disruption of the country, Waller argued that we must devise sensible plans to help the veteran adjust, and the last section of his book specifies such a program.

The nightmares of mass insurrection and of mass domination by ex-soldiers that he conjures up are interesting, but proved to be poor prophecy. He saw correctly the socialization process, the differing values of army life, and the bitterness of veterans, but because he so often sensed the problems of individuals rather than of social structures, he failed to grasp both the flexibility of people and, more important, the institutional patterns of American life that smooth such transitions, fit persons quickly into groups that control them by adequate compensations and punishments, and reassert the strength of civil values which had been, after all, the major content of these men's lives prior to war service. In fact, America absorbed the veterans just as it has assimilated most of the other malcontents, radicals and reactionaries, and crackpots it has produced in abundance. This country has been continually in turmoil, but over a century ago De Toqueville saw how its social patterns allowed relatively free expression, and eventual compromise and absorption, of dissidence.

But if the book is sociologically simple and prophetically wrong, it is moving. Waller demands understanding and compassion for these men, and gains his end because he makes the reader sense what the soldier feels. He recreates the soldier's emotional experience so that the reader may also get that experience inside himself. He gives the stage now and then to Ernest Hemingway, Erich Maria Remarque, or Jules Romains, for they had been there and could recreate it as it really was. In this book, Waller expressed his humane values rather than his concern for cool scientific analysis.

He had always imagined what it might be like to be famous, and he could now play the role of the public figure, cajoled to make speeches or pronouncements and flattered into writing yet another article. In fact, he seemed not to need much persuasion; almost every request of which we have a record seems to have met with his acceptance. The only sour note for him was that Dixon Wecter also published a book on the veteran problem, and with a more arresting title, *When Johnny Comes Marching Home*, just before Waller's book. Worse than the undoubted damage to the sales of his own book, Norman Cousins invited Wecter to review Waller's book for the *Saturday Review*.

In the last months of his life, speech followed speech as he traveled over the country to bring his message to all who would listen. He spoke for the disabled veteran, pled with women to give sympathy to their returning men, and urged programs of physical rehabilitation and government grants for soldiers. To help them further, he even argued that women should get out of the factories and go back to their hearths, where they could do their proper job of bearing children and caring for their husbands. Barnard students expressed great displeasure at finding such a reactionary on their emancipated campus. Nevertheless, even this exhortation was part of his concern for the returned soldier: he should receive sensible, compassionate and special treatment, not only because he might otherwise be a political threat, but more fundamentally because he plainly deserved it.

Fame can lead into new and interesting worlds, from the cocktail parties of the literati to the back rooms of the Mafia. Waller loved to see new worlds and accepted with glee all invitations. In 1945, he reported to his friends some of his encounters with what he called "the Wall Street boys." With gusto he described being conducted by private elevator to a private dining room, delighted to find himself the center of attention in a group of powerful people who represented some of the very forces he occasionally attacked. These men may have thought that the returning veterans could be used and manipulated politically, and Waller was certainly the most conspicuous spokesman for the veteran at that time. He seemed to understand what veterans wanted, and how their allegiance could be captured. At the same time, "the Wall Street boys" were doubtless convinced both by Waller's personal magnetism and his analyses of propaganda that he knew how to mold public opinion.

How many such meetings took place is not now clear, though it is certain that Waller had no political program, and was not capable of a sustained dedication to a line of political activity. Moreover, it is even more likely that he explored this set of ideas and relations because it was his first opportunity to observe the capitalist in his native lair. He could use them more easily than they could use him (following his Principle of Least Interest), because he cared little about them or their goals. They were, however, interesting specimens.

It is also possible that his reports to his friends exaggerated the political interests of these "Wall Street boys," since he would be delighted at hinting to his liberal cronies that he might become a tool of the reactionaries. At least one of his friends thought that these corporation leaders only wished to hire him as a consultant to advise them on a sensible personnel program for the returning veteran.

Along with these activities, Waller was pursuing a small-scale career as editor and businessman. Like most professors who suppose that mere intelligence is sufficient capital for business success, Waller caused little stir with his financial achievements. His first business venture had taken place at Pennsylvania State. (He mentions the possibility of an investment in the winter of 1936–37 in one of his letters to Josephine, but we have no evidence that she knew he had actually made the gamble.) He became a partner in Cordon Press, which had been founded in 1937 by Joseph C. Palamountain, a former teacher of French who had failed to take a Ph.D. at Harvard (a not uncommon background for bookmen of the 1930's). After Granville Hicks had left the *New Masses*, he advised his old friend Stanley Burnshaw to go into publishing. Burnshaw talked with several men on the Macmillan college department staff about this possibility, and a few, including Palamountain, seemed willing to leave in order to found their own company, and before long the details of the new company were being worked out.

The Cordon people supposed, correctly, that they could sell shares to college professors. The social psychologist Theodore Newcomb (1903–   ), then at Tulane, took a $5,000 share along with Waller, and other colleagues joined to make up the required capital. (It must be inserted here as a caveat, that although some of our sources assure us that Waller actually made the investment, others—and we, the editors—remain somewhat skeptical. Prior to his Columbia job, his salary had averaged slightly more than $3,000 annually during the eight years since receiving his Ph.D., and during that period he had moved three times. He had inherited no money. Children had arrived, and his letters reveal a constant shortage of money. Perhaps his "investment" was actually a share in lieu of future royalties on his new book, *The Family*. Perhaps, on the other hand, our doubts reflect merely the failure of those living in an affluent age to comprehend how people in a poorer one managed to save enough to make investments.)

When Waller came to New York, he was fascinated by publishing, and made innumerable suggestions to Burnshaw, who was then the dominant editor in the new company. He would call by telephone and say, "Reporting for duty at Cordon Press." He was a literary man, and took pleasure in this close involvement with the making of books. Before long, however, he had filed suit against Palamountain and was in the midst of an internal battle over control of the company. He sided with Burnshaw against Palamountain, and of course lost, because the latter controlled most of the proxies. In the course of the squabble, Palamountain sought support from the other shareholders, and made disparaging remarks about Waller's conduct as secretary during a meeting of the board of directors. He charged that Waller had doctored the minutes. In 1939 Waller sued Palamountain and two of the directors for libel in the Supreme Court of New York State, and won. He enjoyed both the battle and the victory.

As a result of the battle, both Burnshaw and Donald Ambler left the company, or were severed from it, and began The Dryden Press. Waller was given a few token shares in the new company (later bought back by the partners), but most important he was made sociology editor. He enjoyed working with manuscripts, corresponding with potential authors, and talking over plans for future expansion. The company was successful, both financially and esthetically (of the first twenty books chosen by the American Institute of Graphic Arts for recognition, four were designed at Dryden), but unfortunately Waller did not live long enough to share in what would have been his increasing editorial royalties on the sociology books under this imprint.

In one of his attempts at popular writing, "Life in Suburbia," Waller makes fun of the commuter's life in phrases reminiscent of those used by people who have in recent years fled the suburbs to return to the city. The time wasted in traveling, the separation of home and work, the inefficiency, are viewed with a jaundiced eye. Yet, after his first year in New York City, he chose to move to a suburb called Radburn (Fairlawn, New Jersey), praised by Lewis Mumford as a wisely planned community. Waller explained that he had been taken in by a clever realty salesman, but in fact he made no effort to leave, and it is clear from his Pennsylvania State letters and later ones during his Columbia period that he considered living in the city to be intolerable.

American scholars at times envy what they believe is the old ideal of the German professor's family life. According to this myth, the entire household was organized around the professor's needs. Since he was presumably a great mind, his reading and thinking should not be disturbed. Children tiptoed when he worked, and were grateful if he took them for a short walk before dinner. He needed vacations even if they did not. Even such rest periods were planned mainly for his benefit, although others were often permitted to go along.

Whatever the prevalent nostalgia for this style, assuming it ever existed, some American scholars (and Waller among them) have created a native equivalent, perhaps closer to the pattern of the hard-working American businessman. In this pattern, the professor works extremely long hours both in his office or laboratory and at home. His family does not try to serve him and his needs, but neither do they make great demands on him. Instead, they lead relatively independent lives, calling on his services but seldom. He comes into the house and leaves it without disturbing its daily processes much. He trips to Washington to confer about grants or to serve on a granting committee, and they think about it no more than they do about his commuting to the city. If the electrical system fails, or the car breaks down, he does not drop his work to take care of such chores, or any others, but expects his competent wife to handle the problem. Now and again, his wife reminds him that they owe social obligations, and he takes part in the dinner she arranges, perhaps even for the evening playing the role of the charming host who is a dedicated family man.

After his failure in marriage with the bewitching but volatile Thelma, Waller had married a lively and intelligent but nonintellectual woman with a sensible perspective, one who knew what he needed and wanted. She admired him greatly, and could see through his little pretensions without cruelly making fun of them. She was, as one of their friends put it, a woman in her own right. In the exasperation of a woman running a household with three active children she could express her doubt that he was really a family "expert," but she could accept serenely his habit of going to his study to work all evening after he had been working in New York all day.

Waller served on the school board in Radburn because the community was constructing its first school building and he believed it was the duty of those who understood education to accept responsibility in these areas. However, his interest in children as individual human beings did not match his keen interest in adults. (His interest in his own children increased as they grew older.) Josephine, like many professors' wives, claims that he really "knew nothing about babies." It is, indeed, striking that the sections in *The Family* on parenthood and children are not only relatively short, but are not much enriched by wise insights drawn from his own experience. He admired Cooley's ability to learn about all children from watching his own, but could not match it. His sister-in-law was once surprised at his apparent interest in the antics of her children, but later suspected (because she read his books) that he was simply gathering data.

Waller was not a permissive parent and—as he comments himself about parents—to some extent imitated his own father's hard-mouthed discipline with children. Consistent with his personality but not his discipline, he tried to persuade them to be as iconoclastic as he was about traditional beliefs. He would even expect them at times to show off for visitors by expressing their disbelief in the goodness of the church, the dedication of clergymen, or the sacredness of the flag. And he succeeded in imbuing them with his own love of learning.

In the last period of his life, of course, Waller saw his family less often, but his friends (both students and colleagues) continued to drop in at his Radburn home for evenings of casual or serious explorations of people and ideas.

Although his energies were fully deployed in his speaking and writing for the veterans' cause, his teaching and duties as chairman, and his editing, Waller had many other writing and research aims in view for the near future. He had agreed to collaborate on two books, an elementary text with his friend and former student Seth Russell, and a book on social psychology with S. Stansfeld Sargent, a Barnard colleague. He did not believe that Russell would do much actual writing, but had great faith in his keen pedagogical judgment, his accurate appraisal of what would generate excitement and understanding in the student. Sargent later published (alone) a textbook on social psychology.[97] In emphasizing the interdisciplinary approach of this work, he writes that whatever he achieved through this perspective was inspired by Waller.

Although he left no unpublished writings on the topics, Waller's thinking was increasingly turned toward problems in political sociology, social planning, and social control. As one aspect of this growing interest, he talked both informally and formally about the possibility of applying sociological knowledge to the practical problems of both business and politics.

As noted earlier, he had a lifelong concern with the general problems of scientific methods, and the technical difficulties of a scientific sociology. The papers he left suggest that he was aiming eventually at a monograph that would deal with a wide range of issues in this vexing area, most of which remain as unsettled now as when he died.

Much more developed was his unpublished sociological analysis of higher education. He had been collecting materials and writing on this subject since his Pennsylvania State period. All of this remained at the stage of first drafts, but we have included some of

97   *Social Psychology* (New York: Ronald Press Co., 1950).

his unpublished work in the present book. In preparing *The Academic Man,*[98] Logan Wilson writes,

As you can surmise . . . I got some good leads from Waller and even had the benefit of looking at some random, unpublished notes of his which he had jotted down over the years.[99]

The sections we now have are more systematic, and clearly are only part of a larger manuscript, now lost or incomplete. However, he intended to complete this work. Somewhat more doubtful as a firm goal was his investigation of what Erving Goffman has called "total institutions"—what Waller called "institutions of segregative care"—such as insane asylums, prisons, reformatories, convents and monasteries, and military schools. He had seen the similarity of social patterns in agencies that attempt to mold a total environment for its inmates, whether they enter voluntarily or under duress. He had sponsored or directed several such studies, beginning while he was at Pennsylvania State. It is unfortunate that no manuscript of his remains on this subject, since his writing was usually more probing when he could startle the reader by describing the profane elements in the sacred, or the ritualized aspects of the secular.

During the last year of his life, the popular demands for Waller as a lecturer and writer became even greater. Little time could be allocated to the various projects he planned. He was moving at such a rapid pace that some of his friends were concerned about his health. Shortly before his death, he had complained of chest pains and had seen a doctor, who gave him a clean bill of health.

We must, however, record a minor mystery about his physical health. To at least one of his close friends, he claimed for years that he was living on borrowed time, and even hinted that he might have been injured in World War I. Even if he did believe that his heart was inadequate, Waller would have been unwilling to play the role of the "weak heart" person. He enjoyed instead both keeping fit and telling others about it. He presented himself as

[98]   *Academic Man* (New York: Oxford University Press, 1942).
[99]   Personal correspondence.

physically tough and virile. A high energy person, he would have been unable to let others view him as delicate or incapable of physical strain. His wife Josephine believed that he did know he was turned down by the U.S. Military Administration because of his heart, but also believed this came as a surprise to him. Yet, as we noted before, after that examination he bragged to Stanley Burnshaw how fit he was. Unable to unravel all these somewhat inconstant strands, we simply report them.

The circumstances of his death, like those surrounding many of the important transitions in our lives, were trivial and anticlimactic. He carried a heavy suitcase to the Columbia University subway station, where he was to meet his son Peter. Father and son were planning to travel to Chicago for another of Waller's speeches. Peter arrived at the subway entrance and found a crowd gathered around his father's body. For all his assiduousness in keeeping fit, and despite the repeated examinations that (he claimed) disclosed no pathology to account for his intermittent heart pains, he had died of a heart attack.

As one of Waller's friends wrote later, speaking for most of his colleagues and perhaps all his friends, "It's always the wrong one."

I. Methodology

1

ON CHARLES HORTON COOLEY

1940

THERE HAVE BEEN a few men in history who have raised themselves above their fellows, not by deeds, but by their ability to know and to express what goes on in the human mind. Charles Horton Cooley was one of these. He did not build a better mousetrap, and the world beat no path to his door, but he contemplated his own soul and saw the world reflected there.

Most of us do not know what goes on in our minds. Perhaps it has never occurred to us to wonder how it feels to be ourselves. At best, our knowledge of our own inwardness is confused; it may be rich enough, but it is chaotic. We need a man of genius, a certain peculiar kind of genius, to tell us what we think when we do not quite know what we think. He takes our half-formed ideas and gives them back to us clear and hard and definite; he captures the feeling-states and impressions that are too swift for us and shows us their anatomy. Such men are rare and valuable. They live forever because the human race cannot afford to let them die. They prove that the human mind does not change much from age to age.

Cooley's gift was introspection. He was no scholar compiling footnotes and references and he was not a philosopher in the formal sense. He was a seer. He was a man who used his own mind as a broad highway into the mind of the human race, and a man who

---

Reprinted from the Introduction to *Charles Horton Cooley*, by Edward C. Jandy (New York: The Dryden Press, 1942), pp. 1–6. © 1942 by Edward C. Jandy.

loved to express his thoughts well. He became a sociologist because the developing science of sociology gave him free scope for the kind of thing he wanted to do. He was once an economist. He might well have become a philosopher or a psychologist. In another society, he might have preferred to make his contribution as an essayist.

Only a man who lived Cooley's life, and had his kind of personality, could have seen the things that Cooley saw. He discovered the first principles of human nature, principles which the rest of us can understand well enough now that he has stated them; but the man who discovered them would have to be a little inhuman. If I say Cooley was inhuman, I do not mean that he was cruel or unkind, but merely that he shared very little in some aspects of our human fellowship. Cooley's mental isolation was, I believe, an essential precondition of the discovery that we know nothing certainly of one another, that one's knowledge of others is mental and imaginative, and that society and the individual are one, and our minds all one woven texture. Whatever the reason, he saw these things; he saw them first, and we must copy him, we who follow after.

The faculty of introspection was, of course, not Cooley's only gift. He had a fine, constructive imagination as well. He perceived the psychic fact and perceived in his imagination the wider configuration of which this fact was a part. He was always trying out ways of conceiving things, trying to make sense of the world. His thought covered a great portion of the whole range of human life. But he never wrote unless he had something to say.

. . . Cooley . . . was one of the great men of his generation and possibly one of the great minds of all time. His life and his work had their own peculiar character. Everything about him was touched by his idiosyncrasy. He was not a mass man: he was a representative man, the sort of man of whom his master, Emerson, might have delighted to write. Cooley thought that he gave his mind over to good masters, and they made something of him. I do not think that was quite the way it happened. Cooley had the kind of mind that required great masters, and he found them. A really good mind can never tolerate mediocrity in its teachers.

Cooley spent nearly all his life in a little midwestern town, and he made his living by teaching students who were probably much more fascinated by his eccentricities than his organic view of society. He had few friends or associates; a very few, his family, a handful of trusted colleagues, and Emerson, and Thoreau, and Goethe, one or two others. A narrow life, but deep. And it gave him plenty of time to think.

. . . Cooley's thought ranged over many subjects, and all of it was significant. It is odd, when one thinks of it, that his genius so seldom missed fire and so seldom repeated itself. . . . Cooley stated things so well, and with such economy of expression, that it would be impossible to say his thoughts over in fewer words or different words without losing something. . . . His thoughts were all an organic whole; every part depended on every other. "Cut these words, and they will bleed."

. . . The story of Cooley's life and work is certain to have a bad effect upon young students. The moral is poor, if not negative. Cooley's life teaches us that a man must follow his own interior demon, step to the music he hears, and never mind if others hear a different drummer. A student of human life need not work very hard, or travel far, or bustle about; he may read what he likes and enjoys and therefore he may skip most of what his professional colleagues have written. He need not know very many people, and as for those he does know, it is just as well sometimes not to listen when they talk. To be like Cooley, one takes his time, his ease; he reads great books and reflects upon them, and from time to time he gathers the harvest which comes all untended to his hand. So must you act, says Cooley's life in letters large as day; so must you act, aspiring young man to whom your elders have told that fable of ninety-eight percent perspiration; act so; be like Cooley, and your name will live forever—provided that you are a man of genius.

It is no use whipping the muse, no use trying to write better than you can, no use trying to be profound if you are not profound. No one can be Cooley but Cooley himself. That bothers people. There is no royal road to Cooley's kind of wisdom. In fact, there does not seem to be a road of any kind. Cooley was a man of genius. He had a method, but he did not transmit it. He described his method accurately enough; he "saw life clearly and saw it whole"; he perceived social facts in his imagination; he kept trying to imagine how it would feel to be somebody else. The trouble is that when most people try to use Cooley's methods the results are not very gratifying. Let them try, and let them come to their foreordained failure. Or let them try some other useful but easier sort of social investigation. Make scholars of them and let them pile up facts. Some day another Cooley will come, perhaps a tougher-minded one who knows more of the world, and he will take up where the original Cooley left off. Meanwhile, it is our task to keep the flame of Cooley's thought alive.

. . . I do not believe that Cooley was solipsistic. . . . I think that Cooley's writings show that he understood perfectly the problem which he faced. He abhorred pedantry and would no more have taken the space to discuss such a side issue than he would have thought it desirable to declare that he did not really believe in Santa Claus or go on record concerning the composition of the moon. And as to those discussions the philosophers have held as to whether Cooley was an idealist or something else, I feel sure they do not matter. Cooley was a philosopher, but not that kind of philosopher. He was a man writing books about human life, telling what it feels like to be a human being, trying to make sense of our scattered and contradictory world. . . .

2

INSIGHT AND SCIENTIFIC METHOD

1934

I PROPOSE in this paper to state some methodological implications of the *Gestalt* principle of insight. This is the doctrine that mental events do not occur as separate and discrete sensations, but in organized wholes, and that there is, in some cases, a direct perception of the causal interdependence of events.[1] That we ex-

Reprinted from the *American Journal of Sociology* 40, no. 3 (November 1934) : 285–97.

[1] The definition of insight has presented some difficulty to writers of the Gestaltist school. Insight is apparently that which enables us to perceive certain parts of our perceptual world as cohering with each other, or, in the more complex case, to perceive directly the causal interdependence of two or more processes. Insight in time configurations frequently assumes the form of comprehension in terms of process and function. Kohler says that insight "does not mean more than our experience of definite determination in a context, an event or a development of the total field; and in the actual cases there need be nothing like an invention, or a new intelligent achievement, or so forth. A total field would be experienced *without* insight, if all its several states, wholes, attitudes, etc., were simply given as a pattern, in which none was felt directly to depend upon any other and none to determine any other (Wolfgang Kohler, *Gestalt Psychology*, p. 371). Again, Kohler says, "There is no mere sequence of indifferent events, connected indirectly. Each phase of what happens grows out of its predecessors, depending upon their concrete nature. And the subject, whose experiences are an expression of this developing context in the brain-field, will experience the development, along with its 'referring to,' 'depending upon,' 'away from,' and so forth, that is, with *insight*" (*ibid.*, p. 390).

perience causal determination in a sensory context is the basic assumption of this paper. Whoever points out the implications of a premise does not need to commit himself to the premise. The *Gestalt* theory of perception is but one of many theories, and it would be difficult to establish that it alone is true. The use of the insight concept in the present paper is simply to serve as an organizing principle for some methodological notions which are more difficult to state in a different frame of reference.

Methodology must rest upon certain assumptions concerning the external world and the nature of the perceiving mind. As to the external world, all schools of scientific methodology grant the postulate of determinism. All schools likewise find some way of treating sensory data as more or less true representations of the world of reality, whatever that reality may be thought to be. There is less agreement concerning the nature of the perceiving mind, and widespread disagreement as to the method by which we can definitely establish the existence of a causal relationship.

The doctrines of Karl Pearson, as expressed in *The Grammar of Science,* have had some effect upon methodological speculation in the social sciences. Pearson assumes that the elements of experience are sensations which have no inherent connection with one another; this is typical of a whole school of methodology of which we take Pearson as an outstanding example. Having thus fractured his experiential material, he is forced to achieve some extraordinary intellectual gymnastics in order to put it together again. How establish the fact that the external counterpart of one of these discrete sensations is the cause of the external counterpart of another discrete sensation? Pearson is logical. There is, he says, no *real* cause in the universe as we experience it; cause comes before, and effect after, in an invariable sequence. One never establishes a causal relationship with certainty; one establishes only a probability that an ascertained event will be followed by another ascertained event. A certain sequence has been observed *n* times in the past; weigh against that the negative cases and compute the probabilities. There is no cause, and statistics is the way to find it. This epistemological system has been used as the basis of a rationale of statistical method; on the basis of the Pearsonian notion of cause some statisticians falsely claim that theirs is the only road to scientific truth.

Let us state the assumptions of our own methodology and examine its implications. *Gestalt* doctrine regards sensations as false abstractions from phenomena. Perceptions assume the form of configurations, and some degree of insight into causal processes is usually involved in a perceptual configuration. Cause is an elementary datum of experience; extra-mental manipulations are therefore not necessary to establish a relation of cause and effect. The relationship of cause and effect usually assumes the form of a configuration in time. This theory enables us to avoid the ultimate nonsense of Pearsonian methodology, the doctrine that a statement of a causal relation is really only a statement of relative probabilities. If one perceives a single instance correctly, he can generalize from that instance. When an instance in which a causal relation has been observed is followed by another instance in which this relation is not present, one needs to refine his observation and to restate the conditions under which his generalization is valid.

The Pearsonian methodology rests upon the assumption that sensations are discrete units and have no order in themselves; given this principle, the whole incredible artificiality of method must follow. If, however, cause is an elementary datum of experience, extramental procedures for establishing a relationship of cause and effect are of less importance than what happens in the mind; what is really needful is to experience phenomena with insight.

Science is man's attempt to understand his universe. One focuses his attention upon various aspects of phenomena, attempting to perceive with insight. The advancement of science depends upon the search for insight. The mind of man is a tiny pencil of light exploring the illimitable dark. Causal relations are an inseparable part of experience, to be treated as real because experience must be treated as real; we may seek to refine our perceptions of cause, but we cannot reject them without rejecting our whole world of experiential reality.

If cause is an elementary datum of experience, then the thing to do is to experience it. The essence of scientific method, quite simply, is to try to see how data arrange themselves into causal configurations.[2] Scientific problems are solved by collecting data and by "thinking about them all the time." We need to look at strange things until, by the appearance of known configurations, they seem familiar, and to look at familiar things until we see novel configurations which make them appear strange. We must look at events until they become luminous. That is scientific method. Quantification is not the touchstone of scientific method. Insight is the touchstone.

In the social sciences, we may proceed to obtain insight in three distinct ways:

1. By direct study of human and interhuman behavior in order to perceive with insight. It is difficult to maintain this objective and external approach to human behavior because of the ease with which interpretations based upon sympathetic insight (Type 3) creep in.

2. We may obtain insight by studying certain symbols abstracted from reality and supposed to stand in a constant relation to it. These symbols are usually numerical.

3. We may obtain insight through sympathetic penetration. This insight is based upon the fact that the behavior of others, either directly perceived or mediated to us through language or mathematical symbols, starts certain mental processes in ourselves. This kind of insight is peculiarly liable to error, but of all kinds of insight it is the most significant.

These methods of obtaining insight are of course only analytically separable. All three are used at different stages of every research procedure. The behaviorist cannot dispense with sym-

2   Herbert Blumer seems to be very close to this point of view in the following passage: "What is needed is observation freely redirective and flexible in perspective. Scientific observation, as I understand it, is just this. It places emphasis on exploration, turning over and around, looking intently here and there, now focusing attention on this, now on that. It is flexible scrutiny guided by sensitized imagination. One sees it clearly in the work of Darwin who, incidentally, used neither instruments nor mathematics" (Herbert Blumer, review of Lundberg's *Social Research*, *American Journal of Sociology*, XXXV, No. 6 [1930], 1102).

pathetic insight. Introspection, properly a method of studying phenomena directly, is most useful as an approach to the minds of others. The statistician must usually draw more or less upon sympathetic insight for the interpretation of his phenomena.

Apparently it is possible to offer a valid explanation of the principal methods of science in terms of the search for insight, and to subsume each of these methods under one of our three headings.

In studying any set of phenomena directly, we pass them before our eyes in the attempt to discover recurrent patterns and, if possible, to make out the entire configuration of events. Sumner's study of customs may be taken as a good example of the use of this method. These recurrent patterns gradually crystallize into concepts. Concepts result from the capacity of the mind to perceive the similarity of configurations perceived in succession. Concepts may be defined as transposable perceptual patterns to which we have given names. Imagination is often called into play to fit together pieces of configurations, to perceive with insight configurations of events which have not actually been present to the senses.[3] A high degree of insight into causal relations is implicit in the scientific concept. A concept must be transposable not only from one set of phenomena to another but also from one mind to another. The most effective way to communicate concepts is always to de-

---

3   Herbert Blumer ("Science without Concepts," *American Journal of Sociology*, XXXVI, No. 4, 515–33) has defined the concept in terms of the assistance which it renders in filling in the gaps and open spaces of perception. It is true that the concept does this, but this aspect of the concept should be interpreted rather as imagination, which is the tendency of the mind to complete a configuration when only its rudiments are presented to consciousness. Blumer's view apparently bears the earmarks of sensationalistic psychology, as do most other interpretations of concepts. A concept is not necessarily a construct, and not even scientific concepts are always and necessarily constructs; although the physiologist would have occasion to frame a number of constructs in order to understand the physiological processes of a dog, yet it is likely that the physiologist's concept of a dog as a dog is not much further removed from sensory data than the layman's concept of a dog. The scientific concept often is a construct, a configuration whose rudiments are present to the senses, whose totality is the work of the imagination. Blumer's discussion of this type of concept is particularly enlightening.

scribe or to point to phenomena and to give to each configuration of events its name. All directed thought is conceptualizing activity. An unfortunate circumstance is that communication often breaks down, so that one acquires names without their attendant perceptual patterns. There is abundant evidence in sociological literature that many of our colleagues have learned words without perceiving processes, so that they literally do not know what they are talking about.

Experimentation may be classified as a mode of getting insight through the direct study of phenomena. Experimentation is not a method of establishing causal relations by mechanical manipulation or numerical criteria, for experimentation grows out of pre-existing insight and is useful only in so far as it leads to the acquisition, refinement, or verification of insight. The experimental procedure enables us to isolate one causal mechanism and to observe it in standardized form, to repeat it over and over, or to repeat it with variations until we obtain insight. Any other trained observer may repeat the experiment and get the same result, and the same insight; the ultimate test of the experiment is the ability of different observers to obtain the same insight. Experiments are meant to be repeated. Also, it is pre-existing grasp of causal processes and functional connections which makes an experiment critical or significant. Further, an experiment always flows out of empirical insight as to suspected causal relations and relevant variables; the experiment succeeds if it is based upon good insight, and it usually fails if it is based upon false insight. No virtuosity of technique can compensate for want of understanding.

The application of insight as the touchstone of method enables us to evaluate properly the rôle of imagination in scientific method. The scientific process is akin to the artistic process; it is a process of selecting out those elements of experience which fit together and recombining them in the mind. Much of this kind of research is simply a ceaseless mulling over, and even the physical scientist has considerable need of an armchair. Constructs so formed must be conformable to reality, must be internally consistent, and as far as possible consistent with other members of the same system.

A second method by which insight may be derived is that of the study of symbols derived from phenomena. We shall consider particularly quantitative symbols, although all reports furnished by others would strictly come under this heading. We have ruled out the justification of statistical method which makes counting of cases a condition precedent to establishing a causal relationship; with this must go the belief that what is not quantified is not science. But statistical method remains immensely important in any system of methodology. We do not deny the validity of statistical method, nor contemplate a limitation of its field, but the rationale of statistics which we here present may strike some as strange.

It is submitted that statistical method is successful as a means of discovering truth when it is used to subserve insight, and that it fails when it is used without insight or in such a manner as to obstruct insight. Statistical enterprises depart from pre-existing insight, and are only worth while if they lead to further or more accurate insight. The valid uses of statistics seem to be: (1) to treat mass phenomena, (2) to give objectivity to social investigations by substituting the study of quantitative symbols for the direct study of social phenomena, (3) to sum up and to check partial insights, and (4) to determine the relative numerical importance of known causal configurations.

1. Probably the best use of statistics is for the study of various kinds of mass phenomena. In certain classes of phenomena, the important facts are numerical relations; this is the case with the unemployment problem. Sometimes, too, social facts are so widespread that they cannot be directly studied but must be converted into figures and studied in this symbolic form. As social centralization increases this will be increasingly important. But mass phenomena must be studied until they are seen to fall into a pattern, and until one glimpses, at least, the causal interdependence of parts; they must be studied, in short, with a view to obtaining insight. It is noteworthy that some of the most illuminating studies of mass phenomena would not pass the Pearsonian tests of scientific truth; the parts are quantitative and to some extent repetitive, but the whole is a single case study. Much of what we know about

human ecology is as yet generalization from a single case. In the study of mass phenomena, it is well to insist that there can be no talk of a causal relation unless a definite causal pattern appears.

2. Statistics may give added objectivity to social investigations by substituting the study of quantitative symbols for the direct study of social phenomena. If we are to have an objective social science, we must utilize statistics in this manner wherever it is possible to do so. Social phenomena are so emotionally toned that even the most impartial observer may well doubt whether he has interpreted them without bias. Perhaps this is how it comes about that even those researchers who say the most unkind things about statistics are overjoyed when the turn of events makes it possible for them to quantify their results. It is clear, however, that the use of quantitative symbols by no means guarantees objectivity, for faulty insight underlying the investigation or prejudice in the interpretation may vitiate the entire research. And if symbols are substituted for reality, it is well to remember that a generalization tends to be significant only as an interpretation of that order of phenomena from the study of which it emerges. A study of marriage statistics is not a study of marriage, and all too commonly fails to reveal anything concerning marriage.

3. There is also partial insight which reveals causal processes inconclusively; this appears where we are not able to analyze or control our phenomena properly, and must therefore deal with a nucleus of interlocking and perhaps interfering causal processes. Statistics may be used to refine such fragmentary insight, as a means of gaining control over phenomena of multiple causation. Psychologists, when they are not able to set up their experiments in such a way as to control all the variables, attempt to gain additional control through statistical technique. Statistics may also be used as simple statements of fragmentary insight, or as signposts pointing to undiscovered causal processes.

4. A most important use of statistics is in determining the relative numerical importance of known causal configurations. It would be interesting, and possibly of some importance, to know how many small men have developed the state of mind known as the inferiority complex; only statistics can tell us. The question-

naire, for all the absurdities that unintelligent persons have committed in its name, has served the social sciences well, and its principal utility comes under this heading. The questionnaire is oriented by the empirical insight of the person who frames the questions, and it can seldom reveal anything that was not implicit in those questions; it can rarely, therefore, discover anything new, although it has considerable value in the testing of hypotheses. The greater the quantitative value of the questionnaire, the more nearly defined and interchangeable its units, the more completely it must fail to reveal previously unsuspected connections of cause and effect. However, it is of great practical and administrative importance to know which causal relations are most frequent, for in administration we must always play the main chance; statistics can help us to find the main chance.

It is insight, then, that makes the statistical method work. Our case will be stronger if we can show that when statistical method fails, it is from lack of insight. Bungling statisticians commonly misuse their methods in such a way as (1) to give an unreal conclusiveness to results that are in no sense final, (2) to obscure the dynamic or functional connections in the living material which is the object of research, or (3) to lead research away from the fundamental issues of science toward those relatively meaningless things which are accessible to quantitative techniques.

1. One may, through a statistical organization of his materials, give to them an appearance of order, exactness, and finality that is unintentionally deceptive. There is something certain-seeming in a neat row of figures, something that tempts to dogmatism. The gravamen of this charge is that we may rely upon figures to the neglect of other methods which might bring us into closer contact with our problem. A similar self-deception often occurs when we think we have measured something. Quantification in the social sciences is not often genuine. Typically we have an approximate figure which stands in an unknown relationship to the unknown which we are trying to measure. Thus we use divorce rates as a measure of marital maladjustment, death rates as a measure of ill health, insanity rates as a measure of mental ill health, various figures as indices of the crime rate.

2. Statistical organization of materials may obscure the dynamic connections within them. A science that deals with life must be concerned with process. No statistical organization, however refined, can give us a view of process; it can give only a view of the ends of process. One has often the feeling, when he is confronted with the results of such an elaborate study as Dr. Hamilton's research in marriage, that at least as significant an accounting of marriage might have been made by throwing away all the material which Dr. Hamilton finally saw fit to use and using the material which he no doubt threw away. We become museum keepers when we become mere custodians of facts. What we need is a conception of process, a conception of change, which is something a statistical demonstration often fails to give. Statistical organization involves classification. Classification is grouping like things together. But like things may have in fact no relation to each other. The very process of classification, necessary to statistical treatment, must inevitably destroy certain functional interconnections.

3. Partly as an incident of the inevitable obscuring of functional and dynamic connections, and partly for other not wholly unconnected reasons, the practitioners of quantitative methods have commonly felt a strong impulsion away from the significant central problems of science toward those peripheral phenomena which permit of quantitative study. To be sure, the quantitative approach, used unimaginatively, leads to a mere enumeration of facts, perhaps significant and perhaps not, but demonstrable and ascertainable, concerning certain traits and attributes, and it therefore leads away from a real coming to grips with the dynamic facts of function. Thus the intelligence testers know every fact connected with intelligence except what it is. It is easy, too, to write a chapter concerning sex differences, but it is not easy to show the meaning of those differences in terms of function.

Our third source of insight is sympathetic imagination. The social sciences differ from the physical sciences in that our knowledge of human beings is internally as well as externally derived. Cooley has stated it well:

[Sympathetic penetration] is derived from contact with the minds of other men, through communication, which sets going a process of thought and sentiment similar to theirs and enables us to understand them by sharing their states of mind. This I call personal or social knowledge. It might also be described as sympathetic, or, in its more active forms, as dramatic, since it is apt to consist of a visualization of behavior accompanied by imagination of corresponding mental processes.[4]

This is the scientific method that consists of imagining what it would be like to be somebody else. It is characteristically an interpretation of the behavior of others in terms of purposes and emotional states imputed to them. Insight of this kind is wrongly called introspective, for introspection is a mode of studying phenomena at first hand, while this kind of insight is derived from imagination which makes use of introspection as a clue to the mental states of others.

Sympathetic insight furnishes indispensable clues to human nature, so that what we can find out by behavioristic study must usually seem flavorless by comparison. Behavioristic study is indeed possible only by the most extreme effort of the will, for it is difficult to exclude sympathetic insight from descriptions of behavior, and probably no behaviorist has as yet been able to avoid the occasional use of "introspective" terminology. This kind of insight has two unfortunate limitations: It is exceedingly liable to error, and it is not surely cumulative because it is often incommunicable. These defects cannot be minimized. Those who think that science must be exact will consider it impossible to found a science upon the sands of sympathy and imagination, and perhaps they will be right. Such persons will prefer insight based upon the direct study of phenomena and the study of numerical symbols. But it remains true that nearly all of the things that people most want to know about other people are accessible only through sympathetic imagination. Perhaps we must say with Cooley, "I do not look for any rapid growth of science that is profound, as regards its penetration into human life, and at the same time exact and indisputable."[5]

The literary form which most usefully condenses and organizes

---

[4]   C. H. Cooley, "The Roots of Social Knowledge," *Sociological Theory and Social Research*, p. 290.
[5]   *Ibid.*, p. 296.

sympathetic insight is also an art form, the case study. The case study presents and attempts to communicate both insight derived from behavioristic study and insight of the sympathetic kind. As a combination of "scientific" and artistic insight, the case study is subject to peculiar perils. It is undeniable that every investigator tends to see in a case the things that he is looking for. Whatever its other merits, a highly valued conceptual framework is here undoubtedly a disadvantage, and this is the reason why social investigators who carry a slender load of concepts sometimes go so surprisingly far; they have no preconceptions as to how things are going to shape up. Without concepts as an aid to observation we could see almost nothing, and yet concepts hinder us from seeing things afresh. A value of the life-history document prepared by a person innocent of sociology is its freedom from indoctrinated observation. Many efforts which masquerade as case studies are not case studies at all, but merely the results of informal questionnaires, or schedules, with the results organized by persons rather than by questions; they are not case studies as regards new insight, because the investigator does not get any insight or record his phenomena in such a way as to allow his readers to get it. They are spurious case studies, and their principal use is a quantitative one, for they do make it possible to estimate the relative importance of known causal patterns. As a matter of literary technique, most so-called case studies fail of their purpose because of their conceptualized form. The way to communicate insight is not to verbalize it in the form of an abstraction but to describe or to point out phenomena. The difference between a good novel and the ordrinary case study is that the novel describes false or non-existential phenomena to communicate true insight, while the case study conceptualizes true phenomena to communicate no insight.

It is of some importance to deal with the view that the procedure of collecting a number of case studies renders the process "informally" statistical. This is not necessarily true. An interviewer may wish to subject a number of persons to study simply as a means of learning to see his cases with a high degree of structuration, so that he has more complex and workable insight into every case from having seen the others, and there may be in all this no numerical implication. The procedure does in fact often become informally statistical, but it need not become so. It is an artistic process. Men who can produce good case studies, accurate and convincing pictures of people and institutions, are essentially artists; they may not be learned men, and sometimes they are not even intelligent men, but they have imagination and know how to use words to convey truth. Some of the most significant books in the field of sociology have been written by men who could never be brought to understand the distinction between form and content of social processes.

Our view of scientific method as a struggle to obtain insight forces the admission that all science is half art. All science depends upon perceptions reconstructed and fitted together in imagination, upon an artistic re-creation of events. This holds a *fortiori* for sociology, for sociology must also include imaginative insight. The sociologist must strive to understand the scattered bits of human experience, and then he must try to put things together. There ought to be a place in the world for the sociologist who is also an artist. For in the past we have had to depend upon three sorts of lying prophets for our interpretations of social institutions: upon men of affairs, who lie like Ananias in their own interest, or lie as advocates do to prove their cases; upon literary men, who lie like Baron Munchausen, primarily to amuse, or from sheer lack of mental discipline; and upon scholars, who lie at second hand by quoting something somebody else has said that is not so.

That there can be false insight is a point that has already been conceded. It is possible to perceive causal relationships that do not exist. But the remedy for false insight is not quantification or any mechanical test. Quantification will merely facilitate the elaboration of the error, and experiment will project it into another realm. The one and only remedy for false insight is true insight. There seem to be three criteria of truth in the insight method, and we may characterize them as artistic, systematic, and pragmatic.[6]

6   The artistic criterion includes agreement of (trained but unindoctrinated) observers, wealth of inference, and everything that determines whether or not the whole of a theory presents a convincing picture of some part of the jig-saw puzzle of society. We should restrict the systematic criterion to considerations of internal consistency. The pragmatic criterion is, of course, control.

Insight is the unknown quantity which has eluded students of scientific method. That is why the really great men of sociology had no "method." They had a method; it was the search for insight. They went "by guess and by God," but they found out things. They strove to perceive with insight.

II. Social Problems

3

SOCIAL PROBLEMS AND THE MORES

1936

I

THE TERM *social problem* indicates not merely an observed phenomenon but the state of mind of the observer as well. Value judgments define certain conditions of human life and certain kinds of behavior as social problems; there can be no social problem without a value judgment.[1] When our attitude toward a phenomenon is involved in our concept of it, logical difficulties arise which can only be avoided by shifting to an inclusive point of view which enables us to study both the thing and our attitude toward it. It is the purpose of the present paper to suggest such a point of view for the study of social problems.

Various attempts to treat social problems in a scientific manner have proved useless because they have dealt only with the objective side of social problems and have failed to include the attitude which constituted them problems. The attitude, the value judgment, is the subjective side of the social problem, and its existence renders meaningless any purely objective açcount of social

Reprinted from the *American Sociological Review* 1, no. 6 (December 1936) : 922–33.

[1]   I accept as best and clearest the definition of social problems given by L. K. Frank: "A social problem, then, appears to be any difficulty or misbehavior of a fairly large number of persons which we wish to remove or correct, and the solution of a social problem is evidently the discovery of a method for this removal or correction." (L. K. Frank, *Social Problems; Amer. Jour. Sociol.*, 30, Jan. 1925, 463.) Throughout this paper I have drawn heavily upon Frank's fundamental discussion.

problems. In spite of all attempts to define social problems objectively and denotatively, value judgments inevitably intrude themselves into the discussion. Indeed, value judgments must be
brought in somehow, for there is no other way of identifying a
condition as a social problem than by passing a value judgment
upon it. Because they have failed to define clearly their object of
study, which is properly the condition called a social problem in
relation to the attitude of the person who considers it a problem,
sociologists have failed to achieve a scientifically defensible treatment of social problems.

Two errors, both of which stem from failure to take the inclusive view of which we speak, vitiate the work of those who have
tried to deal with social problems scientifically. (A) In attempting
to exclude value judgments from their discussion, they have unwittingly ruled out the essential criterion by which social problems
may be identified. Value judgments are, therefore, brought into
the discussion by some trick of words or by some error of interpretation which is necessary, if the discussion is to make any sense
at all. Evaluative elements are present in a concept by implication,
as in the case of the culture lag concept,[2] or the definition of some
concept such as social pathology, social psychiatry, or social disorganization is shuffled so that it includes the necessary value judgment,[3] or, as in social planning, value judgments are assumed
throughout the whole discussion but are not necessarily in it.

[2]   See James W. Woodard, "Critical Notes on the Culture Lag Concept," *Social Forces*, 12 March, 1934, 388–398. In this article Woodward
points out implicit evaluations in the concept of cultural lag. This evalua-
tional element detracts from the usefulness of the concept only when one
pretends to use it in a purely objective fashion.
[3]   Note the value laden terms in which social organization and disorganization are defined by Queen, Bodenhafer, and Harper: "When there
is a state of affairs or a trend of events characterized by harmony, team-
work, understanding, approval, and the like, we may speak of organization." (S. A. Queen, W. B. Bodenhafer, and E. R. Harper: *Social Organization and Disorganization*, Thomas Y. Crowell and Co., New York, 1935,
p. 4.) Parenthetically, the above statement as it stands is far from true,
for conflict is not synonymous with disorganization; conflict is frequently
an inherent part of the social structure and one which contributes to its
stability and permanence. The concepts of organization and disorganiza-

(B) Having first ruled out the only thing which all social problems have in common, the fact that someone has passed a value judgment upon them, writers then endeavor vainly to find some other principle which will enable them to treat all social problems together. Some thread of theory is obviously necessary for purposes of logical presentation, but the principle involved is never quite adequate to the task it is called upon to perform; the resulting monographs expound admirably the relationship of social problems to culture lag, social disorganization, and so on, but do not constitute complete treatments of social problems. To take the concept of social disorganization as an example, it is clear that this concept explains much in the field of social problems, but does not explain all. Many of the conditions which we customarily treat as social problems spring from the very nature of the social organization, and not in any imaginable sense from disorganization. Poverty of the wage-earner, sometimes called the basic social problem, is necessitated by facts which lie deep in the present economic system and in the relation of social classes to one another. Substandard housing, likewise, is the natural and inevitable result of institutions and practices of long standing, and cannot be explained in terms of social disorganization. The same is true of many other social problems.

II

If we are to treat social problems scientifically, we must try to understand why we consider them problems. We must subject to analysis our judgments of value as well as the social phenomena upon which these judgments are passed. We may do this by applying the concept of the mores to the problem of social problems as we have defined it. Social problems exist within a definite moral universe. Once we step out of our circle of accustomed moralities, social problems cease to exist for us. Likewise, if we consider the possibility of revolutionary change, social problems lose most of

---

tion lend themselves readily to this type of confusion, being intensely subjective in nature, since what one person sees as disorganization may appear to another merely a more complex form of organization.

their complexity. A simple formulation of our standpoint, which we advance as roughly accurate for most social problems, rests upon the assumption of two conflicting sets of mores. Social problems result from the interaction of these two groups of mores, which we may call the *organizational* and the *humanitarian* mores.[4]

The organizational, or basic, mores, are those upon which the social order is founded, the mores of private property and individualism, the mores of the monogamous family, Christianity, and nationalism. Conditions of human life which we regard as social problems emanate from the organizational mores as effective causes. Indeed, the fact that a certain condition is in some sense humanly caused is an unrecognized but essential criterion of the social problem. We are all, as Galsworthy remarked, under sentence of death, but death is not a social problem; death becomes a social problem only when men die, as we think, unnecessarily, as in war or by accident or preventable disease. Not all the miseries of mankind are social problems. Every condition which we regard as a social problem is in some sense a result of our institutions or we do not concern ourselves with it.

Alongside the organizational mores there exists a set of humanitarian mores; those who follow the humanitarian mores feel an urge to make the world better or to remedy the misfortunes of others.[5] Probably the humanitarian impulse has always existed, but it has apparently attained group-wide expression at a relatively late period in our history, following the breakdown of primary group society. Social problems in the modern sense did not exist when every primary group cared for its own helpless and unfortunate. Social problems as we know them are a phenomenon of secondary group society, in which the primary group is no longer

[4]   I have limited the present paper to a discussion of the interaction of these mores at the present time. A lengthier treatment of the subject would have to pay considerable attention to the historical interrelations of these sets of mores.

[5]   While an explanation in terms of psychopathology would account for the fact that certain persons rather than certain others are ones to pass judgments, we must assume humanitarian mores in order to account for the fact that anyone passes them.

willing and able to take care of its members. It was this breakdown which called group-wide humanitarianism into existence; it was this situation which brought it about that we were asked to feel sympathy for those whom we had never seen. Humanitarian mores are frequently expressed, for they are highly verbal, and they command the instant assent of almost any group.

The formula which crystallizes in our minds as we approach social problems from the angle of the mores is this: Social problems are social conditions of which some of the causes are felt to be human and moral. Value judgments define these conditions as social problems. Value judgments are the formal causes of social problems, just as the law is the formal cause of crime. Value judgments originate from the humanitarian mores, which are somewhat in conflict with the organizational mores. Social problems are moral problems; they are like the problems of a problem play. The existence of some sort of moral problem is the single thread that binds all social problems together. Any important social problem is marked by moral conflict in the individual and social conflict in the group. It is thus that the strain for consistency in the mores expresses itself.[6]

When someone has expressed a value judgment upon some condition of human life which originates from the organizational mores, and begins to reflect upon possible courses of action, he is at last in a position to understand the sense in which social prob-

[6] I should not like to be understood as making a claim for the originality of this conception of social problems. My interpretation is apparently not very far from Sumner's. L. K. Frank, in the paper quoted and in some other writings, appears to have anticipated my statement almost completely. Burgess makes use of a similar conception in one of his papers. (See E. W. Burgess, "Social Planning and the Mores," *Pub. Amer. Sociol. Soc.*, 29, No. 3, 1–18.) In numerous writings Woodard has attacked the same problem by means of a different type of analysis; I have in fact borrowed some terminology and certain interpretations from him. The Marxian conception of dialectic seems closely related to my interpretation; so, I am informed, are certain passages of Bergson. It appears, then, that a great many thinkers have converged upon what is essentially the same interpretation, a fact which should serve, at any rate, to give the interpretation a certain added cogency.

lems are complex. For the same mores from which the deplored conditions originate continue to operate to limit any action which one takes in order to remedy them. Frank illustrates this limiting action of the organizational mores by showing how difficult it would be to explain our housing problem to a man from Mars.

We should have to delegate an economist, a lawyer, a political scientist, a sociologist, and a historian to explain about the system of private property, the price system, popular government, congestion of population, transportation, and so on. And when they had severally and jointly expounded the complexities of the situation, pointing out that we cannot just build houses, but must rely upon individual initiative and private enterprise to enter the field of building construction, that we must use the "price system" to obtain the needed land which is someone's private property, to buy the necessary materials and to hire the skilled labor, that we must borrow capital on mortgages to finance these expenditures, paying a bonus to induce someone to lend that capital and also pay interest on the loan, together with amortization quotas and then we must contrive to rent these dwellings in accordance with a multiplicity of rules and regulations about leases and so on—after all these sundry explanations showing that to get houses built we must not infringe anyone's rights of private property or freedom to make a profit, and that what we want is to find a way of getting houses without interfering with anyone's customary activities, our visitor would suddenly exclaim, "Yes, I begin to see; have you any other such difficult problems, for this is exceedingly interesting?"[7]

In every social problem seek the moral problem; try to discover the complex processes of conflict, supplementation, and interference in our own moral imperatives. That is the principle which should guide the sociologist as he seeks to study social problems scientifically. Let us attempt to sketch the outlines of this conflict of mores with regard to a few typical social problems. Poverty is a social problem, when it exists in the midst of plenty, or in a world in which universal plenty is a technological possibility. The value judgment passed on poverty defines it as at least in part socially caused and as something which ought to be remedied. A simpleton would suggest that the remedy for poverty in the midst of plenty

[7]   L. K. Frank, *op. cit.*, pp. 465–466.

is to redistribute income. We reject this solution at once because it would interfere with the institution of private property, would destroy the incentive for thrift and hard work and disjoint the entire economic system. What is done to alleviate poverty must be done within the limits set by the organizational mores.

A slightly different type of conflict appears when a value judgment is passed, not upon the conditions of someone's life, but upon his behavior. An unmarried girl has a baby; her family and community take harsh and unreasoned action against her. The humanitarian comes in to save the pieces, but he cannot make things too easy for the girl or try to convince her family and community that she is not guilty of moral turpitude for fear of encouraging illegitimacy and injuring the morality upon which the monogamous family is founded. Likewise, venereal disease becomes a social problem in that it arises from our family institutions and also in that the medical means which could be used to prevent it, which would unquestionably be fairly effective, cannot be employed for fear of altering the mores of chastity. The situation is similar when it is a question of adjusting family relationships; Kingsley Davis has supplied a penetrating analysis of the "family clinic" as an agency operating within a circle of conflicting moral demands.[8]

Confusing conflicts of mores appear in those situations, frequent enough in unemployment relief, in which human misery and misbehavior are intermingled. When people suffer privation, the humanitarian mores dictate relief. If these people are willing to work, if the old live in strict monogamy and the young do not contract marriage until they are off the relief rolls, if they obey the law, if they do not conceal any assets, if they spend absolutely nothing for luxuries, if they are grateful and not demanding, if the level of relief does not approach the income of the employed, relatively few objections are raised to the giving of relief. But let any of the above violations of the organizational mores defining the situation of the recipient of charity arise, and the untrained investigator will quite possibly cut off relief in a storm of moral indignation. Herein he is

[8]   Kingsley Davis, "The Application of Science to Personal Relations, A Critique of the Family Clinic Idea," *Amer. Sociol. Rev.*, 1, April, 1936, 236–247.

in agreement with the moral sense of the greater part of the community. The trained social worker attempts at this point to bring the investigator over to a more broadly humanitarian point of view.[9]

It is necessary to remember that in all this the humanitarian is simply following his own mores, which he has received irrationally and which he obeys without reflection, being supported in this by the concurrence of his own group. When the social worker says, "One must not make moral judgments," she means that one must not make moral judgments of the conventional sort, but that it is perfectly all right to pass a moral judgment on the cruel judge or to hate the man who hates the negro. Often the humanitarian has all the prejudices of his society upside down, and one who talks to him is reminded that there is still "a superstition in avoiding superstition, when men think to do best when they go furthest from the superstition formerly received." Among the sociologists, those who teach so-called "attitude courses" are particularly likely to fall into this type of confusion.

A few further complications may be noted. The humanitarian often argues for his reforms on the basis of considerations which are consonant with the organizational mores but alien to the spirit of humanitarianism; he advocates a new system of poor relief, saying that it will be cheaper, while really he is hoping that it will prove more humane. As all of us must do sometimes, in order to communicate truth he has to lie a little. Great confusion is caused in the field of criminology by shuttling back and forth between practical and humanitarian universes of discourse. Orthodox economists have recognized the humanitarian impulse in an almost perverted manner; they owlishly assure us that prevalent economic practices are not what they seem to be, but are in the long run ultra-humanitarian.

Certain implications of this interpretation of social problems on the basis of conflict in the mores seem very clear. I should venture to suggest the following points:

---

9   For a delightful discussion of a number of these situations, see the column, *Miss Bailey Says*, edited by Gertrude Springer, in *The Survey*.

(1) The notion of conflict of mores enables us to understand why progress in dealing with social problems is so slow. Social problems are not solved because people do not want to solve them. From a thousand scattered sources the evidence converges upon this apparently unavoidable conclusion, from the history of reform movements, from the biographies and autobiographies of reformers, from politics, from the records of peace conferences, from the field of social work, from private discussions, and even from the debates of so-called radical groups. Even those who are most concerned about social problems are not quite at one with themselves in their desire to solve them. Solving social problems would necessitate a change in the organizational mores from which they arise. The humanitarian, for all his allegience to the humanitarian mores, is yet a member of our society and as such is under the sway of its organizational mores. He wishes to improve the condition of the poor, but not to interfere with private property. Until the humanitarian is willing to give up his allegiance to the organizational mores, and in some cases to run squarely against them, he must continue to treat symptoms without removing their causes.[10]

Frequently the liberal humanitarian is brought squarely up against the fact that he does not really want what he says he wants. The difficulty which he faces is that the human misery which he deplores is a necessary part of a social order which seems to him good. A cruel person may amuse himself at the expense of humanitarians by suggesting simple and effective means to secure the ends which they believe they value above all others, or a cynical person may use this device to block reform. The means suggested, if adequate to the ends, are certain to involve deep changes in our society, and their costs terrifies the humanitarian so that he feels

---

[10]   Frank makes his intelligent Martian say: "If it is not indelicate of me to remark, every social problem you describe seems to have the same characteristics as every other social problem, namely, the crux of the problem is to find some way of avoiding the undesirable consequences of your established laws, institutions, and social practices, without changing those established laws, etc. In other words, you appear to be seeking a way to cultivate the flower without the fruit, which, in a world of cause and effect is somewhat difficult, to say the least." (*Op. cit.*, p. 467.)

compelled to make excuses. The pacifist is sincerely concerned about war, and he will even assent to the general proposition that permanent peace requires, among other things, a redistribution of world population. But suggest that the United States should make a start by ceding the Philippines and Hawaii to Japan and opening its doors to Oriental immigration, and the pacifist usually loses heart! Indeed, one wonders whether there are many pacifists whose pacifism would not be shattered by a Japanese invasion of Mexico or Canada. The pacifist does not really want peace at its necessary price; he wants peace with the continuation of things in the present order which necessitate war. He wants a miracle. Lincoln Steffens tells how the shrewd but illiberal Clemenceau defeated Wilson by showing him the cost of peace; the incident is valuable, at any rate, as showing how the two men might have behaved.[11] Professing to be completely in sympathy with Wilson's ideals, Clemenceau stated that peace would involve the loss of colonies; the French would have to come out of Morocco; the United States would have to surrender island possessions, give up spheres of influence, abrogate the Monroe doctrine, and so on. When Wilson replied that America was not ready to go quite so far, all at once, Clemenceau retorted that in that case the conference did not want peace, but war, and that the best time for France to make war was when she had one of her enemies down. One is reminded of Bacon's saying, "For it is the solecism of power to think to command the end, and yet not to endure the mean."

When one considers the conditions under which the humanitarian impulse comes to expression, he must realize that the urge to do something for others is not a very important determinant of change in our society, for any translation of humanitarianism into behavior is fenced in by restrictions which usually limit it to trivialities. The expression of humanitarian sentiments must remain almost wholly verbal, and because of this situation which is inherent in our acquisitive and possessive society: No one loses by giving verbal expression to humanitarianism or by the merely

[11]   Lincoln Steffens, *The Autobiography of Lincoln Steffens*, pp. 780–781.

verbal expression of another, but many would lose by putting humanitarianism into practice, and someone would certainly lose by any conceivable reform. From the powerful someone who is certain to lose comes opposition to reform.

For the person who makes his living by practicing humanitarianism, the professional social worker, there is small opportunity to participate in social change in any important or fundamental way. The private agency depends for its support upon voluntary contributions, and the contributions of the rich greatly outweight those of everyone else. The social worker earnestly follows the humanitarian mores, and passes value judgments upon conditions of human life which originate from the organizational mores, but he dares not attack those organizational mores directly and effectively, for the people who pay his salary and in countless ways assist him in his work of mercy are the persons who profit from the continuation of things as they are. An analysis of the board of directors of a private agency, and of the list of large contributors, will usually reveal among these "angels" a large enough sprinkling of persons who own slum tenements, profit from sweated labor, speculate in real estate in various not too ethical ways, and make lucrative deals with the government, to block effectively or very greatly to hinder any attempt to change the conditions of the masses. The wives of predatory business men may have their pet charities, but they are not going to subsidize a revolution.[12] Lincoln Steffens found that it was ultimately not the worst people but the best people who blocked reform. Nor does the social worker who is attached to a governmental agency labor in an ideal situation. He does not have to carry rich patrons around on sofa pillows, but he has to work for politicians, for politicians who have no understanding of the fine points of social case work and a very great understanding of the necessities of practical politics.

(2) The conflict of motives with which we face social problems produces a lack of wholeness in our mental processes concerning them. Although sociologists have studied social problems for many

---

[12]   See Maria Rogers and Edward J. Fitzgerald, "Social Work is Futile," *The American Mercury*, 32, July, 1934, pp. 265–273.

years, they have produced astonishingly little systematic thought concerning them. Sociologists have displayed a considerable tendency to take over the formulations of social workers. Let us attempt a brief critical analysis of the mental product of the social worker. The mental processes of social workers as a group may perhaps be described as aim-inhibited. The profession lacks a philosophy, and lacks it precisely because some generations of social workers have defined their task narrowly in terms of a half-understood interaction of conflicting sets of mores. When one has accustomed himself to the thought that he can carry any proposed scheme only a certain distance, when one has formed the habit of breaking off any action, or speech, or thought, when it reaches a point where it may offend someone important, he loses the faculty of carrying mental processes through to completion. The task determines the content and organization of the mind to a considerable degree; the task which the social worker sets for his intelligence is to work for social amelioration and yet remain within the bounds of the basic mores. He must, therefore, keep his mental processes fragmentary. Other characteristics betray the useful inability of even very intelligent social workers to draw obvious conclusions. There is overemphasis of the individual causes of poverty. There is the tendency to regard social problems as the problems of poor people exclusively. Euphemisms becloud the premises and the conclusions of the social worker to an amazing degree, and only a few of the boldest escape the tendency to speak in riddles. The function of these euphemisms is of course to prevent another from drawing for the social worker the conclusion which he so carefully avoids stating. Following those fads which always flourish where a basic philosophy is lacking, social workers seize upon various harmless proposals—case work, psychiatry, social security, and other assorted brands of salvationism—and magnify their importance until they seem like things worth dying for.

My remarks are not intended as a criticism of social work; they are directed merely at the ideology of social work. The social worker has perfected an adjustment to the situation presented by the conflict of mores, and I do not deny that he performs a certain function in a world that is imperfect and is not likely to get any better very soon. I am simply analyzing the moral blockings which prevent the social worker from thinking incisively. Many sociologists are caught up in an almost identical situation, especially those who specialize in the study of social problems. And such moral disunity effectively robs of significance the work of a great many brilliant men in our field.

(3) The humanitarian and organizational mores are somewhat in conflict with one another, but they are also related in another way. These two sets of mores are complementary parts of the same culture configuration, related parts of a single organic whole. The organizational mores produce conditions which call the humanitarian spirit into activity; at the same time humanitarianism takes care of certain exigencies in such a way as to decrease the probability of sudden, violent changes in the organizational mores; the "pathos manipulation," to employ the phraseology of a colleague, of the social worker and the reformer enables the existing culture configuration to persist unbroken. Here we are brought sharply up against the inescapable problems of value which are implicit in the evolution-revolution antithesis.

III

Almost everything that has been said or written concerning social problems has been oriented from the point of view of the humanitarian mores. Making use of one verbal trick or another, sociologists have found excuses for importing into our science almost the whole of the humanitarian ideology with all its self-contradictions and illogicalities. Such practices give color to the belief that sociologists are "fake professors of a pretended science." Pretended scientists have lost themselves in the mazy interrelations of the humanitarian and the organizational mores, when they should have been following a third set of mores, the scientific. The duty of one who wishes to adhere to the scientific morality is clear enough. He must study the processes of social change of which the struggles to deal with social problems are a part. The scientist must completely eschew all moral judgments, those which emanate from humanitarianism as well as others.[13] He must completely subordinate all other values to that of intellectual and scientific integrity.

The urge for social betterment is itself a part of the dialectic of social change which the sociologist sets out to study. The sociologist must investigate the growth and functioning of the humanitarian mores, as well as the operation of those mores from which the conditions which we call social problems result. He must trace the complex patterns of facilitation and interference which characterize the interaction of these mores. He must discover the long run as well as the short run interactions of humanitarianism and individualism, and ascertain to what extent they tend to interpenetrate. He must study the cultural and psychological background of reformers. He must attempt to forge a really comprehensive theory of social change; he must do more fundamental thinking than has yet been done as to the relative importance of compromise and of intransigent struggle in social change.

[13]   I am inclined to agree with Woodard that this formulation does not exclude all evaluations. Woodard argues that the scientist should not pass moral judgments (and this includes judgments emanating from the humanitarian mores), but points out that in a functional science some sort of judgment of value is not only appropriate but altogether unavoidable. He suggests that the sociologist may essay "inductive appraisals of functional appropriateness," based upon his special knowledge of social processes, of the interrelations of human beings and institutions, and his grasp of the organismic unity of society; such judgments are non-moral in nature, and are in fact the best possible safeguard against moral judgments. Cf. James W. Woodard, "Critical Notes on the Nature of Sociology as a Science," *Social Forces*, 11, Oct. 1932, 28–43.

4

ADDENDUM TO THE PHILOSOPHY
OF HISTORY

A CURIOUS FACT about human history is that in the thousands of recorded crises which the race has endured the right side has nearly always won. History, especially the new history, does not always say this right out, and yet it is there somehow, and one who reads the record with an ear for overtones can hear it.

It is curious when one thinks about it that right should almost without exception triumph over wrong. It certainly demands explanation. Were the wicked always weak? Or the weak wicked? It seems incredible that the strong should always be also the just, and yet there are the facts. Whenever mankind has stood at the crossroads, it has somehow taken the right turn. The Greeks beat off the Persians, which was fortunate for us, as anyone must admit, since otherwise we should all be Orientals. Cicero, after prodigious talk, finally managed to conquer Catiline, who was a rotter by any standards. Christ died on the cross but on the third day he rose again. Judas Iscariot went and hanged himself. We Europeans beat off the Moors. We did not succeed in our enterprise with regard to the Holy Sepulchre, but the episode was fortunate none the less in its effect upon the growth of modern civilization, and after a while we decided that the Holy Sepulchre did not matter so much after all. The Commoners at length defeated the Stuarts and established the foundations of free government. We Americans overcame the English. The North battered the slave-power

Previously unpublished.

of the South into submission. The same providential hand has guided us in the internal struggles of our country. At various times in our history the people have seemed to be on the point of yielding to some demagogue and yet somehow they never have for any length of time. Justice has sometimes been balked or delayed, but apparently it has always triumphed in the end. Right has usually prevailed over wrong. It seems providential, somehow.

Of course some of the crises of history were more or less spurious. Subsequent history would have turned out about the same if they had been decided differently. The United States might have become a great and democratic nation if the colonists had not beaten the English. The slaves would probably have been freed, in time, if there had never been a Civil War. Perhaps Bryan would not really have ruined the country if he had been elected. We may allow for these spurious crises. True crises still remain in plenty. Why is it that we see so clearly as we read history that the right side always won? A number of reasons suggest themselves.

The right side always won because the victors lived to tell the tale. History was written by the victors for the victors. We have never heard Catiline's side of the story. All that we know of him we know through his enemies. The victors in any struggle are by definition those who in the end manage to establish a new consensus favorable to themselves and to their point of view. Naturally history justifies them. "God will pardon you," said the cynic. "That is his trade." The philosopher of history must say something like this to the statesman. The first lesson of history is that the statesman who wishes to be well thought of by posterity must be successful. He must win. Beyond that it perhaps does not greatly matter what he does. He may rob, murder, assassinate, and oppress; if he destroys the old order and establishes a new consensus of his own, his place in the memory of mankind is secure. History will justify his deeds, for that is the way of history.

The essential rightness of the historic process is, however, more than an illusion produced by the fact that the victors manage to establish their consensus and to destroy the view of things previously established. We must reckon with the further fact that history takes up where the crisis ends and builds upon its results.

However immoral the outcome of the crisis may seem from the viewpoint of moral principles previously accepted, the life of man produces a new system of right based upon the way in which it did in fact turn out. However the old values may have suffered, society founded on the new set of conditions soon produces a new system of values. "The whole history of mankind," says Sumner, "is a series of acts which are open to doubt, dispute, and criticism, as to their right and justice, but all subsequent history has been forced to take up the consequences of those acts and go on."[1]

Anything that is wrong is wrong at some particular place and time, and then only for a little while. If the wrong persists, it soon becomes right. Perhaps the evil that men do lives after them, but it does not long remain evil. A new system of right is founded on the newly established scheme of things. Once a new organization of society has been established, the force or fraud, the violation of previous values which may have been involved begin to matter less and less. Soon all those who have been wronged have died, and with them the wrong itself dies. There may be new wrongs, but that is a different matter. Soon a new system of right develops, and the dislocation involved in attempting to right the old wrong might well be a greater wrong than the one it was intended to redress.

One reason why a new system of right arises is that men arrange their lives on the basis of the newly established scheme of things. A new state has been established, no matter how. When its citizens buy its bonds there comes to be a certain rightness in continuing that form of government. New territory is somehow acquired and opened for settlement. Investors and settlers crowd into it, and at some point the new system of right prevails over the old. When this occurs, of course, is a matter of judgment. Practical sense recognizes the validity of these claims established by use. We Americans took our country from the Indians by ruthless methods, but no one proposes to give the land back to them. One does not often hear anyone propose to give California back to Mexico.

When this problem of right and wrong in historical perspective is translated into sociological terms, it becomes very simple. The

[1]   W. G. Sumner, *Folkways*, p. 66.

mores, the basic customs of the society, can make anything right. All right and all wrong is in the mores; nothing can be either right or wrong except on the basis of the mores. Every institution, every society has its rationalizers to defend it and its code to justify it. When the society is changed, there is always a violation of the existing moral consensus, but a new moral consensus at once arises to justify the change. And so it seems to us that every change that has been made in the past was a just one. We do not, and could not if we would, examine the conflicting value systems which would have arisen if the event of various historic crises had been different.

Anthropology has familiarized us with the facts that nearly every people considers its moral code superior to all others. Ethnocentrism is the name applied to this bias which exaggerates the importance of one's own group and the rightness of its mores. If we apply this notion of ethnocentrism to historic process, we understand why our own epoch seems better than any other, why the whole course of human history seems an unending struggle upward to ourselves, and why everything that contributed to bringing about our present morality seems right. History has always taken the right turn, because it could not take a wrong turn. Whatever turn it took would now seem right to us because it led us where we are. Mankind has travelled a devious road from nowhere to now, but it was the right path because it led us to the glorious present.

The attitude of the group toward its history is analogous to that of the individual toward his own past. "I wouldn't go through it again for anything on earth, but I wouldn't take a million dollars for the experience," declares the soldier returned from the wars. The married man is glad that he is married with a great part of his mind, the bachelor is equally pleased that he has remained single. The religionist is grateful for the pious upbringing that made him what he is. "There but for the grace of God" is a formula of thanksgiving. All of us, in our hearts, and often not without reservations, are glad that we are not as other men. "I am loyal to the past because the past is me."

The historian necessarily writes in an ethnocentric perspective. He is a member of a group. He is steeped in the folkways and mores and values of that group. He cannot avoid feeling that all that has gone into the making of his own group has been more or less good. But if the event of various historic crises had been different, the society in which the historian grew up and for which he wrote would be different, and he would still write of these events in the same complacent way.

It may be said that the new historian writes with objectivity of the past, and is not open to the criticism here put forward. It is true that historical writing has made great strides, but it may well be doubted that the historian has emancipated himself from the mores of his own time and place, or that indeed he has ever made any serious attempt to do so. Scientific history has been very successful in one respect: It has torn down the fictions or false beliefs which people manufacture in time of crisis and by which they then live and act, and has thereby prevented these false beliefs from becoming permanently a part of the fabric of the historic record. It was necessary for the American colonists to have certain beliefs about the English in order to be able to struggle against the English. It was necessary for the North to have certain beliefs about the South and for the Allies to believe in German war guilt. In each of these cases the scientific historian steps in to restore the matter to a truer perspective. The historian can write with some detachment and devotion to truth of conflicts past and gone. He is not under the sway of the passions which activated the participants in those old struggles. But can he avoid the subtler influence of the fact that these bygone conflicts have formed the society in which he lives, from whose point of view he evaluates the succession of past events?

It seems unlikely that the historian should be any more able to escape the influence of the morality of his own society than any other social scientists. It can even be argued that he ought not to try to escape it, for though our morality is relative to time and place and circumstance, it is still our morality and we have to live by it. But when all is said, it seems that there is perhaps a case for introducing into historical writing a heightened awareness of the manner in which our morality influences our judgment of the past events which have made that morality.

5

CRITICAL NOTES ON THE COST
OF CRIME

(with E. R. Hawkins)
1936

A CONSIDERABLE LITERATURE on the cost of crime is already extant. Much of this literature is wholly fallacious. Most of it is misleading in its general implications. Only a very small part of it is written with any conception of the methodological difficulties inherent in the problem. It is strange that so many pages of printed matter should have been produced with such a small expenditure of reflective thought. It is the purpose of the present paper to test the truth of some of the premises of this literature by economic analysis and to point out a new direction of investigation....

Some Crime Economically Productive

An assumption underlying discussions of the ultimate cost of crime, frequently explicitly present in the discussion, is that labor of criminals and of those who are paid to struggle against criminals is lost to "productive" labor. Many more or less eloquent passages from the pens of leading criminologists could be quoted to this effect. Nowhere does one find a statement of the fact which is very clear to the economist, that the distinction between crime and "productive" labor is a moral and not an economic distinc-

Reprinted from the *Journal of Criminal Law and Criminology* 26 (January 1936) : 679–94, with elisions. By special permission of the *Journal of Criminal Law, Criminology and Police Science* (Northwestern University School of Law) © 1936, Volume 26, Number 5.

tion.[1] The economist is not supposed to allow moral considerations to intrude themselves into his analyses. He may not approve of advertising, he may not approve of sweatshop labor, he may not approve of the life which human beings must lead "back of the yards" because of large-scale meat-packing, but he is not supposed to allow such considerations to enter into his analyses of the process of production and utilization of goods and services. The sober economist is therefore obliged to point out that much crime is economically productive. The prostitute, the pimp, the peddler of dope, the operator of the gambling hall, the vendor of obscene pictures, the bootlegger, the abortionist, all are productive, all produce goods or services which people desire and for which they are willing to pay. It happens that society has put these goods and services under the ban, but people go on producing them and people go on consuming them, and an act of the legislature does not make them any less a part of the economic system.

Reasoning based upon this false distinction sometimes leads to ridiculous misapprehension of economic concepts. "Our national income," remarks a popular orator, "is only seventy billion, and if we spend ten billion for crime, that leaves only sixty billion for legitimate industry." Criminologists do not fall into this error, and yet there is some reason to believe that it underlies some of their reasoning. Obviously the national income is not expended in that way. In estimating what the automobile industry produces annually, one takes the sum of money expended for automobiles as a measure of the value produced by the industry, and says that the

---

[1]   This distinction between economic and moral considerations has been hard won even among economists. John Stuart Mill, in his *Principles of Political Economy*, i, 3, sec. 5, said: "The annual consumption of gold lace, pineapples, or champagne, must be reckoned unproductive, since these things give no assistance to production, nor any support to life or strength, but what would easily be given at less cost." In the Eighth Edition of his *Principles of Economics*, 1920, Alfred Marshall made a considerable concession to the exclusion of ethics from economics: "It is true that all wholesome enjoyments, whether luxuries or not, are legitimate ends of action, both public and private; and it is true that the enjoyment of luxuries affords an incentive to exertion, and promotes progress in many ways" (p. 66). But note the word "wholesome"!

industry contributed so much to the national income. We must treat economically productive crime in the same way. The sums of money diverted to bootleggers must be added to the national income, not subtracted from it.

Crime and Economic Waste

It is usually taken for granted that enormous wastes are connected with crime. It does not seem possible to question the truth of the statement, but a careful analysis of the relation of crime to economic waste, and of the meaning of this waste in our economic system, has been wanting hitherto. The interrelations of law, crime, and waste are very complex and it is not easy to frame an ordered conception of them. There are many kinds of waste and they impinge upon the law in different ways. Waste may be defined as a net loss of utilities, which may be brought about by a destruction of utilities or by creation of utilities with a greater expenditure of economic resources than would be necessary whether under this economic system or another. Four general statements may be made: 1. Many crimes involve destruction of utilities. 2. Some crimes cause wastes that have been specifically outlawed. 3. Some crimes effect saving of wastes required by law. 4. Some crimes effect a saving of the wastes of competition.

1. Physical destruction of property frequently occurs because of the haste and irresponsibility of the criminal. For example, a box-car thief may carelessly damage much of the contents of the car. A safe-cracker may ruin a five-thousand dollar safe to obtain a few hundred dollars. Such destruction is a loss to society and to the individual owner, and is not even partially offset by a gain to the criminal. Similarly, stolen goods frequently suffer a shrinkage of value even though not physically destroyed. The value of a car is lessened by the common practice of car thieves of "stripping" the car and selling the parts. Stolen goods are frequently put to a lower use than that intended, with a consequent shrinkage in value.[2]

[2]   Such shrinkage, however, can be assessed only in terms of lowered market value, if the goods are resold. Even though the criminal uses the stolen goods carelessly or assigns them to lower uses, he may derive greater utility from them than the original owner.

2. In the cases noted above waste is incidental to the crime. Some actions, however, are criminal because they violate specific laws against certain types of waste. Waste of natural resources and wild life has come within the jurisdiction of law through regulations aiming at conservation. Some of the New England states have found it desirable to conserve the lobster business by making it illegal to retain lobsters of less than a certain size. This regulation has been to the advantage of lobster men and has been for the most part observed. Yet there has grown up a flourishing illegal business in "short lobsters."

Again, illegal oil drilling is a crime that prevents the curious picture of restoring a waste that has been outlawed. The same may be said of violations of the fish and game laws. Violations of the N.R.A. codes' provisions against wasteful methods of competition may also be cited, if convictions are upheld by the higher courts in cases now pending.

3. Contrariwise, some crimes effect a saving of wastes that are required by law. A certain mine is operated to remove and put on the market a one-foot vein of coal. In mining this coal it is necessary to cut out and throw away a much larger vein which cannot be put on the market because it is below the ash fusion point required by the state law. Otherwise this is excellent coal; it might be used for domestic purposes, would be mined very cheaply, etc. It can never be mined now, according to experts. This is a waste required by law, avoided by the crime of "coal bootlegging." Bribery of police officials to evade the requirements of ordinances is sometimes cheaper than compliance. Presumably some social end is served by the ordinance, and the social loss of the evasion may be greater than the individual gain of the briber. Yet it is to be suspected that many ordinances are enacted that do not serve social ends commensurate with the cost involved, and that some of them even have been passed to create opportunity for "shake-downs." It may conceivably be argued that such ordinances themselves constitute crimes, and that the cost of complying with them or evading them alike is a cost of crime; such a view would involve a conception of crime that would be acceptable to the welfare economist but rather novel to the penologist.

4. Some criminal activity illegally effects a saving by reducing

the wastes of competition. In the main, our automatic economic mechanism relies upon the self-interest of producers and consumers to achieve maximum utilization of economic resources. Yet social waste may follow from the self-seeking activity of individuals. In our individualistic economy these wastes inherent in competition have not been subjected to much regulation until comparatively recent times. Indeed, in the endeavor to enforce free competition, government has forbidden businessmen to regulate competition for the reduction of wastes. Some of the most conspicuous wastes involved in free competition are duplication of capital equipment, cross-hauling, and competitive selling effort. Many associations and combinations of producers have had as their purpose, at least in part, the reduction of these wastes. Thus, the American Malt Company effected a saving in salaries and cross-freights, the United States Leather trust effected savings by using bark lands nearest the various plants, the American Tobacco trust spent far less in advertising than the constituent companies after dissolution, the whiskey and sugar trusts saved by closing some plants and running the others continuously and to capacity. Examples could be multiplied. Yet most of these trusts and associations have been declared illegal, in violation of the Sherman Act.

Other business men have sought to eliminate the wastes of competition by less formal and more clearly criminal methods. Dorr and Simpson have observed that racketeers frequently do not force themselves upon business but are invited by business itself.[2]

In an earlier study, Landesco says, "The racketeer does not always impose himself upon an industry or an association. He is often invited in because his services are welcome."[3]

This fact suggests that the racketeers are in reality performing some kind of valuable function. That function is in part the reduction of the wastes of competition. It has long been recognized that unrestrained competition may not be the life of trade, but the death

[2]   Dorr, Goldthwaite H., and Simpson, Sidney P., *Report on the Cost of Crime and Criminal Practice in the United States*, prepared for The National Commission on Law Observance and Enforcement, p. 410.
[3]   Landesco, John: *The Illinois Crime Survey*, Part III, *Organized Crime in Chicago*, p. 982.

of trade. Our economic system, having as its keystone the legal guarantee of the freedom of contract and individual enterprise, makes possible in many fields a continual influx of aspiring entrepreneurs possessed of little capital and vast ignorance. Not knowing their costs, such entrepreneurs are frequently price-cutters selling below their true total prime and supplementary costs. True, they are ultimately forced out of business, thousands of them annually. But there are always others to take their places. The net result is that there are always sufficient numbers of such entrepreneurs to dislocate and disorganize the industry. Their operations result in a net social loss, even though they sell at lower prices, because the economic resources employed by them are true costs that must be paid by somebody. They unproductively lose their own capital, and when they are finally forced out of the field they typically leave behind them credit losses that become part of the cost of doing business of those who supply them. . . . It is no coincidence that the rackets have been most significant in those fields that are most harassed by entrepreneurs of this sort by reason of their easy access to those of small capital and competence. Witness the rackets in the fields of laundry, cleaning and dyeing, drug stores, grocery stores, etc. Nor is it a coincidence that the gunmen are often associated with the larger and more substantial business men in these fields. These are business men who have large capital investments to protect, who intend to cover their costs and stay in business.[4] A dictatorship of force is set up to impose upon

---

[4]   Landesco's comment is particularly revealing. He says: "The Chicago Laundry Owners' Association, doing finished work, has always opposed these little fellows who can start up with nothing." (Landesco, John, *op. cit.*, p. 983.)

Again, we read: "The Chicago Hand Laundry Owners' Association are 'little fellows' who send their work to large wet wash laundries and upon return iron it, return it to the customer and collect. They do a 'drop' trade, which means that the customer drops his bundle at their store and comes in to get it. This organization was originally formed by Hirschie Miller as an aid in organizing the inside laundry workers. In this instance Gorman was not invited in, but the Laundry Owners' Association sent him to take these 'little fellows' in hand, relieving Hirschie Miller. But Gorman has not worked to the entire satisfaction of the Laundry Owners' Associa-

competitors a schedule of prices at which they must either cover their costs and permit others to do so, or be driven out of business by the loss of their price appeal. In the distribution of milk the same effect has been achieved by regulations necessitating expensive equipment. These regulations, fostered by big distributors, discourage small distributors from entering the field. An interesting parallel is found in the fact that chief support of the N.R.A. dictatorship of prices and costs is given by the largest and most highly capitalized businesses. The analogy may be pursued further. In a sense the N.R.A. also represents the use of compulsion for the purpose of controlling the disorganizing forces of unrestrained competition.

A case similar to the one outlined above is to be found in the familiar circumstance of too many enterprises in a given field or locality, none of them cutting prices below costs, but all of them operating at unduly high cost by reason of spreading their overhead over too small a volume of sales. The overhead of each one of these enterprises is a cost which must be borne by the consuming public. A socialistic society would immediately eliminate such needless duplication. It is conceivable that the racketeer may produce the same beneficent effect by the use of his bombs and intimidations. A frequent clause in the code of racketeering aims at a restriction of the number of enterprises in the field and a prohibition of new enterprises. The result is a greater sales volume for the remaining enterprises, which enables them to allocate less overhead to each unit of sales, and provide for the racketeers' tribute and their own usual profits without raising the price to consumers.

It is interesting to note that in this case competition would produce the same effect if it worked perfectly. The theory of pure competition contemplates no such waste as is involved in the ob-

---

tion, because he has permitted new 'little fellows' to start as long as they did not open places of business too near association members. He was always partial in designating wet wash laundries to receive work from those 'little fellows' to the exclusion of certain other wet wash laundries. He then permitted a group of hand laundrymen to establish a new wet wash laundry (a new competitor for the 'big fellows'). In this new laundry he took a fair size amount of stock as his share." (*Ibid.*, pp. 984–985.)

served fact of needless duplication of stores and other enterprises. In the theory of pure competition, any one enterprise could immediately gain all the business of its rivals by a slight reduction in prices. Price competition would continue until there would remain in each field only enterprises operating at the size of greatest efficiency and lowest average cost. The reason that this does not happen is that competition is not actually pure, but is tinged with monopoly elements. Each seller who has a trade mark, or a place of business different from others by reason of its location, atmosphere, or personality is a monopolist in the sense that he is the only one selling precisely that bundle of utilities. His customers cannot be taken from him *en masse* by a slight price differential. Instead, varying numbers of customers would shift at different prices, depending upon the degree of consumer preference. This is just another way of saying that the seller can dispose of different quantities at different prices, instead of an unlimited quantity at the market price and none above the market price, as would be the case in pure competition. It is to these monopolistic elements that we must attribute the excessive number of enterprises, each with its own more or less loyal clientele.

Shifting and Incidence of the Cost of Crime

Such fragmentary examination of the shifting and incidence of the cost of crime as have been made are rather unsatisfactory. Dorr and Simpson, for example, say:

The racketeer exacts tribute from his immediate victims and in some cases the matter ends there. In such case, in the absence of monopoly conditions, the immediate victim cannot pass on his loss to the purchaser of his wares or services, and it is he who is out of pocket.[5]

This statement is diametrically opposed to the usual economic analysis, which holds that in the absence of monopoly conditions such costs, like taxes, *must* be passed on by the seller, and would be borne by him only if monopoly were present. The confusion

5   Dorr and Simpson, *op. cit.*, p. 410.

arises from the common mistake of regarding our actual system as one of pure competition, whereas in reality it is tinged with monopolistic elements. The theory of monopolistic competition outlined above provides us with the correct attack on the problem. Each monopolistic competitor, having an individual market demand curve, has the option of selecting the price along that curve which, considering sales volumes at that price and unit costs at that volume, will yield him the greatest profit. This price need not be equal to average cost, since by definition the enterprise is monopolistic to a degree, depending on the degree of consumer preference, and presents difficulties to anyone who might otherwise, attracted by high profits, attempt to enter the same market. It is quite possible for the seller of a product differentiated by trade mark, location, or atmosphere, to continue operating above costs permanently, or as long as the consumer preference lasts.

This suggests that there is a fallacy in the popular belief that the seller must pass the costs of racketeering along to the public because he is operating at cost and cannot bear them himself. It is possible and probable that the consumer is spared the cost of racketeering in some instances because the merchant bears it. The merchant would bear the costs if the shape of his demand curve indicated that an attempt to raise prices to cover the added cost would lower his sales volume sufficiently to lower his total revenue by more than the amount of the racketeer's tribute. The more cognizant of his best interests the merchant, the more this would be true. This principle would apply also for a whole industry. If the cleaners and dyers of a particular city attempt to use a gunman-enforced price schedule that is too high, they will quickly discover that loss of sales volume to substitutes will decrease their total revenue.

This happened to the barbers and cleaners of Chicago. When Chicago cleaners raised their price to $1.75 and more for cleaning a suit of clothes they suffered such diminution of demand that ultimately the racket broke. It is even conceivable that a racket would *lower* prices in an industry, in two ways: (1) by increasing sales volume for the smaller number of permitted enterprises, thus permitting prices at a point of lower marginal cost; (2) by taking price-fixing discretion out of the hands of many partial monopolies and concentrating it in the hands of the broader monopoly, which, through the hiring of expert advice, is better able to select the price of maximum returns in competition with other industries and substitutes.

A final comment may be made. Even in cases where the consumer does pay the cost of racketeering, because of the shape of the demand curve, the matter is by no means ended there. If consumers as a class pay more for this particular commodity, they have less to spend for other commodities. In a sense, other industries really pay for the cost of racketeering. More, a reallocation of economic resources may be involved. The consumers who pay more to the racket-ridden industry are not precisely the same as those who previously patronized it. Some, the marginal buyers, shift to substitutes with the price rise; the substitute commodities are actually benefited by racketeering. Tracing the numerous strands of social effect becomes an extremely difficult and complex proceeding. Enough has perhaps been said to indicate that the problem is by no means so simple that it can be dismissed by adding up the sums racketeers receive.

Much the same principles apply to other crimes commonly listed in computations of the cost of crime. Loft robbery, truck hijacking, etc., are properly regarded as constituting costs of the industries involved. Usually the losses are made truly costs of the entire industry by the device of spreading those losses over the entire group by means of insurance. What is not recognized in such computations is that the losses may not be borne by the consumers entirely, but to some degree by the businessmen. Take the case of robbery of silk from trucks or lofts. Certainly such loss raises the cost of silk to the merchant. It does not, however, proportionately raise the price of silk dresses sold by a smart store or trademarked with a prestige brand, if any part of the previous price had gone toward payment for the atmosphere or prestige of the brand or store. The seller would have previously fixed his price at the point which would give him the greatest aggregate revenue. He would again do this. If his demand curve were a straight line, the rise in price would be exactly half the increase in marginal cost. If marginal costs were constant, which is not improbable for realistic volume ranges, the increase—price would be exactly half the insurance cost per unit of sales.[6] If marginal costs were decreasing, the price would increase more than half the insurance costs. If marginal costs were increasing, the price would increase less than half the insurance costs. If the demand curve were not a straight line, the effect of the crime cost in raising price would be greater the more concave is the demand curve, and less the more convex the curve.

The simplest case, that of a straight demand curve and constant marginal costs, may be illustrated with a chart (Fig. 1).

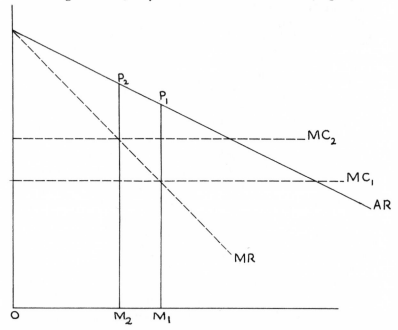

Fig. 1.—AR represents average revenue; MR, marginal revenue; MC, the original marginal cost and MC2 the marginal cost increased by crime cost (or insurance) of a constant amount per unit. In accordance with the principle of pricing at the point at which MR=MC, M_1P_1 will be the original price and M_2P_2 the price resulting from the added cost burden. In this case the rise in price is half the rise in marginal cost. It is assumed that the AR curve does not change.

[6]   For the somewhat intricate geometrical proof of this statement, the reader is referred to Robinson, Joan: *Economics of Imperfect Competition*, London, 1933, II, 5.

Crime an Integral Part of Economic System

Without in the least apologizing for crime as a moral phenomenon, we are forced to the conclusion that it is an industry like
other industries, bound together in inextricable interdependence
with all the other institutions and activities by means of which
man makes a living. Sutherland has made some extraordinarily
penetrating comments on "the pervasive nature of criminality";
he shows that crime permeates the whole of our economic structure.[7] But even professional and avowed crime is an integral part
of the economic system. As an industry, it gives direct employment
to thousands of persons who would otherwise be in competition in
the labor market; indirectly, it contributes to the financial welfare
of those who supply it with equipment and those who benefit by
the spending of the spoils. Most immediately, it supports the manufacturers and sellers of the weapons and tools of criminals and
policemen, the landlords who rent houses of prostitution and offices
of private detective agencies, and a host of others. More remotely,
the most diverse and respectable industries are involved through
our delicate interlocking exchange mechanism. The automobile
manufacturer, for example, need draw no distinction between cars
that are wrecked by criminals, through carelessness or intent, or
"stripped," for the parts, and those that wear out in the normal
duties of producing utilities for law-abiding citizens. Wastes involved in crime are as useful from the producer's point of view as
legitimate consumption.

People depend upon crime for a living who do not realize what
they owe to the bootlegger and the pimp. The "decent elements"
in the community derive from the conditions that produce sordidness and crime the income that enables them to struggle against
sordidness and crime just as the druggist's wife puts in the collection plate on Sunday the quarter that bought the ginger ale for
someone's Saturday night spree. Upon this paradox, reform movements have often broken, for in proportion as reform movements
succeed they "hurt business," and in proportion as they hurt business they lose support! Nor is the opposition to reform solely a

7   Sutherland, E. H., *Principles of Criminology*, pp. 31–38.

selfish action on the part of the interests immediately affected. If it were somehow possible to eliminate all crime suddenly, the effect on our entire economic structure would be as disastrous as the collapse of any other industry of similar magnitude. The repercussion would be the same in kind, if not in degree, as that which typically follows a great war.

It would be a false inference to conclude that efforts to reduce crime should be halted. Realistically, we know it to be extremely improbable that the fight on crime could succeed completely and quickly enough to cause serious dislocation of industry. This disrupting effect is purely a phenomenon of the short run. In the long run, no economic system can prosper by "making work." The "creation of purchasing power" by unproductive work is fundamentally fallacious, despite the widespread currency of the belief to the contrary. If crime were suddenly to be eliminated, there would begin immediately a shifting of the factors of production. The length and severity of the period of readjustment would depend solely upon the degree of mobility or immobility of those factors. For example, if safe-cracking could be entirely prevented, manufacturers of safes would suffer a loss of business, which would be spread to other industries because of the decline in the personal incomes derived from the safe-manufacturing. But those who formerly purchased replacement safes would be enabled to buy other goods in an equal amount, possibly from the safe-manufacturers themselves if they shifted in appropriate fashion. The net gain would lie in the additional goods which would be bought instead of replacement safes.

Several of the credits on the economic balance-sheet of crime are not purely short-run, but are more permanent in their nature. Activities that are legally criminal but economically productive of utility must be regarded as credits even in the long-run view. So also must the various crimes that involve savings of the wastes of natural resources and of the other wastes caused by free competition. It is not argued that these credits can be even approximately assessed for proper cancellation against the economic debts of crime. We can measure some elements of the cost of particular crimes, but we cannot measure the cost of crime.

The significant point to be emphasized by the present analysis is that instead of attempting to discover the cost of crime, an enterprise foredoomed to some absurdity, we need to study the economic effects of crime. We need to know the nature and magnitude of the probable immediate results of a crime crusade. We need to be more cognizant of the permanent consequences of crime as an organic part of our society. How does crime operate to introduce expensive goods to new price classes? What is the effect of crime in redistributing the national income? What unintended consequences for the larger social order have such crimes as bank robbery, embezzlement, counterfeiting, and racketeering? Who pays for goods that have been stolen or destroyed; what problems of shifting and incidence appear? What are the roots of crime in legitimate business? These, it seems to the present writers, are some of the significant questions that arise from a study of the cost of crime. It is within the power of the human mind to answer them.

III. The Family

6

THE RATING AND DATING
COMPLEX

1937

COURTSHIP MAY be defined as the set of processes of association among the unmarried from which, in time, permanent matings usually emerge. This definition excludes those associations which cannot normally eventuate in marriage—as between Negro and white—but allows for a period of dalliance and experimentation. In the present paper we propose to discuss the customs of courtship which prevail among college students.

Courtship practices vary from one culture group to another. In many cultures marriage eventuates from a period of sexual experimentation and trial unions; in others the innocence of the unmarried is carefully guarded until their wedding day. In some cultures the bride must be virginal at marriage; in others this is what she must not be. Sometimes the young are allowed no liberty of choice, and everything is determined for them by their elders. Sometimes persons marry in their own age group, but in other societies older men pre-empt the young women for themselves. Although there are endless variations in courtship customs, they are always functionally related to the total configuration of the culture and the biological needs of the human animal. It is helpful to remember that in a simple, undifferentiated, and stable society a long and complex process of choosing a mate is apparently not so

Reprinted from the *American Sociological Review* 2, no. 3 (October 1937) : 727–34.

necessary or desirable as in our own complex, differentiated, and rapidly changing society.[1]

The mores of courtship in our society are a strange composite of social heritages from diverse groups and of new usages called into existence by the needs of the time. There is a formal code of courtship which is still nominally in force, although departures from it are very numerous; the younger generation seems to find the superficial usages connected with the code highly amusing, but it is likely that it takes the central ideas quite seriously. The formal code appears to be derived chiefly from the usages of the English middle classes of a generation or so ago, although there are, of course, many other elements in it.

The usual or intended mode of operation of the formal mores of courtship—in a sense their "function"—is to induct young persons into marriage by a series of progressive commitments. In the solidary peasant community, in the frontier community, among the English classes of a few decades back, and in many isolated small communities in present-day America, every step in the courtship process has a customary meaning and constitutes a powerful pressure toward taking the next step—is in fact a sort of implied commitment to take the next step. The mores formerly operated to produce a high rate of marriage at the proper age and at the same time protected most individuals from many of the possible traumatic experiences of the courtship period.

The decay of this moral structure has made possible the emergence of thrill-seeking and exploitative relationships. A thrill is merely a physiological stimulation and release of tension, and it seems curious that most of us are inclined to regard thrill-seeking with disapproval. The disapproving attitude toward thrill-seeking becomes intelligible when we recall the purpose of such emotional

---

[1]   James G. Leyburn quotes an old-fashioned Boer mother who said, "I am sick of all this talk of choosing and choosing. . . . If a man is healthy and does not drink, and has a good little handful of stock, and a good temper, and is a good Christian, what great difference can it make to a woman which man she takes? There is not so much difference between one man and another." (*Frontier Folkways*, p. 129) Such an attitude was possible in Boer society as it is not in ours.

stirrings in the conventional mores of courtship. Whether we approve or not, courtship practices today allow for a great deal of pure thrill-seeking. Dancing, petting, necking, the automobile, the amusement park, and a whole range of institutions and practices permit or facilitate thrill-seeking behavior. These practices, which are connected with a great range of the institutions of commercialized recreation, make of courtship an amusement and a release of organic tensions. The value judgment which many lay persons and even some trained sociologists pass upon thrill-seeking arises from the organizational mores of the family—from the fact that energy is dissipated in thrills which is supposed to do the work of the world, i.e., to get people safely married.

The emergence of thrill-seeking furthers the development of exploitative relationships. As long as an association is founded on a frank and admitted barter in thrills, nothing that can be called exploitative arises. But the old mores of progressive commitment exist, along with the new customs, and peculiar relationships arise from this confusion of moralities. According to the old morality a kiss means something, a declaration of love means something, a number of Sunday evening dates in succession means something, and these are enforced by the customary law, while under the new morality such things may mean nothing at all—that is, they may imply no commitment of the total personality whatsoever. So it comes about that one of the persons may exploit the other for thrills on the pretense of emotional involvement and its implied commitment. When a woman exploits, it is usually for the sake of presents and expensive amusements—the common pattern of "gold-digging." The male exploiter usually seeks thrills from the body of the woman. The fact that thrills cost money, usually the man's money, often operates to introduce strong elements of suspicion and antagonism into the relationship.

With this general background in mind, let us turn to the courtship practices of college students. A very important characteristic of the college student in his bourgeois pattern of life. For most persons, the dominant motive of college attendance is the desire to rise to a higher social class; behind this we should see the ideology of American life and the projection of parents' ambitions upon children. The attainment of this life goal necessitates the postponement of marriage, since it is understood that a new household must be economically independent; additional complications sometimes arise from the practice of borrowing money for college expenses. And yet persons in this group feel very strongly the cultural imperative to fall in love and marry and live happily in marriage.

For the average college student, and especially for the man, a love affair which led to immediate marriage would be tragic because of the havoc it would create in his scheme of life. Nevertheless, college students feel strongly the attractions of sex and the thrills of sex, and the sexes associate with one another in a peculiar relationship known as "dating." Dating is not true courtship, since it is supposed not to eventuate in marriage; it is a sort of dalliance relationship. In spite of the strength of the old morality among college students, dating is largely dominated by the quest of the thrill and is regarded as an amusement. The fact that college attendance usually removed the individual from normal courtship association in his home community should be mentioned as a further determinant of the psychological character of dating.

In many colleges, dating takes place under conditions determined by a culture complex which we may call the "rating and dating complex." The following description of this complex on one campus is probably typical of schools of the sort:

X College, a large state-supported school, is located in a small city at a considerable distance from larger urban areas. The school is the only industry of the community. There are few students who live at home, and therefore the interaction of the young is but little influenced by the presence of parents. The students of this college are predominantly taken from the lower half of the middle classes, and constitute a remarkably homogeneous group; numerous censuses of the occupations of fathers and of living expenses seem to establish this fact definitely. Nevertheless, about half of the male students live in fraternities, where the monthly bill is usually forty-five or fifty dollars a month, rarely as high as fifty-five. There is intense competition among the fraternities. The desire for mobility of class, as shown by dozens of inquiries, is almost universal in the group and is the principal verbalized motive for college attendance.

Dating at X College consists of going to college or fraternity dances, the movies, college entertainments, and to fraternity houses for victrola dances and "necking"; coeds are permitted in the fraternity parlors, if more than one is present. The high points of the social season are two house parties and certain formal dances. An atypical feature of this campus is the unbalanced sex ratio, for there are about six boys to every girl; this makes necessary the large use of so-called "imports" for the more important occasions, and brings it about that many boys do not date at all or confine their activities to prowling about in small industrial communities nearby; it also gives every coed a relatively high position in the scale of desirability; it would be difficult to say whether it discourages or encourages the formation of permanent attachments. Dating is almost exclusively the privilege of fraternity men, the use of the fraternity parlor and the prestige of fraternity membership being very important. Freshman men are forbidden by student tradition to have dates with coeds.[2]

Within the universe which we have described, competition for dates among both men and women is extremely keen. Like every

[2]   Folsom, who has studied this same process, has come to essentially similar conclusions concerning the exclusion of certain persons from the dating process: "This factor is especially prominent in state universities with a vigorous fraternity culture and social stratification. Such institutions are attended by students from an unusually wide range on the social scale; there is a tendency to protect one's social ranking in college through a certain snobbishness, and there is also a great drive toward social climbing. Fraternities are important agencies in this struggle for prestige. The fraternities and sororities apply considerable pressure to the 'dating' of their members. One gets merits, whether formally recorded or not, for dating with a coed of a high-ranking fraternity, demerits for association with a non-fraternity person. The net result of this competition might seem to be to match each person with one of fairly equal rank, as happens in society in general. But there is another result. It is to discourage matching altogether among the lower ranks. The fire of competitive dating burns hot at the top, smoulders at the bottom. The low-ranking student often has more to gain by abstaining from dating than from dating with a person of his own rank." (J. K. Folsom, *The Family*, p. 341.)

other process of competition, this one determines a distributive order. There are certain men who are at the top of the social scramble; they may be placed in a hypothetical Class A. There are also certain coeds who are near the top of the scale of dating desirability, and they also are in Class A. The tendency is for Class A men to date principally Class A women. Beneath this class of men and women are as many other classes as one wishes to create for the purposes of analysis. It should be remembered that students on this campus are extremely conscious of these social distinctions and of their own position in the social hierarchy. In speaking of another student, they say, "He rates," or "He does not rate," and they extend themselves enormously in order that they may rate or seem to rate.

Young men are desirable dates according to their rating on the scale of campus values. In order to have Class A rating they must belong to one of the better fraternities, be prominent in activities, have a copious supply of spending money, be well-dressed, "smooth" in manners and appearance, have a "good line," dance well, and have access to an automobile. Members of leading fraternities are especially desirable dates; those who belong to fraternities with less prestige are correspondingly less desirable. I have been able to validate the qualities mentioned as determinants of campus prestige by reference to large numbers of student judges.

The factors which appear to be important for girls are good clothes, a smooth line, ability to dance well, and popularity as a date. The most important of these factors is the last, for the girl's prestige depends upon dating more than anything else; here as nowhere else nothing succeeds like success. Therefore the clever coed contrives to give the impression of being much sought after even if she is not. It has been reported by many observers that a girl who is called to the telephone in the dormitories will often allow herself to be called several times, in order to give all the other girls ample opportunity to hear her paged. Coeds who wish campus prestige must never be available for last minute dates; they must avoid being seen too often with the same boy, in order that others may not be frightened away or discouraged; they must be seen when they go out, and therefore must go to the popular (and expensive) meeting places; they must have many partners at the dances. If they violate the conventions at all, they must do so with great secrecy and discretion; they do not drink in groups or frequent the beer-parlors. Above all, the coed who wishes to retain Class A standing must consistently date Class A men.

Cressey has pointed out that the taxi-dancer has a descending cycle of desirability. As a new girl in the dance hall, she is at first much sought after by the most eligible young men. Soon they tire of her and desert her for some newer recruit. Similarly the coed has a descending cycle of popularity on the campus which we are describing, although her struggle is not invariably a losing one. The new girl, the freshman coed, starts out with a great wave of popularity; during her freshman year she has many dates. Slowly her prestige declines, but in this case only to the point at which she reaches the level which her qualities permanently assure her. Her descent is expedited by such "mistakes," from the viewpoint of campus prestige, as "going steady" with one boy (especially if he is a senior who will not return the following year), by indiscretions, and by too ready availability for dates. Many of the girls insist that after two years of competitive dating they have tired of it and are interested in more permanent associations.

This thrill-dominated, competitive process involves a number of fundamental antagonisms between the men and the women, and the influence of the one sex group accentuates these. Writes one student informant, a girl, "Wary is the only word that I can apply to the attitude of men and women students toward each other. The men, who have been warned so repeatedly against coeds, are always afraid the girls are going to 'gold-dig' them. The coeds wonder to what degree they are discussed and are constantly afraid of being placed on the black list of the fraternities. Then too they wonder to what extent they can take any man seriously without being taken for a 'ride.' " Status in the one-sex group depends upon avoiding exploitation by the opposite sex. Verbatim records of a number of fraternity "bull sessions" were obtained a few years ago. In these sessions members are repeatedly warned that they are slipping, those who have fallen are teased without mercy, and others are warned not to be soft. And almost all of the participants pretend a ruthlessness toward the opposite sex which they do not feel.

This competitive dating process often inflicts traumas upon individuals who stand low in the scale of courtship desirability. "While I was at X College," said a thirty-year-old alumnus, "I had just one date. That was a blind date, arranged for me by a friend. We went to the dorm, and after a while my girl came down and we were introduced. She said, 'Oh, I'm so sorry. I forgot my coat. I'll have to go get it.' She never came down again. Naturally I thought, 'Well what a hit I made!'" We have already seen that nonfraternity men are practically excluded from dating; it remains to note that many girls elect not to date rather than take the dates available to them. One girl writes as follows: "A girl's choice of whom to fall in love with is limited by the censorship of the one-sex group. Every boy that she dates is discussed and criticized by the other members of the group. This rigid control often keeps a girl from dating at all. If a girl is a member of a group in which the other girls are rated higher on the dating scale than she, she is often unable to get dates with boys who are considered desirable by her friends. In that event she has to decide whether to date the boys that she can and choose girl friends who would approve, or she must resign herself to not dating."

Since the class system, or gradient of dating desirability on the campus, is clearly recognized and adjusted to by the students themselves, there are interesting accommodations and rationalizations which appear as a result of inferior status. Although members of Class A may be clearly in the ascendant as regards prestige, certain groups of Class B may contest the position with them and may insist upon a measuring stick which will give them a favorable position. Rationalizations which enable Class D men and women to accept one another are probably never completely effective.

The accommodations and rationalizations worked out by one group of girls who were toward the bottom of the scale of campus desirability are typical. Four of these girls were organized in one tightly compact "bunch." All four lived off campus, and worked for their room and board. They had little money to spend for clothes, so there was extensive borrowing of dresses. Members of the group co-operated in getting dates for one another. All of them accepted eleventh hour invitations, and probably realized that some stigma of inferiority was attached to such ready availability, but they managed to save their faces by seeming very reluctant to accept such engagements, and at length doing so as a result of the persuasion of another member of the bunch. The men apparently saw through these devices, and put these girls down as last minute dates, so that they rarely received any other invitations. The bunch went through "dating cycles" with several fraternities in the course of a year, starting when one of the girls got a date with one member of the fraternity, and ending, apparently, when all the girls had lost their desirability in that fraternity.

Partly as result of the unbalanced sex ratio, the boys of the group which we are discussing have a widespread feeling of antagonism toward the coeds. This antagonism is apparently based upon the fact that most of the male students are unable to date with coeds, at least not on terms acceptable to themselves. As a result of this, boys take great pride in the "imports" whom they bring in for house parties, and it is regarded as slightly disgraceful in some groups to date a coed for one of the major parties. Other men in the dateless group take on the role of misogynists—and read Schopenhauer.

During the winter term the preponderance of men assures to every coed a relatively high bargaining power. Every summer witnesses a surprising reversal of this situation. Hundreds of women school teachers flock to this school for the summer term, and men are very scarce; smooth, unmarried boys of college age are particularly scarce. The school-teachers are older than the boys; they have usually lost some of their earlier attractiveness; they have been living for some months or years within the school-teacher role. They are man-hungry, and they have a little money. As a result, there is a great proliferation of highly commercialized relations. The women lend their cars to their men friends, but continue to pay for repairs and gasoline; they take the boys out to dinner, treat them to drinks, and buy expensive presents for them. And many who do not go so far are available for sex relations on terms which demand no more than a transitory sort of commitment from the man.

The rating and dating complex varies enormously from one school to another. In one small, coeducational school, the older coeds instruct the younger that it is all right for them to shop around early in the year, but by November they should settle down and date someone steadily. As a result, a boy who dates a girl once is said to "have a fence around her," and the competition which we have described is considerably hampered in its operation. In other schools, where the sex ratio is about equal, and particularly in the smaller institutions, "going steady" is probably a great deal more common than on the campus described. It should be pointed out that the frustrations and traumas imposed upon successful candidates by the practice of "going steady" (monopolistic competition) are a great deal easier to bear than those which arise from pure competition. In one school the girls are uniformly of a higher class origin than the boys, so that there is relatively little association between them; the girls go with older men not in college, the boys with high school girls and other "townies." In the school which is not coeducational, the dating customs are vastly different, although, for the women at least, dating is still probably a determinant of prestige.

True courtship sometimes emerges from the dating process, in spite of all the forces which are opposed to it. The analysis of the interaction process involved seems to be quite revealing. We may suppose that in our collegiate culture one begins to fall in love with a certain unwillingness, at least with an ambivalent sort of willingness. Both persons become emotionally involved as a result of a summatory process in which each step powerfully influences the next step and the whole process displays a directional trend toward the culmination of marriage; the mores of dating break down and the behavior of the individuals is governed by the older mores of progressive commitment. In the fairly typical case, we may suppose the interaction to be about as follows: The affair begins with the lightest sort of involvement, each individual being interested in the other but assuming no obligations as to the continuation of the affair. There are some tentatives of exploitation at the beginning; "the line" is a conventionalized attempt on the part of the young man to convince the young woman that he has already at this early stage fallen seriously in love with her—a sort of exaggeration, sometimes a burlesque, of coquetry—it may be that each person, by a pretence of great involvement, invites the other to rapid sentiment-formation—each encourages the other to fall in love by pretending that he has already done so. If either rises to the bait, a special type of interaction ensues; it may be that the relation becomes exploitative in some degree and it is likely that the relationship becomes one in which control follows the principle of least interest, i.e., that person controls who is less interested in the continuation of the affair. Or it may be that the complete involvement of the one person constellates the other in the same pattern, but this is less likely to happen in college than in the normal community processes of courtship.

If both persons stand firm at this early juncture, there may ensue a series of periodic crises which successively redefine the relationship on deeper levels of involvement. One form which the interaction process may assume is that of "lover's quarrels," with which the novelists have familiarized us. A and B begin an affair on the level of light involvement. A becomes somewhat involved, but believes that B has not experienced a corresponding growth of feeling, and hides his involvement from B, who is, however, in exactly the same situation. The conventionalized "line" facilitates this sort of "pluralistic ignorance," because it renders meaningless the very words by means of which this state of mind could be disclosed. Tension grows between A and B, and is resolved by a crisis, such as a quarrel, in which the true feelings of the two are revealed. The affair, perhaps, proceeds through a number of such crises until it reaches the culmination of marriage. Naturally, there are other kinds of crises which usher in the new definition of the situation.

Such affairs, in contrast to "dating," have a marked directional trend; they may be arrested on any level, or they may be broken off at any point, but they may not ordinarily be turned back to a lesser degree of involvement; in this sense they are irreversible. As this interaction process goes on, the process of idealization is re-enforced by the interaction of personalities. A idealizes B, and presents to her that side of his personality which is consistent with his idealized conception of her; B idealizes A, and governs her behavior toward him in accordance with her false notions of his nature; the process of idealization is mutually re-enforced in such a way that it must necessarily lead to an increasing divorce from reality. As serious sentimental involvement develops, the individual comes to be increasingly occupied, on the conscious level at least, with the positive aspects of the relationship; increasingly he loses his ability to think objectively about the other person, to safeguard himself or to deal with the relationship in a rational way; we may say, indeed, that one falls in love when he reaches the point where sentiment-formation overcomes objectivity.

The love relationship in its crescendo phase attracts an ever larger proportion of the conative trends of the personality; for a time it may seem to absorb all of the will of the individual and to dominate his imagination completely; the individual seems to become a machine specially designed for just one purpose; in consequence, the persons are almost wholly absorbed in themselves and their affair; they have an *egoïsme à deux* which verges upon *folie à deux*. All of these processes within the pair-relationship are accentuated by the changes in the attitude of others, who tend to treat the pair as a social unity, so far as their association is recognized and approved.

7

BARGAINING AND EXPLOITATIVE
ATTITUDES

1938

THE LOVER is not insane—and yet not sane. He is under the sway of his passions, but he has moments of lucidity, and he sometimes displays a sort of lunatic ingenuity in gratifying his desires. The ordinary unmarried person is not a lover, but he knows that he is capable of becoming one. He longs for this fulfillment at the same time that he fears it and dreads it as he fears and dreads to die.

. . . The sentiment of love arises in a definite social situation. It is always associated with other sentiments. One who falls in love and marries does more than fulfill his biological destiny; he makes certain decisions as to his future social and economic position in the world. When one marries, he makes a number of different bargains. Everyone knows this and this knowledge affects the sentiment of love and the process of falling in love. Let us then examine the ideology of bargaining. Now bargaining is giving a *quid pro quo* and is perfectly in accord with the mores upon which our society is founded. But what if the something which one is supposed to give for something be withheld? We have then exploitation, a practice which is contrary to our mores. Yet there is a powerful impulse toward getting something for nothing, and bargaining tends to go over by imperceptible stages into exploitation. This, too, we must analyze. . . .

Reprinted from *The Family* (New York: The Cordon Company, 1938), chap. 10, with elisions.

The Bargain of Marriage

Two kinds of bargains are struck in the courtship process: bargains which have to do with marriage, or with relations which are thought of as leading to marriage, and bargains which have to do merely with the conditions of association outside of marriage. The kind of bargaining which has to do with marriage has had a long history, and folk wisdom recognizes its importance. As in dating, so in marriage one gets about what he deserves according to the accepted standards of the group. In the simple, homogeneous group, this is very clear. In modern society, groups are confused, and cultural imperatives are in conflict, and therefore the nature of the bargaining process is more complex and its outlines are confused. Further, the current emphasis upon marriage for love causes the bargaining element to be concealed, and yet no thoughtful person will contend that it is not present; indeed, it may be argued that the transition from the old arranged marriage has brought the bargaining attitude into the love relation more explicitly, for previously the families bargained, but now everyone must higgle for himself.

The traits which determine whether one will win, place, or show in the marriage competition are such things as family background, economic power, education, and personal qualities such as age, beauty, and sexual attractiveness. For the woman, it is very important that she should not be above a certain age at the time of her first marriage. Economic power is a more important determinant of a man's marriageability than of a woman's in dowryless America. In every group and class of society, the qualities which determine eligibility for marriage are different from those which are considered important in other groups, but it seems certain that there are always more or less recognized standards, and that one does well or badly by himself with reference to those standards. It would be interesting to trace the variations in marriage bargains which are produced by variations in each of our factors. But this would be long; let us take a single factor as an example. A woman's age is important in nearly every group. Age means less to the modern maid than it meant to her grandmother, but a great deal of the old attitude is left. . . .

Courtship Bargains

The ultimate bargain of the courtship process is marriage, a bargain to end all bargaining, but there are many intermediate bargains which have to do with the conditions of association in courtship. Nor should it be thought that these types of bargains are wholly unrelated. . . . Women are ready to marry at an earlier age than men; because of this fact, and because in our culture a woman gains a certain status and security by marriage, there arises sometimes a bargaining process between man and woman in which the man attempts to get sexual gratification from the woman without marrying her or making a public, enforceable promise to marry her, and if possible without telling her that he loves her in a serious way, while the woman holds out for the conventional values of sentiment and the wedding ring. It may occur that the woman gives up the hope of marriage altogether, and accepts such association with a man as she can get, more or less on the man's terms, or it may happen that she will consent to extra-marital relations because of the fear that the man will break off the relationship, but while she consents to the relationship on this basis she hopes that it will eventuate in marriage—as indeed it often does.

Bargaining and the Conditions of Love. If anyone should inquire how this bargaining aspect of courtship and marriage is psychologically possible in view of the strength of the emotions involved, it does not seem difficult to give a satisfactory answer. We must think of the tendency to fall in love as a coiled spring mechanism which is partially counterpoised by other attitudes and habits. The tendency to love is released only when certain conditions are satisfied and when other attitudes facilitate rather than inhibit its expression. Thus the young man of good family may be greatly attracted to the chorus girl, and may consider marrying her, but in another part of his larynx are other and different subvocal responses, and it usually does turn out otherwise. Or a girl may be ever so impressionable and sexually responsive, but manage to sell her virtue dearly none the less because other attitudes are operative in her mind to keep her from yielding completely under circumstances which are not wholly favorable.

The importance of this perfectly normal inhibition of the formation of love attitudes by class attitudes and familial attitudes has apparently escaped most commentators altogether and yet it operates in almost every case. In the well-organized person of the upper middle class, any suspicion of marrying for money would be unjust and psychologically incorrect; it has been said of the men of certain families that none of them marry for money, but when the time comes for them to fall in love and marry they manage to fall in love with wealthy girls. Certainly some such regulative device is part of the normal pattern of female love in bourgeois society. There are certain economic conditions of a woman's love. Indeed, there must be such conditions if the woman is to avoid the tragic inconvenience of poverty. For there is this difference between the man and the woman in the pattern of bourgeois family life; a man, when he marries, chooses a companion and perhaps a helpmate, but a woman chooses a companion and at the same time a standard of living. It is necessary for women to be mercenary.

In the usual case, the tendency to love lies latent in the individual for a considerable number of years, never attaining its fullest possible intensity of expression. When the time has come for the man to marry, the brakes are automatically released, and he begins his career of emotional involvement with the accelerating momentum of a car rolling downhill. We must assume some such hypothesis to account for the fact that people can at length become very impatient in their desire for that which they have previously so long and so patiently awaited. When the time comes, when all the conditions are satisfied, such persons give themselves as fully as they are able in the relationship. In this analysis, which perhaps fits some cases closely, we must allow for the fact that the majority of persons probably present a less pleasing picture. In the first place, the capacity to love is permanently injured in many because they love when the necessary conditions are not present; they love before they are able to consider marriage; they love too well and too easily, and in consequence they suffer certain traumas which permanently interfere with the development of favorable love attitudes and their expression—all this, of course, in terms of the conventional mores. In the second place, it need not be assumed that love is anything like a pure emotion for the majority of people. The glamour of class, the lure of wealth and power, the pleasant feeling of being envied by others are for many people important elements in the only kind of love of which they are capable.

Definition of Exploitation

Let us now consider the emergence from the complex bargaining process which we have described of definitely exploitative attitudes. The word *exploitation* is by no means a desirable one, but I have not been able to find another which will do as well. In the dictionary definition of exploitation as an "unfair or unjust utilization of another" a value judgment is contained, and this value judgment is really a part of the ordinary sociological meaning of the term. I shall attempt to employ this judgmental term without applying any judgment of my own. One may properly use the term to denote the sort of utilization of another which, in accordance with conventional standards, would be called unjust or unfair.

There are many kinds of exploitation, as many as there are standards of just and fair utilization of others. The kind of which we are now speaking is delimited and defined by a value judgment emanating from the organizational mores of the family. According to the moral standards which are still formally in force, courtship is a process in which every step is a commitment of the whole person, and the whole process of interaction moves rapidly toward total involvement and total commitment in marriage. The situation on the basis of which we adjudge exploitation to be a wrong is one in which, in ordinary language, a kiss means something, a declaration of love means something, a number of Sunday evening dates in succession means something, the acceptance of expensive entertainments and presents means something, and these meanings are enforceable by customary law. We now face a situation in which these meanings have disappeared and one person seeks to derive thrills from the person or the body of another without any involvement of his own personality. Now certainly there can be no "injustice" or "unfairness" in the fact that these conventional meanings are absent from the relationship; injustice arises when they are present for one and not for the other, or when one person deceives the other about the presence or absence of these meanings. The classic example of exploitation is that of the man who "takes advantage" of a girl by seducing her on the promise of marriage. The girl who "leads a man on" for her own pecuniary or social advantage furnishes the opposite type of exploitation. Each plays upon the morality of the other without fulfilling his own commitments in terms of that same morality. This is the *raison d'être* of the value judgment on exploitation.

The great prevalence of exploitative relations today is thus a result of a transition in morality. For if the conventional meanings, the commitments and sentimental involvements are absent from the minds of both parties, then there is clearly no exploitation. With the increasing individuation of the time, there is a tendency for the sex behavior of the unwedded to lose its implication of total involvement. The old morality, however, is still strong, and perhaps no person of our time is really emancipated from it. There is a strong impulsion toward individualized behavior, and a powerful back-pull toward sentimental involvement in the older mode. It is this confusion of moralities, this unstable equilibrium of the mind, this incredibly complex interweaving of sentiment and objectivity which makes the realistic study of courtship so difficult.

Factors in Exploration

The factors in the social situation of the unmarried which facilitate the appearance of exploitative attitudes seem to be the following: the dominance of the thrill, the association of unmarried persons of different social classes, the association with one another of persons of the same class, but varying degrees of dating desirability, courtship traumas and frustrations, and the influence of one-sex groups. It should be emphasized in the beginning that much of what we are forced to treat as exploitation is not conscious or intended, but a result of attitudes which are early implanted and automatically called into play by certain situations; the moral problem of the *mens rea* is a problem for others, not for us, for we avoid it by refusing either to approve or disapprove of the practices. It must be equally emphasized that much exploitation is conscious and intended, and we must never forget that a great deal of exploitation is planned which never actually takes place.

Because we have already discussed the thrill at some length, we need not go into it much farther. The point seems to be clear. Thrill-seeking is not necessarily exploitative. It is a violation of the organizational mores of the family consequent upon the increasing individuation of secondary group society. So long as both persons treat a relationship merely as one of thrill-seeking, the relationship is individuated and in a sense immoral, but not exploitative. As soon as a coed has learned that she must neck for her movie, she has begun to become individuated. In relations outside the circle of primary contacts, each person feels a strong impulsion —almost a necessity—to exact a *quid pro quo*. Thrills cost money —usually, the boy's money, but dating is also expensive for the girl; each must get his pound of flesh or feel that he has been cheated. Such depersonalized relationships, however, are exceedingly unsatisfactory to persons who have been reared in our culture. It is difficult even to get a thrill with no sentimental involvement on either side. Frankly thrill-seeking relationships, therefore, are very unstable. They may break up of their own weakness from sheer disinterest. Or both persons may go on directly from thrill-seeking to uninhibited courtship, building up sentimental involvement gradually. Or each may attempt, by a pretended emotional involvement, to constellate in the other a different moral attitude and thus to exploit him; this seems to be the usual course, and we must later study the process in which true courtship develops from these tentatives of exploitation.

Social Class. When individuals of different social classes are thrown together, certain violations of the mores appear. This is a principle as old as the class system of society. The relations involved are individuated relations which verge upon the exploitative. Typically, the men of the upper group make use of the women of the lower group for relatively irresponsible sex gratification. In the South, white men use negro women, and this has been going on long enough and extensively enough to inject a sizable amount of white blood into the American Negro. Many similar phenomena occur in the North, though they are usually limited to young, unmarried persons. College boys in the big cities frequently consort with girls of the working class for sexual purposes; often there is a well-recognized meeting place and a customary routine of amusements for such "pick-ups." Often "Charity girls" live in the rooming house districts of the city; they are recruited from the large number of women who are paid just a little less than they need to live, and who associate with young men who are paid somewhat more but not enough for marriage. Floyd Dell has pointed out that in groups where sexual betrothal exists, young men frequently make use of the custom to exploit their partners.[2]

It would be difficult to say to what extent such relations are definitely exploitative. In return for the prestige which such association can give them, and in return for certain luxury amusements, and also as an acceptable outlet for their own impulses, women accept such relations in which the responsibility of the man is sharply limited. Although the formal mores put the responsibility for these marginally exploitative relationships upon the man, we must not forget the counter-exploitation of the woman. Contemporary literature has familiarized us with the social type known as the "gold digger," the woman who exploits the man on the basis of her sex-appeal. Anyone who is willing to do a little exploring in night-clubs, cabarets, taxi-dance halls, and girls' dormitories will have no difficulty in discovering women of this type.

Courtship Desirability. The relative position of two persons in the "rating-and-dating" scale may also determine a pattern of exploitation similar to that which goes with differences of social class. A boy and girl are thrown together. They are of the same general class standing, but one stands recognizably higher in the scale of courtship desirability than the other. The more desirable person has many more opportunities for courtship associations than the other, and both recognize that he could, if he wished, "rate" someone more desirable. An interaction ensues based upon

[2]   Floyd Dell, *Love in the Machine Age*, Farrar & Rinehart, 1930, pp. 163–164. It seems likely that such exploitation is usually by boys of the girls' own class, and that girls who associate with men who are markedly above them in the class system do not usually expect marriage.

the fact that the person in the higher position has little motivation to continue the relationship while the other desires its perpetuation intensely. Control of the relationship follows the principle of least interest, and the relationship, if it is continued, comes to give the dominant partner everything that he desires of such a relationship (and what he may desire is by no means limited to sexual demands) while the other partner gains nothing but the continuance of the relationship. . . .

Exploitation of this sort is very often unintended. It just happens and often it happens because the exploiter is a person of facile sympathies. A "high-minded" young woman was the belle of a certain small town. One of her admirers was a small, partly bald and thoroughly unprepossessing young man who served as minister in one of the churches. The girl did not love him, did not even like him, and she decidedly did not want to become a minister's wife. After a time, she refused to have anything further to do with him; she made this decision many times, but was never able to stick to it. He continued to plead for the continuation of the relationship on any terms whatever, and in order to influence her he did many difficult favors for her and spent a great deal of money on presents. Because of her sympathy for the man, as she said, she could not always refuse his well-intended offers, and because of pity and a sense of guilt she could not always refuse to see him. Yet she was so little at one on the matter, so ashamed to be seen in his company, that when she appeared on the street with him she always managed to be about three steps ahead of him, a physical withdrawal which admirably symbolized the relationship. The relationship dragged on in this manner for a number of years until she fell really in love with someone else and gained the courage to break off the affair ruthlessly. This affair seems to be typical of a certain class; we recognize as familiar the facile sympathy for another which enables one to take something which she wants, the ego-wound involved in associating with a person of inferior status, the symbolic withdrawal from identification with that person, injuries worked upon the inferior because of this motivation, and the final ruthless break.

Age. Age is a factor which affects one's bargaining power in such relationships very decidedly. The usual pattern here is that the young woman, taking full advantage of her youth and beauty, exploits the older and probably wealthier male. The taxi-dancer, according to Cressey, can make a living by means of her catch-penny tricks until she reaches the age of twenty-eight or thereabouts, and then she must take up another way of life. The "kept women" and "gold diggers" of Park Avenue are young women who live by exploiting middle-aged men. In *Big Blonde* Dorothy Parker has given us a picture of such a woman when she has reached an age at which she can no longer command her price. Indeed this pattern is so very common that it is usually assumed that a young woman who marries an older man is marrying him for his money; this assumption is often inaccurate because after all there are father fixations. In all of this it should be understood that the price is not always paid reluctantly; often the bride is urged upon the exploiter by every means of persuasion which the exploited can employ. The older male is frequently more than willing to pay a high price for the favors of a young woman; he offers the price gladly while he asks only that he be permitted to cherish his illusions. The opposite type of exploitation, that of the older woman by the younger male, appears to be much less common in American society. . . .

The Influence of One-Sex Groups. In our society adolescents associate freely in one-sex groups. These groups, of which the gang is only one of the many possible forms, nourish a public opinion which greatly encourages the exploitation of the opposite sex. To some extent, the status of a boy in the group of boys depends upon seductions which he has succeeded in bringing off, or which he claims to have brought off, and contrariwise upon successfully defending himself against attempted exploitation by girls. In this group, the boy who gets his way with women is admired, and the one who falls in love is a fool and a fair mark for all kinds of obscene humor.

This attitude seems to exist in all classes. A few years ago a young steel worker of Gary was on trial for his life, accused of murder while attempting rape. A conversation of a few days before the crime weighed against him heavily. In the fiercest possible language he had expressed his determination to seduce the girl or "beat hell out of her." Such a conversation could just as well have taken place among the boys in an expensive private school or between brothers in a college fraternity. I have in my files extensive records of "bull-sessions" taken down verbatim by a member of a certain fraternity; in these unplanned and undisciplined conversations this same attitude comes constantly to the surface. The boys brag endlessly of their sexual exploits, detail the means for effecting seductions, declare their intention of bringing some affair to a successful conclusion by fair means or foul. The fraternity attitude toward love is perhaps typified by the fact that it is regarded as a very good joke to purloin the loved one's picture from a brother and to enshrine it in an unseemly place. This is the tone of the mono-sexual group, and interaction processes in such a group operate powerfully to enforce the exploitative attitude; I have already pointed out that this, too, is an idealization of women, and of a kind which coexists with the other sort of idealization. . . .

The role of the member of the one-sex group is considerably altered when it becomes known that he has fallen in love. He is frequently the center of an extreme unfavorable type of interaction, if the group happens not to approve of his love choice; in fraternity groups, the brothers hold councils and lay deep plans to save some brother from his thralldom. The lover is in almost any case the butt of many jokes, and yet the attention which he receives is not altogether ill-intended, nor is the lover wholly displeased by it. For though the lover is regarded as ridiculous, he is also an object of envy, and he usually realizes his position. And the teasing which he must endure serves only to remind him of the pleasant state of his emotions, unless it exceeds the conventional boundaries. In groups of girls, the position of the person in love is one which confers more outright distinction and exacts fewer penalties than appears to be the case with boys.

Comments and Conclusions

This view of courtship as a process in which bargaining and exploitative attitudes appear may strike the reader as completely unrelated to the attitudes of actual persons. It is true that

I have tried to give numerous examples, and those of the commonest sort, but someone will be sure to say that those examples are very atypical cases, and that the persons who have been cited are not persons who have the usual standards of morality. I should reply to this for that these notions of bargaining and exploitation have their clearest expression within the framework of the conventional mores. Dozens of proverbs display the importance of the marriage bargain for folk-wisdom. "There's no old foot but there's an old shoe to fit it." "It would have been a shame to spoil two families." "She flew all over the flower garden and lit on the manure pile." And as to the bargains of courtship, there is the cruel assumption of moral persons that a man who can enjoy a woman physically outside of marriage will not marry her. Even the most gracious of the young woman's advisers may counsel her a little cynically about courtship bargaining. Must a girl pet? "Yes," says the mellow and courteous Mary Perin Barker, "if she is not clever."

A more serious criticism is perhaps that my theory of courtship attitudes does not make sufficient use of psychoanalytic concepts. This was no inadvertent admission, but the result of an attempt to state a fairly complete theory of this phase of courtship interaction in specifically sociological terms. Young persons being constituted as they are develop under the conditions of association in the courtship period the attitudes which I have tried to describe. It happens that I have directed my own analysis at the interaction process of courtship; I recognize the necessity of supplementing this analysis by pointing out how these processes are related to the inner nature and the developmental history of the participants. Here the psychoanalytic contributions are much in point. It is obvious that the exploitative attitudes which arise in the courtship process are based upon something in the previous experience of the individual; these attitudes could not be developed if they were not already present in the personality in germinal form.

8

COURTSHIP AS A SOCIAL PROCESS

1938

Interaction of Idealizations

ONCE a courtship passes its earlier stages, an interaction of idealizations takes place which carries the couple farther and farther from contact with reality. At the outset A and B see one another without the intervention of any other screens of idealization than are produced by conventional attitudes toward the opposite sex, and by a certain irreducible over-valuation of the sex object; allowance must also be made for the petty frauds which young persons conventionally perpetrate upon one another, mostly in matters of no importance. Jack sees Betty as a woman, and with all the apperception mass which thousands of statements about women have given her in his eyes; he sees her as a young man necessarily sees a woman, as the possessor of the beauty that dwells in his beholding eyes; he sees her dressed in the borrowed finery of a fraternity sister and decorated by the beauticians, but he sees her more clearly and judges her more justly than he will ever do again—that is, if he likes her.

As the love relationship develops, A idealizes B, replacing the actual B to a considerable extent with a creature of his own imagination. . . . Because of this idealization of B, he displays to her only a limited segment of himself; he puts his best foot foremost and has his shoes shined beforehand; he tries to be in her presence the sort of person who would be a fit companion for the sort of person he thinks she is; all of this facilitates the idealization of A

Reprinted from *The Family* (New York: The Cordon Company, 1938), chap. 11, pp. 271–77.

by B, and B in turn governs her behavior in such a way as to give A a false impression. This interaction, aided by the mounting strain of sex pressure, leads to the cumulative idealization of the courtship period. It should also be pointed out that the illusions which young persons have concerning one another contribute their part to make the experience of a love affair a gratifying ego experience. The man considers some woman a distinctly unusual representative of her species, and is correspondingly flattered by the fact that she has chosen him of all the men in the world.

The lover's wish to explain himself, to reveal his shortcomings and to receive forgiveness in advance for all the sins he will commit in later life—these things have their reason-for-being in this interaction of idealizations. Realizing that the girl he loves has idealized him, the lover is troubled, and he tries to persuade her that he is not what she thinks he is, but perhaps he never tries very sincerely. The girl assures him that he is not so bad, that his petty vice do not matter by comparison with his great and obvious virtues, and she recites a catalogue of her own evil deeds. But no one is an effective devil's advocate when he himself is to be canonized, and the result of this process is to bind the couple together. The scrupulous character of these mutual confessions indicates a nicety of moral feeling in the other, as the ready forgiveness bespeaks a magnanimous spirit. In other ways, as well, those who are in love try to bring their relationship into adjustment to reality; it is doubtless the realization that he is not what the woman thinks he is that prompts the lover's typical insistence that he wishes to be loved for himself alone (whatever that may mean) and not for this quality or that. The psychoanalytic experience which takes place at this phase of the love affair is doubtless of great importance in cementing the relationship. There is catharsis and a resulting intense transference in these long rambling conversations of lovers who are never at a loss for something to say to one another.

Pair Unity

As a courtship proceeds, a special rapport develops between the two people. This rapport is, of course, a purely psychic thing, but there is always an attempt to objectify it in some way. As a result of conversations and experience, there emerges a common universe of discourse characterized by the feeling of something very special between two persons; the importance of this something special is clear in the statement of denial, "There is nothing between us." There is a strong impulse to symbolize this something between in a tangible way. A boy and girl have a date and they hear some particular song, or sing it, and that is their song from then on. They soon develop a special language, their own idioms, pet names, and jokes; as a pair, they have a history and a separate culture. They exchange rings or some other articles as soon as possible, striving to make tangible and fixed that elusive something between.

As a relationship develops, the pair tends to become fused into an increasing compact social unity. The characterization of a love affair as an *égoïsme à deux*, egoism of a pair, is apt. It occurs almost inevitably that the lover is likely to forget his duties in other relationships. He is especially likely to use his friends rather ruthlessly in the furtherance of his love affair, feeling that they have as great an interest as he in that which is after all uniquely his own concern. On the psychological side, the emergence of the pair as a social unit is attended by the process of sentiment-formation, or, if one wishes, transference. It is also important that because of the newness of the emotions and the habits involved in a love affair they demand a great deal of attention; attention is almost completely centered upon the pleasing and novel relation, and all the other concerns of the person suffer correspondingly.

When the relationship begins to be recognized by others, certain readjustments of the relation itself and of the relation of both persons to others are necessitated. When others approve of the affair, they tend to treat the two as a unit, to think of them together, and to arrange for them to be together; this introduces a new element of responsibility and stability into the relationship. The expectations of friends which constellate themselves about an affair change its inner nature subtly but effectively. When the affair comes to furnish an outlet for the desires of match-making friends and mothers, it loses some of its exciting novelty but gains stability and security. When others disapprove and oppose, the effects are almost unpredictable. There seems to be a tendency for such outside opposition to strengthen the unity of the pair temporarily, but perhaps at the expense of its lasting stability.

Mutual Identification

One result of the recognition of an affair by outsiders is that each member of the pair comes to regard himself as identified with the other to some extent. It is perfectly normal for the feeling of self-hood to include such intimate relations, and for the individual to feel that his status depends upon the status of the other person. It is partly from this feeling of identification that there arise those very common attempts to make the other person over. There are certain faults which the eyes of affection do not see, but one may sometimes see them through the eyes of others, and because he wishes others to think well of a person he may attempt to make her over in a pattern of perfection. Identification thus normally introduces new elements of tension into the relationship. A less normal kind of identification seems also to be common. Thus one finds a number of persons who apparently wish to be the loved object, and strive by imitation of clothes, mannerisms, and the like to accomplish this effect. It is true that one can imitate or even take the role of the other without this desire to be the other; a certain amount of unconscious and conscious imitation is perfectly normal and even has some importance as an adjustment mechanism; we refer here to the definitely abnormal desire to be the loved object. Thus where a girl has a desire to wear a coat like her lover, this possibility is very revealing as to the inner nature of the relationship. Ordinarily love relationships lead to exaggeration of normal sex differences, but here we are faced with the opposite phenomenon. A number of explanations on the basis of psychopathology suggest themselves.

The Principle of Least Interest

Up to this point we have assumed that emotional involvement is mutual, and that both parties fall in love at a fairly even tempo. It does not always happen so, perhaps not even usually. One is reminded of the famous French epigram concerning mutuality, that in every love affair there is always one who loves and one who permits himself to be loved. Even where an affair develops more or less evenly through its various stages, one person usually becomes more involved than the other, and must therefore take the lead in furthering the movement from stage to stage. If there is too pronounced a difference in the tempo of involvement, there is an abnormally great chance that the relation will be arrested on a level of exploitation, or at least at some point at which the person less involved takes the other person very much for granted. According to conventional notions of courtship, the man should first become involved and should take the lead in furthering the affair. If the woman is first involved, she should hide this fact from the man in order to prevent him exploiting her and also to avoid destroying his interest in her as an unsolved problem. It has sometimes been pointed out that the purest type of feminine love is a sort of reflected narcism; the woman loves the man because he loves her; the feminine tendency toward this type of attachment (probably a result of our mores) facilitates the sort of interaction process in which the man takes the lead.

Control in these extra-marital relationships follows a principle which we may accurately, if somewhat ungrammatically, designate as the principle of least interest.[1] That person is able to dictate the conditions of association whose interest in the continuation of the affair is least. This fact has many consequences. In the first place, there is a great possibility that any relationship may be arrested on the level of some sort of exploitation with very unpleasant consequences for one of the parties. Once the relationship has become exploitative, the likelihood that it can progress through other stages is probably decreased, since the exploited one, having lost altogether the power to fight for the control of the relationship,

---

[1]   Cf. Ross's discussion of the law of personal exploitation: "The thing is common and its rule is simple. In any sentimental relation the one who cares less can exploit the one who cares more. In the man-woman relation and the mother-child relation we see this plainly." (E. A. Ross, *Principles of Sociology*, Century, 1921, p. 136. Reprinted by permission of D. Appleton-Century Company.)

does not sufficiently command the phantasy life of the exploiter to cause him to fall in love; the best ally of the exploited, however, is the conscience of the exploiter. It is these exploitative affairs, which steadily decrease in meaningfulness for the exploiter, which lend most support to the conventional mores. In the next place, a realization that premature involvement has its inconveniences and its hardships leads people in the courtship period to resist the development of love attitudes. Finally, the prolongation of some of these unbalanced, least-interest-dominated relationships produces some very unsatisfactory marriages; it seems possible that many of the cases which Jung describes as those of the container and the contained arise less from the factors to which he ascribes them than from the bargaining situation of courtship. A further consequence of the principle is that one who has suffered serious exploitation in one affair may try to be the exploiter in the next.

Further Complexities

The complexities of courtship processes are considerable, and perhaps I am not wrong in believing that women are more clever than men in taking advantage of them. The principle of least interest is true in general; the principle itself explains many courtship phenomena, and the fact that people know this principle explains others. And it is true that exploitation of some sort usually follows the realization that the other person is more deeply involved than oneself. So much almost any reasonably sophisticated person understands. The clever person, in my observation usually a woman, knows how to go on from that point. A girl may pretend to be extremely involved, to be the person wholly dominated by the relationship; this she does in order to lead the young man to fasten his emotions and to prepare the way for the conventional dénouement of marriage, for, in the end, while protesting her love, she makes herself unattainable except in marriage; this is certainly not an unusual feminine tactic and is executed with a subtlety which makes the man's crude attempts at guile seem sophomoric. The less conventional girl may, indeed, after many protestations of love on both sides, permit physical relations, counting upon an extremely adroit manipulation of the young man's conscience to secure her hold upon him. Again and again, the man is caught by his own attempts at exploitation and by his own conflicting moralities; here as elsewhere pride goeth before a fall. In order not to leave a false impression, I ought to say that many women make use of such mechanisms, but few plan to do so or seem to realize exactly what is happening. Women might plan their campaigns so but probably very few do. And yet there seems no doubt that women understand the intricacies of courtship interaction better than men do. If such a book as this were written by a woman, what secrets might she not reveal!

The ego feelings of both parties produce additional complexities. As one undergraduate informant has remarked, "After one or two kisses have been exchanged, each has a basis for the rationalization that it would be unfair to the other to break off an affair that has gone so far and involved the emotions of the other so completely." "Pluralistic ignorance," ignorance by each of the real attitudes of the other, produces many amusing situations. Each member of a pair states to others that he is not very deeply concerned, but hesitates to break off the association because of the possible disorganizing effect upon the other. Of course in such cases we must not forget that each person may be perfectly sincere, having been led by his ego feelings to minimize his own involvement and magnify that of the other. There is also a self-protective element, in that each one anticipates the possible end of the relationship, and seeks to prepare his "alibi" in advance.

Strength of Sentiments Released

When at last the powerful love attitudes are fully released and centered upon a single person—when sentiment-formation overcomes objectivity—for many a person life is out of hand. . . .

9

MARRIAGE SOLIDARITY

1938

THERE are many persons who would never move their fingers toward the button which would wipe out their marriages as completely as if they had never been. Let us remember that there are those who would rather be married than not, and to their present mates. We have usually been inclined to take marriage solidarity for granted, and to devote our efforts of analysis to those conflict processes which run counter to the mores of marriage. This is an unsound approach, for marriage solidarity is a fact requiring explanation quite as much as marriage conflict. We now devote our attention to the factors and processes which make for solidarity.

Pair-centered Interaction

One of the important causes of marital solidarity is the ideal of solidarity. Prior to all marriage interaction is the determination of the individuals concerned to "make their marriage work," and to achieve happiness—if such determination indeed exists. Our culture lays it strongly upon the individuals to form the marriage pair into a solidary group. In the "Whom God hath joined together" formula, it is laid upon those who are not privy to the marriage contract that they must remain outside the sphere of marital interaction. In general, the ideal of solidarity probably

---

Reprinted from *The Family* (New York: The Cordon Company, 1938), chap. 15, pp. 383–402, with elisions.

makes for solidarity. If fissures develop in the marriage, the ideal of solidarity sometimes causes them to become wider.

Park and Burgess have enunciated the important principle that the external relations of the group determine its internal structure. This principle carries us a long way toward the understanding of solidarity in marriage. In and around the married pair there arise characteristic forms of interaction; for the outside world, one type of interaction is the norm, but a quite different type prevails within the group. This is the mechanism by which the assimilation of each to each is effected in marriage.

Let us begin our discussion with an apparent exception. If an observer from another planet came to the earth and visited us in our homes, it would perhaps seem to him that married persons have little interest in one another. When a third person is present, husband and wife direct their attention at him; themselves and their relation they seem to take very much for granted. The whole ritual of deference, politeness, and compliments is likewise mostly for outsiders.[1] This is an enormous break from the interaction of courtship, which excludes outsiders almost completely. It is understandable as an example of the laws of habit formation; when one is forming new habits, he is attentive to them and conscious of them, but as the habits become established, attention moves away from them. In the early months of marriage, the attention mechanism is less often operative in the marriage situation itself, and it is increasingly directed at the outside world. To persons afflicted with the romantic attitude, this comes to be quite a problem.

The direction of attention away from the marriage relationship may usually be taken as an indication that the relationship is on the whole satisfactory, else it could not be taken for granted. (It should be understood that we are speaking merely of a redirection of attention from marriage, not of the flight from marriage contact

---

[1]   Cf. Charles Lamb's delightful essay, *A Bachelor's Complaint on the Behavior of Married People*, in which he states this norm of deference for outsiders. He complains of "the very common impropriety of which married ladies are guilty,—of treating us as if we were their husbands, and vice versa. I mean, when they use us with familiarity, and their husbands with ceremony."

or other forms of avoidance reactions.) And it is very important, likewise, that outsiders assume the marriage relation to be one of amity and accord; this, too, is taken for granted and not commented upon, demonstrations of intimacy being in fact rather bad form. This tacit assumption of an intimacy too great to need any proof and too common to be commented upon is, as we shall see, one of the roots of solidarity.

In yet another way this redirection of the social process operates to create intimacy, though not always the kind of intimacy one desires. When people are together in the courtship period, they are alone together, and others do not intrude upon their privacy, but no one hesitates to intrude upon a married pair. The result is that one sees the mate in his whole circle of routinized relationships; one discovers his personality by learning what roles he plays in all the groups to which he belongs. As life goes on one learns to know the mate by seeing him reflected in a myriad of relationships. Perhaps this is the true meaning of the old saying that one never knows a man until one has eaten a peck of salt with him. What one learns about the mate by seeing him in other relations is not always pleasant; perhaps, thanks to the prior operation of idealization, it is not usually pleasant, but it is always revealing. One learns that one's husband is a sissy, or that one's wife has a reputation for telling lies. Or one discovers some unsuspected quality of greatness in the mate. It may even happen, where one's claim to distinction is based upon qualities not easily perceptible to the ordinary observer, that one cannot possibly evaluate the mate except in terms of his reputation in some specialized group that is qualified to judge. In such cases it is interesting to watch the process in which the wife or husband assimilates the standards of the sub-group and comes to pass judgments on the basis of such standards. Any great variation above or below the norm of respect is certain to have its repercussions in the marriage relation.

There is a sense in which there is a loss of intimacy in marriage; there is at least a kind of intimacy which is sometimes lost. Before marriage one usually talks a bit about himself—quite a bit! Probably this is motivated in part by sex frustration and made possible by the newness of the relationship. After marriage this sort of thing is likely to fall off. There are yearnings and fancies which one will communicate to a stranger but not to his friends. The wife, since she can hardly remain a stranger, can no longer elicit these confidences. Again, the very meaningfulness of the relationship interposes certain barriers, or perhaps it would be more accurate to say that the conditions of meaningfulness interpose the barriers. Many excellent orators do not like to have their wives in the audience when they make speeches. The roles clash. Probably such a man knows that he can never be a hero to his wife, and feels that she will laugh when she sees that others regard him as a hero. We do not have to go very far in the psychoanalytic universe to discover a reason for this in the husband's own desires. Often the reason is merely the husband's desire to make a mother substitute of the wife and to be for her a little boy. A similar clash of roles may be produced by the development of personality after marriage. Where the wife's conception of her husband stabilizes at an early period, as it often does, and he continues to develop in the world outside of marriage, her conception of him rapidly becomes archaic.

In terms of such a differential of communication as we have already hinted at, we may state the whole process of differential interaction in relation to marriage solidarity. There is a whole range of states of mind which are communicable in marriage but not outside of it. When an acquaintance asks, "How are you?" the answer does not call for the slightest bit of introspection, for he expects a stylized response. A witty colleague once characterized a certain hypochondriac by saying that he was the kind of man who, when you asked him how he was, told you. But there is ordinarily no incongruity in the communication of such states of mind within the family. A kind of frank, reasonably complete communication continues in the family which is even moderately well integrated; the poet has referred to wives telling their secrets to their husbands at the midnight hour. The secrets of marriage are among its most important assets, a fact which puts a real obstacle in the way of research in marriage. The similarity of marriage to the analytic situation is here very apparent. Mutual communication gives solidity to the relationship. Completeness of communication in one relationship gives one verbal continence in others. As in the analytic situation, all the old ambivalences arise in the new relationship, and likewise one encounters resistances and other barriers to communication in proportion as the relationship becomes meaningful. Marriage is unlike the analytic situation in that the relationship is usually arrested at some point and there is no breaking of the transference. And—a most important lack— the conscious guidance of a trained analyst is missing.[2]

The Fiction of Solidarity

We must couple with this idea of differential interaction the notion that members of a marriage group are identified with one another and coupled together in the minds of others in a sort of public privacy. I have elsewhere developed this paradox:

For marriage has two elements of strength, the one, that it is private, the other, that it is public, and from neither of these is the group outside altogether excluded. It is a public privacy; privacy is assured and its value enhanced by the public character of the arrangement. This public-private character of the arrangement is a source of both strength and weakness in the institution, and of both happiness and unhappiness for the married. For when a man loves his wife he is proud to have his friends know that she is his; he does not see her faults as people do who do not love her, and he does not realize that most others, if they trouble at all to speak of him as the husband of a particular woman, say, "Well, I'm glad it's he." If he does not love her, he sees her defects more clearly than anybody else, having more opportunity, and more motivation to do so, but he imagines that others see her as he does; thereby his unhappiness is increased. But as love is made stronger when people at large know of it, so its frustration is the more keen if it is glimpsed by persons outside.[3]

2   See Hans von Hattingberg, "Marriage as an Analytical Situation," in *The Book of Marriage*, H. Keyserling, ed., Harcourt, Brace, 1926, pp. 329–347.
3   Willard Waller, *The Old Love and the New*, Liveright, 1930, pp. 106–107. Reprinted by permission of The Liveright Publishing Corporation.

In reasonably sophisticated circles, people usually see the importance of the appearance of solidarity and address themselves consciously to the task of building and upholding a fiction of solidarity even if the reality does not exist. When such a façade is erected before marriage, members of the outer group recognize, perhaps, that the picture does not conform to reality, but they attempt to give no sign of such recognition. Conventionalization and hypocrisy enter here.[4] The fiction of solidarity may arise as a result of the type of interaction which customarily surrounds the pair. One discovers that persons around him assume that he gets on well with his wife, ask him no questions about the details of his married life, and in fact will hardly permit him to impart such details; the flow of self-feeling comes to include the relationship, and presently he is greatly disturbed by any break in the smooth front of the marriage.

Dual Participation

Nor must we forget the dual participation of married persons, around which so much of our social life is organized. To invite one member of a married pair and not the other is something of a breach of politeness in most circles. Married couples entertain other married couples and are so entertained by others. Bridge, the commonest card game, is a game for four people. The stage is set for couple-participation; bachelors and spinsters have difficulty in joining in and married persons without their mates cannot conventionally be included at all.

New problems are occasioned by dual participation, by the fact

---

[4]   Conventionalization arises when we agree to treat a thing as true whether it is or not. Thus in certain circles all women are spoken of as virtuous, although everyone knows that some are not. In other circles, all marriages are spoken of as happy and successful. Conventionalization sometimes assumes an extreme complexity; a person is lying; the other person knows that he is lying; and the first person knows that the second person knows that he is lying; the second person knows that the first person knows that the second person knows that the first person is lying —but neither one breaks face.

that one person is necessarily included in nearly all the social relations of the other. Directions of development are set up in early
marriage which ultimately have profound effects upon the personalities of both husband and wife. For example, let us suppose
that one person greatly excels the other in social facility—a situation which is far from uncommon. One may even say that it usually occurs that one person is superior to the other in conversational ability, social facility, and the aptitude to set the stage for
social interaction. The tendency is for the facile one to do most of
the talking, to make most of the contacts—and with his own kind.
It usually turns out that the one who has the greater original capacity for social leadership continues to develop at an accelerated
pace, while the other person is correspondingly stunted. The facile
member builds up about the pair the type of social interaction and
the kind of social world in which he is at home; it often happens
that this is not the most congenial atmosphere for the other person
—so that he suffocates like a fish from too much air. Such a situation frequently brings out all the positive traits of one member,
while it forces the other to develop negativistic, retiring traits and
attitudes. The relationship of container and contained may arise
from this situation, when one person comes to depend upon the
other for social expression and to have his social contacts filtered
through the other person as a medium. Because of processes which
he himself has initiated, the container is likely to grow dissatisfied
with the contained. In predicting adjustment along this line, it
would be necessary to know a great many details about the personalities, although in most cases the probable course of events is
obvious enough. Two things stand out as important preventives
of this type of marital maladjustment; similarity of cultural backgrounds and interests, and the cultivation of separate social worlds
for married persons.

Social Habits in the Family

The nexus of interaction which is a family may be viewed
as a set of intermeshing, mutually facilitating habits. . . .

Interaction is Continuous

Interaction in the established marriage tends to remain on an even keel, or to continue in the directions which have been set in early marriage. It is perhaps in order to stress the fact that it remains *interaction*. We are accustomed to emphasize the point that the crucial adjustments of a marriage are made in the first few months, and this is a sound principle, but we must not forget that the process of adjustment continues while the relationship lasts, and that many important adjustments are made in the later years of a marriage. One person makes an adjustment, and the other adjusts to that adjustment in such a way as to call for further adjustment of the first person and so on endlessly. Also, the adjustments which are stabilized in early marriage interaction are likely to be very expensive to one person or the other, and the person who forms them may develop unpleasant traits or indulge in outlet behavior which produces a further crisis. Or, after a year or so, a so-called adjustment may become insupportable and have to be changed. The advent of children changes the personality of the man or the woman, and vastly alters the relationship. Success or failure reacts upon the man and upon the wife's estimate of him; his status in the family is likely to be correspondingly changed. It is worthwhile to bear in mind that although the adjustments of marriage are stabilized the adjustment process itself never ceases.

10

MARRIAGE CONFLICT

1938

"KILL THE CAT on the first day and you'll never have any trouble with your wife." So ran the advice which in other days the experienced patriarch gave to the young husband. If we grant the premises, the saying expresses a sound understanding of the realities of marriage interaction. For the start is all-important. With the words, "I now pronounce you," a process begins which will go on, in most cases, "till death do us part." The man and the woman have started on a journey and they cannot turn back. The words "husband" and "wife" soon acquire "meanings" not given in the dictionary definition.

Marriage as an Undefined Situation

In sociological terminology, we may say that every new marriage is an undefined situation. Each individual begins tentatively to explore the behavior possibilities of the situation. Each one tries to find out what he can do and should do and begins to form habits, but neither can stabilize his habits at once because the other person is also carrying on an exploratory process. If the duties and privileges of husband and wife were more exactly defined in our culture, this period of confusion could come to an end in a short time. The fact is that there are few patterns for early marriage interaction, and those which exist are not very helpful.

Reprinted from *The Family* (New York: The Cordon Company, 1938), chap. 13, with elisions.

For guidance in this perplexing situation, the newly married must depend chiefly upon four sorts of existing patterns:

1. There is a tendency for patterns of interaction established in the courtship period to influence marital interaction. Some habits may be carried over into marriage without modification, but these are usually few and unimportant because the environment has changed. Most of the habits of the courtship period are manifestly unsuitable for marriage. Control on the principle of least interest cannot satisfactorily be employed in a relationship in which both individuals have by definition a very important stake. Likewise the idealizations of the courtship period must crumble soon or late. For the most part, habits of the courtship period influence marriage interaction because they continue as demands for activity on the one hand and as expectations on the other, and yet are necessarily reversed. The idealized interaction of courtship cannot continue, and yet most persons expect it to continue. Many important behavior tendencies in both parties have been anesthetized in the courtship period and now slowly return to life. Add to this the fact that after marriage many persons set out to redress the wrongs and remedy the bad bargains of the courtship period, and we have a fairly complete picture of reversals of courtship habits.

2. Many young persons of today discuss their marriage problems in advance, and agree upon a code of marital behavior. They have observed the marriages of their friends and associates, and the spectacle has given them to think. Determined that their own marriage shall not be like the rest, they arrive at a number of clear-cut decisions in advance. Each of them shall have the maximum amount of freedom in the relationship. They shall never let the sun go down on their wrath. When one of them is angry, the other shall hold his temper. If ever they cease to love one another, they shall separate amicably without recriminations. Their naïve faith in the principles and agreements by which they hope to attain marital happiness is amusing and pathetic. Premarital agreements could perhaps be made to work if each person could be a Joshua to his own motives and arrest the processes of change within himself. After marriage each of them will be acted upon by a radically dif-

ferent situation, one for which his experience furnishes no parallel. Each of them will become a different person and will find it difficult to be bound by his own previous decisions. Frequently these very agreements are the cause of conflict later because they are abrogated in practice and one person or the other feels cheated. Often such agreements are merely the rationalizations which enable people to get through the crisis of marriage. And yet we must concede that the people who attempt to define the situation in advance are acting in a sensible way. If they could have more knowledge of the situation they face, their endeavors would not turn out so badly. At present, rules and pre-marriage agreements probably have real utility in preserving the assets of "good" marriages, but are of no use at all in the others.

3. The conventions which govern the marriage situation also furnish certain patterns for marriage interaction. In some cultures, these patterns are very explicit and leave the individual little leeway for his own choices. In our culture, they were once a great deal more explicit than they are at present. Where the married pair formed a part of the larger family, as it did among the Polish peasants, where a stable church and a stable community exerted continuous pressure in favor of the established mores, it could not be said that marriage interaction was guideless. Even under modern city conditions, there are still conventions of marriage, entrenched in the consciences and ego-ideals of the participants, and they influence marriage importantly. But the conventions are in conflict with one another, for the married pair may represent different orthodoxies, and the old orthodoxy is likely to be opposed by the new. And there are many important matters on which the conventions are silent. In such a situation, social definitions break down, and the married pair must work out their own mode of life on the basis of the inner dynamics of their relationship.

4. Many attempts are being made to supply through various channels of education new and more rational patterns of family interaction. To some extent these apply to the troublesome early period of marriage adjustment. A prevalent shortcoming of such educative programs is that they are highly moralistic; they strengthen the hold of the established conventions but make the

inevitable departure from these conventions more destructive when it comes. Educative programs with regard to family life are probably at their best when they liberate the young from conventional patterns which are not workable at the present time, and attempt to equip them with attitudes of tolerance and flexibility and techniques of meeting the crises which are certain to arise. A fundamental limitation of pre-marital instruction or "guidance" is the difficulty of communicating knowledge concerning a certain sphere of social interaction to persons who lack the experience background into which to assimilate such knowledge. A person who has never been married cannot possibly imagine how it feels to be married and no one can tell him. There are, therefore, many generalizations which can be comprehended by the married person with ease—by the unmarried not at all. The systematization of knowledge in sociology may ultimately prove to be a great aid in communicating insight into the married state to the inexperienced. If it does no more, systematic instruction may shorten the period of confusion-delay in early marriage interaction.

After we make due allowance for the patterning of marriage interaction, it remains true that the new marriage is an undefined situation. The social form created by marriage must find its way in a sort of tentative process; it must grow as a grapevine grows, blindly reaching out its tendrils, making many false starts but attaining at last to light and solidity.[1] Like a rat in a maze, each member must try out many patterns of behavior in the new situation. Some patterns will appear highly successful; these will tend to stabilize in the form of powerful habits. Other patterns of behavior will be penalized by conflict or other forms of failure; it is thus that the limits of interaction are defined. A man who moves into a new house must go through a period of tension and attention before he is at home; he must find the switches for the lights; he must learn

---

[1]   The concept of the tentative process and the grapevine analogy are borrowed from Charles Horton Cooley. (See C. H. Cooley, *Social Process*, Scribner, 1918, Chapter I.) Robert Cooley Angell has already called attention to the fact that this concept may be applied to marriage. (R. C. Angell, *The Family Encounters the Depression*, Scribner, 1936, p. 13.)

which is the hot and which the cold water faucet; above all, he must be careful of the cellar stairs. In the end one comes to be at home in a new home. In the end the grapevine finds its way. So with marriage.

The experience of beginning married life is defined in the mind in three different ways, according to the point in time from which one looks at it. One experiences marriage in phantasy long before he experiences it in fact, and afterwards one reworks the marriage experience and every other significant experience in retrospective imagination. One looks forward to marriage for a long time, and this in itself is a factor of the greatest importance in explaining marriage interaction. The little boy announces that when he grows up he is going to marry Jenny Lou, and the young women dream and see visions, and before marriage lovers are much given to imagining things as they will not be. Convention molds this phantasy; literature and the arts furnish many of the materials for it; and deep-lying impulse furnishes its motive power, for phantasy is a tendency to act transformed into a tendency to dream and sent on a long ballistic curve into the skies. Phantasy directed toward the future probably plays a very important part in the clarification and organization of our purposes.

When at length the experience comes of which one has dreamed, it is certain to be affected by the fancies which have been woven about it. Pre-existing phantasy gives depth and meaning to the present experience. It may be that one experiences reality as a fancy come to life, and a delightful sense of unreality pervades the thoughts of one who loves deeply and is recently married. Or it may be that reality clashes with the idea, and one observes with despair the toughness of reality and the frailty of illusion.

The continent of fact is bounded by two oceans of illusion. After the event the marriage experience is redefined by wishful thinking operating through the years. After the years of youth are gone, one views them through a mist of idealization and believes that they were really what one later wishes that they might have been. If the marriage adjustment is favorable, one forgets all the little unpleasantnesses of the beginning, and relives in imagination the early days of marriage as they might have been but were not. If the marriage later fails, one may repress all memory of pleasant things, and redefine the whole experience in terms of the new configuration. This reworking of past experiences helps to make them bearable and gives to them a factitious consistency. It is an obstacle in the way of the scientific investigation of human life.

Honeymoon Interaction

Honeymooners are not always ecstatically aglow, if we can credit the stories that they tell later, but still it is very likely that the honeymoon is the high point of most marriages and of most lives. It is a period of extreme importance for later adjustment. It has been said that marriage is the remedy for the disease of love, a remedy which operates by destroying the love. Often such a process does take place, and it begins on the honeymoon.

I am not using the word "honeymoon" in the conventional sense, to denote a trip to Niagara Falls. The wedding journey is an accident; the honeymoon, as a period in the psychic adjustment of a married pair, comes near to being a universal. The honeymoon lasts while illusion lasts. . . . the imperious drive for sexual fulfillment narcotizes but does not destroy other drives and habits. When one is in love, and in the early days of marriage, nothing else matters. A remarkable euphoria attends this state of mind, and the whole of life tends to be suffused with erotic pleasure. This is necessarily a transitory condition. The psychic honeymoon, which begins when one falls in love, ends when the narcotized habits regain their propulsive power and when the erotic euphoria fades away. Hamilton's study of 200 married persons shows something concerning the duration of the psychic honeymoon. Fifty-seven persons were dissatisfied with their marriages before the end of the first year; thirty-nine more before the end of the second year; twenty-one more admitted dissatisfaction but did not specify the date.[2]

[2]   G. V. Hamilton, *A Research in Marriage*, Boni, 1929, p. 69.

Every crisis of our personal lives is like every other in some respects. In every crisis there is the same preoccupation with the crisis and what it means, the same withdrawal of attention from the world and concentration upon a small circle of interests, and the same inability to grasp the significance of the crisis all at once. There is the feeling of spontaneity and choice which is in no way diminished by the fact that the individual does merely what his culture commands. After the crisis, there is the gradual emergence of a new life organization, a more or less automatic adjustment of life habits, which is not the result of planning but the basis upon which planning and direction will build.

The *égoïsme à deux* of the courtship stage becomes almost a *folie à deux* in early marriage and then subsides to the ordinary form of family egotism. As in every other situation which calls for the reorganization of habits, the run of attention is interrupted and attention is directed at the crucial, problematic, or frustrating point in the situation—here the marriage partner and his desires and expectations. Early marriage is characterized by an abnormal sensitiveness of each person to the moods of the other. If Mary responds to some statement without her usual enthusiasm, her new husband must hold an inquisition there and then to find out what is wrong. The slightest hint of a flaw in the rapport is a calamity which demands the attention of two whole personalities. Each member of the new pair experiences an impulsion to explore the other as fully as possible, to know the other's most minute shading of attitude, and at the same time to reveal himself. This period of absorption in the new relationship is functionally important in enabling the individuals to build up their habits of life together.

The euphoria of the state of being in love characterizes early marriage, in which it serves the function of enabling the individual to accept with equanimity thwarts to his pre-existing habits and denials of his value system, rendering him insensible to the meaning of the changes in his life until new habits have been formed and they have brought into being a new system of values. Likewise the traditional wedding trip, whatever may be said against it on other grounds, removes the person from the environment in which his established habits function and encourages him to concentrate on the formation of new habits.

The dominant motivation of the honeymoon is to widen the area of contact between two personalities. So long as the relationship is new, every contact is pleasant because it is erotically tinged. In the normal course of events, the relationship soon loses its original intensity. Habits of adjustment to the other person become perfected and require less participation of consciousness. Security in love changes the character of the affectional bond. The wide area of the taken-for-granted is a basis of mutual faith and understanding or its opposite. It must be emphasized that this is the normal sequence of events, and that the marriage in which it does not take place is the one which must be branded as pathological. It is the unstable marriage which has the greatest number of high points and valleys.

Burdensome Habits and the Honeymoon. It frequently happens that habits established in the first days of marriage become a burden afterwards. If we examine those marriages which have become burdensome to one or both parties, we often find that these persons live in a habit-cage which they built in their early months together. They once took pleasure in doing certain things together, or one of them took pleasure in some action by the other, and they still continue to do these things which now cause them pain, perhaps reproaching themselves the while because they are lacking in the proper sort of marital sentiment. Collective habits establish themselves very easily because each is motivated by the imagined expectations of the other, and they are often wide of their mark because of the unwillingness of either to break through the circle of pretended enjoyment by a frank communication. Each refrains from frankness because he believes that a delusive rapport is better than no rapport at all. It is worthy of remark that such enslaving habits would not be likely to arise in a culture which rigidly defined the duties of husband and wife. . . .

Opposition of Sensualization and Idealization. . . . The courtship process gives birth to excessive idealizations. In marriage this process is reversed. Idealization is the process of building up an imaginary picture of a personality; from certain rudiments of the configuration of a personality, idealization conjures up the total configuration. We now meet the opposite process in which the imagined picture is overwhelmed by a flood of sensory details.

Before marriage we have our phantasies, to which our frustrated impulses urge us and for which the culture furnishes the materials; after marriage we have the person, which brings with it its own delights, but the phantasy is usually nobler and more kind.

Now gently, now with startling brutality, the real person and the reality of marriage pound at the portals of thought, and at length enter. One may struggle against disillusionment. As a hitherto unperceived facet of a personality reveals itself and destroys an illusion, one may build a mental bulwark about the old illusion or rationalize the new behavior into some sort of agreement with the old configuration. Or one may have recourse to the old and foolish device of attempting to make the other person over in conformity with one's desires. Or one may accept disillusionment and feel that he has been cheated in marriage, not realizing that it is his own imagination that has cheated him. The romantic complex has thus been blamed by many writers for the difficulties and disappointments of marriage.

The impact of one person upon the other is often incalculably heavy. And the marriage situation, aggravated by the extreme intimacies of early marriage, is a crushing weight upon the idealized pictures of marriage. As the area of privacy diminishes, the opportunity for idealization diminishes at an equal pace. As intimacies increase, opportunities for disgusts are multiplied. As personalities become known, imagined accords and agreements are destroyed. As the revelations of the past of the other person proceed, something ordinary replaces the imagined clouds of glory. As we have seen, it is of the nature of early marriage interaction to tend toward an unusual intimacy. It is not surprising, therefore, that the honeymoon so often ends in conflict.

Universality of Conflict

If Romeo and Juliet had lived together long enough, they would probably have had their disagreements like everyone else. For all young lovers know that their passion is without parallel in the history of the human race, and that their marriage will be just like no other, but their life together usually turns out to be just another marriage like all the rest. In our culture we set a high value upon happiness in marriage and we try to believe that a considerable degree of accord is the usual portion of married persons. We are helped to maintain our illusions by the pretenses of married people, for it is regarded as faintly ridiculous not to be happily married, and the fiction of solidarity is, in fact, one of the most important assets of any marriage. And yet we know perfectly well that there is no marriage in which there is not a certain area of conflict and disagreement.

It is perfectly possible for people to quarrel sometimes and yet live happily together. Keyserling has characterized marriage as a state of tragic tension, but tragic is too strong a word, for it is likely that most marriages do not often rise to the heights or sink to the depths of tragedy. Conflict itself is not always an evil even under our marriage mores. As Simmel once pointed out, conflict enables us to support relations which would otherwise be unbearable. Marriage conflict is often the only means by which unworkable schemes can be shuffled off and new ones formulated. Human beings like us of today, who have not been trained to live in a consistent world, probably would not find a relationship from which conflict was absent very interesting or rewarding. Not that conflict gives pleasure in itself, though that may happen too. The pain of conflict is a necessary part of other experiences which are pleasurable. There comes to mind that dictum concerning the pleasure that is distinguished from the sharpest pain only by the fact that one would not part with it for anything in the world. Conflict is not always tragic.

And yet it would be a great error to agree too hastily with the apologists for the family who say that the ivy-çovered old institution is really all right and that the things which seem to be wrong with it are really all right too if we can just understand them. It does seem that the average marriage has a great deal of conflict and that not of a kind which is particularly helpful to the personalities concerned. Most marriages rapidly develop a number of areas of frustrating conflict and many develop such intricate patterns of cross purposes that the persons involved must spend all their energies upon them without deriving from them any pleasure.

Factors in Marriage Conflict

Situational Imperatives toward Conflict. In discussions of cultural definitions as affecting marriage, we generally stop short with the consideration of conflicting definitions. It is also true that conflicts may arise in marriage because of common definitions, because both persons embrace a common definition which facilitates conflict. A prizefight might be a boxing exhibition or a grudge fight, and the difference is in the social imperatives which hedge it about. It is so with marriage; on this point the evidence of cultural anthropology is convincing.[3] Culture may give to marriage in general a prevailing tone of hostility, or it may bring people together in such a way as to minimize conflict. Cultural definitions set the stage for marriage interaction.

The interaction of the courtship period often carries over into marriage in such a way as to make destructive conflict unavoidable. Courtship takes place in a bargaining situation from which exploitative, antagonistic attitudes easily emerge. It leads to a progressive idealization which takes people farther and farther from reality, and makes the ultimate shock of adjustment more severe than it is in other culture. Courtship facilitates a paralysis of other behavior trends in the interest of the satisfaction of one, and these other tendencies must one time come to light. Each person has suffered certain wrongs in the courtship period, and he is likely to set out to redress them after he has gained the security of marriage. It often happens that each member of a pair feels that he has made a bad bargain, but postpones consideration of this fact until after marriage. Or it may occur that some man or woman has been so sought after and pampered in the unmarried state, because of unusual bargaining power, as to be unfitted for any marriage without extensive reconditioning.

Our culture sets the stage for the development in the early months of marriage of patterns of intimacy which will constitute a heavy burden for the pair to carry through life. The honeymoon psychology welcomes any sort of contact with the other person,

[3]   See Margaret Mead, *Growing Up in New Guinea*, Morrow, 1930.

however troublesome or costly to other segments of the personality, but such things cannot last forever; if in addition people have been trained to regard the intoxication of early marriage as the desirable norm of marriage, some mutual disillusionment is inevitable. Likewise the amputation of habits under the ether of the honeymoon is often regretted later. Similarly, the revelations of each to each in the honeymoon period, a practice to which a very powerful and foolishly human impulse prompts us, are likely to be acceptable and assimilable at the time but not later.

The very intensity of the marriage relation in our culture invites conflict. Persons who have never quarreled with their roommates one day find themselves quarreling with their wives. One has a greater stake in a marriage than in any other relationship and therefore he forgets his manners; he forgets them, of course, because he must, because the frustration involved in not speaking his mind is greater than he can bear. When we add to the great intensity of feeling in the marriage relation the fact that no graceful pattern of marital relations is enshrined in present-day conventions, we approach more nearly the understanding of the problem.

Conflict which arises from agreed-upon culture patterns involves a certain amount of rapport, and is not always destructive of marriage. In the balanced ratio of antagonisms and accords which constitutes marriage, such conflicts play their part. Husbands and wives are held together by their bickerings as well as by their high moments. There is a sense in which any established definition of behavior is better than no definition; the established may always be anticipated and adjusted to. In a well-integrated culture, only a minimum of conflict would arise from agreed-upon definitions. In our culture, however, disunity has reached a high point; we teach persons to behave in a certain way in their marriage relations and also to resent such behavior in others. So that the force of cultural conditioning, due allowance being made for the imperative toward peaceable marriage, tends rather to maximate than allay conflict.

Intensity of the Relationship. We have said that the very intensity of the relationship between two persons may be a cause of friction. In other words, two people quarrel because they love one another very much. This seems paradoxical, but it is not. Conflict is a clash of wills. The closer the association between two persons, the greater the hazards which it must run. The closeness or intensity of the relationship not only increases the emotional reaction to a clash of wills; it must also necessarily increase the chance that such a clash will occur. Sociologists have long been familiar with the fact that we often quarrel bitterly with those whose opinions are closest to our own, while we behave quite rationally toward others whose opinions are opposed on all counts; here is the application of this idea to marriage. For "all men kill the thing they love." . . .

In-laws. When a marriage is celebrated, a new group is formed, and each of two established groups gains a member and loses its first claim upon one of its own members. Conflict, overt or covert, between the group and its new member is the traditional issue of the situation.[4] The father and mother of the newly married persons necessarily over-value their own child, and cannot believe that anyone is quite good enough for him; they are therefore highly critical of the newcomer in the group. Likewise, the family group is jealous of the affection which was formerly bestowed within the group and is now supposedly directed at the new member. Every family has its own set of collective representations, traditions, superiority fictions, its own pathos and humor—in short, its own culture—and to this specialized culture the newcomer offers at least the passive resistance of ignorance and is likely to outrage it actively. Cultural differences, great and small, solidify the group against the new member. To this is added the difference in the role assigned to each mate by his own mate and by his parents and in-laws; parents see Mary as a somewhat irresponsible child, but John sees her as a wife and expects her to fulfill the responsibilities of adulthood; from this clash of expectations arises a conflict similar to that between the parent and the teacher. The result of all this is that the parental family exerts a powerful back-pull upon the members of the new family group. The embitterment of one's re-

[4]   Hamilton found that the visiting mothers of ten husbands and eighteen wives were accused of causing trouble. Sisters-in-law were also somewhat undesirable guests. (G. V. Hamilton, *op. cit.*)

lations with his in-laws becomes a cause of conflict with the mate. This phenomenon is greatly accentuated in cross-culture marriages, but it is not solely caused by culture conflict.

The relation of a man to his mother-in-law is traditionally an unpleasant one in our culture, and is without a doubt our most joked-about relationship. The relation of mother and daughter is recognizedly close. And the aging mother has a difficult time in finding a new role and adjusting herself to the fact that her children are now adult and independent. Nor is the relation of the woman to her mother-in-law ordinarily supposed to be a pleasant one. There is a folk-saying that two women cannot live in the same house. The husband's mother is jealous of her son's affection, and relinquishes it with difficulty.

It may be that specifically psychoanalytic factors are at work, especially in the relation between the man and his mother-in-law. The man's mother-in-law, perhaps cut short in her own emotional life, lives vicariously in her daughter, and tends, therefore, to fall in love with her daughter's husband. Her inhibitions lead her to resist any such attachment strongly, and accordingly she turns toward him the hostile side of her ambivalent emotions. On the side of the man, there is apt to be a strong transference upon the mother-in-law as a mother substitute, but ingrained inhibitions lead him to react strongly against this attitude. In addition, the mother-in-law arouses some mental conflict because she resembles the wife in many respects but lacks her youthful charm, and this is a further source of hostility.[5]

The Freudians quite rightly, as I believe, trace the taboos which govern the relation between the spouse and the in-laws to the inevitable conflict in the relation, which people attempt to handle by providing cultural means for its regulation. This seems to be one of the most plausible of the Freudian contributions to anthro-

[5]   For a full discussion of the psychoanalytic factors involved see J. C. Flugel, *The Psycho-analytic Study of the Family*, Woolf, 1929. This problem is also discussed by Brill in "The Only or Favorite Child in Adult Life," a paper in *An Outline of Psychoanalysis*, J. S. von Teslar (ed.), Boni & Liveright, 1924, pp. 134–135. See also Sigmund Freud, *Totem and Taboo*, London, Routledge, 1919.

pology. Apparently the present generation of anthropologists, trained to a wholesale rejection of evolutionary anthropology and of all psychologism, have not quite known what to do with this upsetting bit of insight. The fact seems to be that wherever we have marriage we have a problem of in-law relationships, and that different cultures have handled this problem in different ways. The orthodox manner of handling the relationship in our culture is by imposing the norm of affection upon the new relationship.

Intrusive Factors in Family Conflict. We should also give brief mention to certain intrusive factors in family conflict. By *intrusive factors* we mean to designate those influences which come from outside the family scene and facilitate conflict.

In an integrated culture each institution tends to support all of the other institutions of society. In our society a generation ago we were much closer to an integrated state than we are now, and the threads of religion and community sentiment wove in and out of the fabric of family life and gave it strength. There was nothing which one did from affection but what it was his duty also. To the sentiments of family life the community gave its approval and the church its supernatural sanction. The economic values of family life were not small. In the present social order, these extra-familial bulwarks have been removed from the pattern of family life. The life of the larger group is often divisive in its effect upon the family group.

There are marriages whose internal strength is sufficient to cause them to hold together under any and all circumstances. The effect of adverse external conditions upon such marriages is merely to strengthen them. There are other marriages which would not be satisfactory under any circumstances. The middle group of marriages is the one in which the balance of happiness or unhappiness seems most to depend upon external conditions.

There is an incident in *Eyeless in Gaza* which seems to illustrate the general point in intrusive factors in the love relationship. A man and a woman who are lovers are lying on a roof sunning themselves. An airplane flies over them and a little dog either jumps or is thrown from the airplane. It lands on the roof and dies instantly. Blood splashes over the woman. In horror and disgust the woman leaves and will never have anything to do with that man again. It is difficult to see what Huxley means by relating this preposterous incident, unless he wishes to symbolize the impact of intrusive factors upon a relationship. He has, to be sure, indicated the previously existing weaknesses in the relationship.

Usually the impact of intrusive factors is less tangible than in Huxley's story. A man and a woman are married and the man has helped the woman to build up a number of fictions by which she lives. Their relation is far from perfect, but under ordinary circumstances it might endure. From without there comes a social hurricane which destroys the wife's so beautiful conception of herself, and straightway the marriage breaks up. If the pair had been living in another social milieu, their story might have been different.

The economic situation of the family affects the conflict processes within it profoundly. The long arm of the job reaches into the home and sets husband and wife against one another. Occupations which have a high contact mobility have correspondingly high divorce rates. The person who considers himself a failure in his occupation is likely to compensate by becoming a domestic tyrant. The wife who considers her husband a failure may find her response to him as a lover dwindling along with her respect for him as a man; sometimes the husband projects upon the wife a reproach of this sort when the reproach exists only in his own mind. The number of such cases among relief families is said to have been large in recent years.

Nor must we neglect to mention those families wrecked by success. Financial or business success often brings with it the opportunity to rise to another class and this involves marriage conflict as a result of the conflict of class standards; this is probably the simplest case of those wrecked by success. In other cases, financial success brings out the weaknesses of a marriage by making possible the gratification of wishes which are incompatible with marriage. A considerable number of men are faithful to their wives because of poverty; financial plenty destroys the stability of their marriages. Finally we come to the class of cases described by Freud; there are persons who seem to be able to bear their frustrations as long as they seem to be imposed by poverty or other external circumstances, but when the external obstacles are removed internal limitations of behavior become apparent and neurotic behavior ensues.

Under our present mores, when a slight breach appears in the rapport of a couple, the effect of the group life of the pair is frequently to enlarge the area of disagreement. . . .

11

PROBLEMS OF THE DIVORCÉ

1930

THE WORLD that loves a lover does not love a divorcé, although it may like to read about him in the newspapers. Preference for the tender emotion is not difficult to understand. Love is simple, direct, and beautiful. The lover knows what he wants and goes after it. Frustration, usually the lot of the divorcé, is complicated, circuitous, and ugly. The divorcé does not know what he wants and is not sure that he wants it anyhow. He has got what he wanted and found it was not good for him. The divorcé, further, has rendered himself vaguely indecent by violating a marriage taboo which, although consciously repudiated by the half-enlightened multitudes, yet remains a powerful element in determining their behavior. The very word divorcé, to say nothing of its more vulgar synonyms, smacks of sexual irregularity.

In the explanation of popular prejudice against divorced persons, there is another factor, of the most subtle, to be considered. People do not like divorced people because they have personal problems. A woman may lie, steal, murder, even lose her virtue, and there will still be those who say that there is some hope for her. But let her admit some difficulty in controlling her thoughts and arranging her life and she is forever damned. She has problems, personality problems! Away with her! A man may carry tales, libel, seduce, betray, he may yet rise to a position of power and trust, but if he ever admits any subjective difficulties he is

Reprinted from *The Old Love and the New* (Philadelphia: Liveright, 1930), chap. 1, pp. 3–28, with elisions. By permission of Liveright, Publishers, New York. © 1930 by Horace Liveright, Inc.

branded as an impossible person. It is not a crime to have problems; if it were, the attitude could be faced and evaluated. It is simply impolite, and no gentleman would do it! And then, in these post-Freudian days, there cluster about the person who is not quite at one with himself splotches of masturbation and stains of incest.

The problems that the divorcé must face are of a sort well calculated to make him preoccupied and subjective, and therefore perhaps a bit harder to understand than he would otherwise be. They are of such a compelling nature that his energies are likely to run long in internal channels, so that all his acts are enfeebled with thought. It is not possible to imagine more thorough-going reorganization than is in extreme cases necessary after a divorce. One must reorganize his love life, he must salve over his wounded pride, he must rechannelize his habits, he must reëstablish himself in his social group, and he must settle the conflict with himself, always present, sufficiently well that he can go on living effectively. The divorced woman must in most cases face also the problem of economic rehabilitation; she must learn to pay her own way. The most casual consideration of these necessities of reorganization will suffice to suggest the explanation of the fact that real reorganization is rare.

This process by which one marriage partner is split from the other and learns to live apart is one process. It neither begins nor ends with divorce. Marriage relations are carried over into the post-divorce period, indicating that there is much vitality in a relationship after the legal break has occurred. In other cases, the relationship is dead long before any mention is made of a legal step. It is the process with which we should be concerned, regardless of its location in time and space. And, though it be swift or gradual, this process must always take place whenever a marriage breaks up, and it must include, at one time or at separate times, reorganization along all the lines mentioned. . . .

We may turn . . . to a discussion of certain things which may give clues as to the types of readjustment which will be effected. For as the marriage and the divorce are expressions of entire personalities and are best understood in the light of the entire life-pattern of the person, so is the person's conduct during the period of readjustment governed by the major trends of the personality as brought out by the social situation of which it is a function. Anything, then, that will tell us what sort of people we are dealing with, or that will bring out the essential characteristics of their life-situations, will serve as a key to the readjustment effected after divorce.

One such key is furnished by the reason for the delay, or for wanting to delay, in getting the divorce. It rarely happens that people wake up one morning, find that they want to get divorced, and proceed to consult a lawyer the same day. Such a decision is usually reached after long deliberation, if not debate, in which one or the other of the mates takes the aggressive rôle. Or if there is no discussion, then both know long before the actual break which way things are heading. Usually, however cogent may be the considerations which ultimately carry the decision, there are other reasons which for a time are equally valid and which are opposed. In listening to the narratives of divorced people one is moved to marvel at the powers of the human spirit to take abuse, to suffer punishment in intolerable situations. Making allowance for the fact that they give highly rationalized accounts in which what they have suffered is not minimized, one still must believe enough to wonder why the people did not separate long before they did.

Why was the divorce so long delayed? In the answer to this question lies often the key to the readjustment which the couple effect after the divorce. What was uppermost in their minds while they were yet married will be dominant in their thoughts while they are reorganizing their lives separately. Other things which were unforeseen may come to affect the situation, or those foreseen may not be in fact important, but in general the motives operative in the life-situation before divorce continue to be so in that existing afterward.

If people have hesitated to split their ménage because of a reluctance to let their friends, or enemies, know that all is not well in their lives, then covering up before their friends will be of great importance in their readjustment. In such cases there is often a complete break with all the people who have known them. This desire to avoid having one's friends know the unfortunate truth may arise from fear of a loss of professional or social standing, in which case the attempt will be much more seriously made to hide the real state of affairs from the public. Such pretense is usually transparent, and is at worst considered dishonest and at best pathetic.

If a couple delay to seek their happiness separately because of religion or moral scruples, then religion and conflicts over it will predominate in the period of readjustment. If the reason for the delay is a desire for security on the part of one or both of the mates, then we may expect to find in the period of readjustment a buttressing and intrenching of one's self which is intended to assure security in the possession of such personal assets as the divorce has left untouched. If people postpone making a break with each other because of real affection—and contrary to the general opinion there is a great deal of what is called love which is lost between persons who nevertheless decline to sleep beneath the same blanket—then the marriage partners may expect prolonged agony and anguish and turmoil of spirit on account of mental conflicts which they can never quite solve. All these factors operate to cause people to procrastinate, to postpone, to delay, hoping that after all it may not be necessary, for though people marry in haste they must perforce divorce in a leisurely fashion, and all these factors have an influence on the type of readjustment which people effect after the break. . . .

.   .   .   .

We may arrive at a better understanding of the divorcé's problems of adjustment if we compare them with the problems of people whose situation is similar in some respects but different in others. Such cases, to take only those within the ken of all, are cases. . . . of broken love affairs which did not go to marriage and the cases of those interesting married people who should have got divorces but did not. . . .

Though divorced persons and those who have lost their lovers sometimes take advantage of their common misery to console each other, their problems are really of quite a different sort. They are alike in that both suffer, or may suffer, from the pangs of love which if not unrequited is at least thwarted. The advantage is of course with the person who has lost his sweetheart, for although there may be more idealization in extra-marital than in marital love, there are more guards and more barriers between the persons, so that the relationship is less close. Both may suffer from injured pride; the divorcé, having been injured the more publicly, suffers more. Both suffer from mental conflicts which may in the case of either become very severe, but the advantage is again with the person whose affair stopped short of marriage.

There are certain respects in which the situations of these two sorts of persons suffering from interruptions of their love life are altogether different. One suffers no loss of social standing from the breaking up of an affair which did not proceed to marriage. One's friends often do not even offer to sympathize with one over such a break, there is an element of humor in the quarrels of lovers. The disappointed lover has a great advantage over the thwarted husband or wife in that there is present for him a clear and unequivocal definition of the situation. The break having been made, he should reconstruct, nor does anyone consider it indelicate if he begins that process at once. Further, as the habits of courtship are of but little account by comparison with those of marriage, the penalty for breaking them is less. An additional factor is that since the affair is lighter in its nature, one is more likely to tell just how the break occurred, and is therefore more likely to talk it out, getting what is known as a "catharsis." It seems, however, that it is even more important in these cases who breaks the affair, possibly because, the affair being of a less serious nature, the inner qualms of the one who breaks it are more easily hidden. The one case in which the situation of the divorcé is better than that of the lover who has suffered a disappointment is that of the woman who has lost her virginity to the man whom she is giving up. If she attaches an uncommon value to that physical attribute, she may well grieve over having lost it illegitimately. That, too, is passing, for this fragile thing, virginity, has in these skeptical days a waning value.

We have yet to consider how the situation of the divorcé differs from that of those pathetic persons who ought to get divorces but for some reason will not.[1] The life of persons who live together in

---

[1]   We are not discussing here those married people who separate but refrain from getting divorces. These separations are tantamount to divorces except for the fact that reconstruction by starting another home is im-

marriage, when the rapport upon which the relationship rests is gone, is if anything more effectually thwarted than is that of the divorced person. Divorce is a lump sum, it is said, that one pays for freedom to work out his own life adjustments; since one is never really free, it is a lump sum with continued partial payments. But those who live together when the marriage has become hollow pay and pay and pay, and never stop until they die.[2]

It is amazing how completely a marriage may in fact have ceased to be a marriage and yet remain one in form. The alienation of the marriage partners from each other may be complete, so that there is apparent no vestige of an emotional bond between them. Their estrangement may even be public and admitted. One may satisfy his own desires for status by a public derogation of the other, which represents the opposite extreme to emotional identification with the love object. It may happen that the life of the married ones is completely split, the husband having his friends, his life, his work, his ambitions, dreams, and ideals, from all of which the wife is excluded, she being similarly independent. Under such circumstances it is likely that each will be completely objective about the other. Or, unable quite to break away, and yet unable to solve their elusive incompatibility, they may meet and quarrel, giving vent to their pent-up hate in violent, cathartic quarrels whose periodicity and satisfactoriness to the partners indicate perhaps that in some bizarre way their sex life has been shunted off into that unfortunate channel. . . .

He who explains divorce—and no one has, with all due respect to the present so numerous learned tomes—should also be able to explain why people go on living together, and he who first satisfactorily explains either the one or the other will have explained much. Fear may lead people to prefer the familiar misery of living together to the unknown sufferings of divorce.

---

possible,—a fact not without important consequences, it is true, but one which we may perhaps be permitted to overlook for the time.

[2]   Since this was written a case has been called to our attention in which this was literally true. A man who had hated his wife for many years, but who had not been able to divorce her, lay in his last illness. Whenever his wife passed near his bed he kicked at her. His last agonies were precipitated by one final attempt to express his hate in this fashion.

IV. On Education

12

NOTES ON THE TRANSFORMATION

OF THE TEACHER

A PERSON enters college teaching with a well-formed set
of attitudes. He enters a world in which many, if not most, situations are neatly defined, and he must make constant adjustments
between his definitions and those which his colleagues and his
students stand ready to impose upon him. The attitudes of the
beginning teacher are sometimes only deflected by the situation.
Sometimes they are ruthlessly suppressed by the group and other
attitudes substituted for them. With regard to many situations the
teacher has no attitude at all. In order to understand the professor,
we must know how the college environment acts upon the attitudes
which he brings to his profession.

We are here concerned with the deflection and transformation
of attitudes by the teaching situation. What Znaniecki has attempted to state in *The Laws of Social Psychology*[1] we shall here
endeavor to state concretely. We shall be concerned with changes
which occur almost entirely in the first decade of college teaching. . . .

An attitude undergoes a considerable metamorphosis when it
becomes self-conscious. Social attitudes readily become roles, and
much of human behavior is explicable as the dramatic living out

---

Previously unpublished.

[1]   Florian Znaniecki, The Laws of Social Psychology (Warsaw:
Gebethner & Wolff, 1925; reissued New York: Russell & Russell, 1967).
—Ed.

of conscious or unconscious roles. When people play a certain role in a situation, and receive either approval or disapproval because they play the role, especially if they earn their living by playing the role, they experience a shift of attention which alters the inner nature of the role. . . .

The internal organization of an attitude is further changed when the attitude is expressed in words or deeds, and one learns what others think of a person who displays such an attitude. The change may be a very gradual one.

In a public official an attitude that was once sincere may ultimately become mere attitudinizing. By the expression of an honest belief a man commits himself to a certain position. A group forms about him in the expectation that he will continue to lead them in fighting for this belief. To keep the group together, he must frequently trot out this opinion for exercise and display. After a while he expresses the opinion more or less automatically, more from the expectation of praise than from inner conviction. He becomes the more a hypocrite the more he looks at others' faces when he speaks.

Sociologists who start out as sincere and highly motivated liberals often lose much of their liberal enthusiasm and perhaps transfer their enthusiasm to science. Sociologists usually justify such a change of attitude by saying that when they analyzed their liberal programs more closely, they realized that they needed to know a great deal more about society before prescribing for it; they know now, they say, that they must develop something of a science of society before any really effective program of reform can be worked out. By offering an explanation of the development of the scientific attitude, we do not mean to imply that the above propositions are false; we account for a change of attitude, but do not say that the customary justification of the scientific attitude is false.

Something happens when a liberal becomes a teacher of liberalism; he becomes a teacher more than a liberal and perhaps a teacher and not a liberal at all. To essay a crude analysis: One begins teaching sociology with certain clearly defined liberal ideas and a strong motivation to spread them. One receives favorable or unfavorable recognition as a result of the expression which one gives to these ideas. This recognition deflects one's attention from the ideas to the social situation; one enjoys the role one plays so much that one gradually loses interest in and familiarity with the ideas. Perhaps this early liberalism represented an attempt to talk out one's complexes. It is perfectly possible to talk out one's complexes and partially to cure one's self of the disease of liberalism by talking about it. The college liberal sometimes finds that he has no very strong motivation to continue with the kind of talk by which he has gained his present status. He formalizes his role and plays it with increasing distaste. Perhaps his work is such that he feels called upon to issue certain humanitarian exhortations from time to time; but he finds himself emotionally dry, in the same situation as the minister of the gospel who has preached himself out and needs new stimulation for his spiritual life. There are other factors involved. Part of the motivation of rebellious liberalism is one's own insecurity and lack of recognition; it sometimes happens that a sociologist makes satisfactory progress in his profession and needs this no longer, so that one more emotional spring has dried up. Liberalism, in so far as it represents rebellion against the established and accepted, is peculiarly likely to be rebelled against when it becomes the established mode of a group. Further, the work of the teacher necessitates social distance, often requiring the teacher to limit himself to facts and to avoid emotion. There is considerable pressure upon the young sociologist from his sociological colleagues who want him to be scientific, who indoctrinate him with the notion that only a very foolish sociologist passes value judgements. Doubtless some of these factors had something to do with the tendency of the young sociological liberal to contrast and analyze arguments for and against war rather than to take a strong stand against it.

By a similar process reformatory zeal of a more dynamic sort is sometimes shunted off into science. Mr. A. was for some years an agitator and social reformer. At the time of the Farmer-Labor party, he threw himself into the campaign with selfless fervor. His candidates were nearly all defeated and he felt that there was little value in efforts to ameliorate the condition of mankind. He returned to school to take graduate work and became greatly interested in the development of a science of society. He wished this science to be built upon a solid base, so that it could not be destroyed by changes of fortune, and he felt that this could best be done on the basis of quantitative method. He received favorable recognition for his first few papers on quantitative methods, and transferred his motivation almost completely to the development of that phase of science.

This metamorphosis of reformatory energy is of course in perfect accord with Dewey's theory of the instrumental character of thought. All social science may be said to flow out of thwarted, or impeded efforts to make the world better. The reformer meets with a check, and stops to think the situation over. Perhaps he decides that he can best serve humanity by spending his life in thinking the situation over. As a result of his new role of the student, he acquires a new life purpose, which is perhaps checked in its turn by the realization that he can never understand the whole of the life of man, and he specializes in some one field in which he spends his life in trying to develop a method.

If there seems a reasonable chance of overcoming opposition, the attitudes of the courageous man are stiffened by opposition. To stiffen an attitude is, of course, to effect a real change in it, and usually to increase its importance in the scheme of personality. Direct attack may cause one to come to defend that which he might otherwise be willing to discuss critically, and awareness that others regard one as a representative of a particular school of thought may encourage one to identify himself with it. "When I was taking graduate work at Chicago," writes one informant, "I did not identify myself with the Chicago system of sociology or feel called upon to defend it. I accepted it and was trying to learn it. There was so much about the Chicago system of thought that I had not learned, that I should not have dared either to defend it or criticize it when others were present who knew it better. When I transferred to another graduate school, I met Mr. Y., who immediately began to attack the Chicago school of sociology, and, as I thought, to ridicule me as a representative of it. He was joking, but he soon got me into a state of mind where I was not joking. I regarded myself as the chosen defender of the Chicago system; I forgot that I did not know very much about the system of thought, and I set out to prove its superiority to all other systems, and the superiority of systematic to unsystematic thought in general. It was not until I was removed from this situation that I regained perspective."

College teaching furnishes a refuge for many persons who are not able to face reality. These are the tender-minded, for whom any contact with things that are sordid and brutal and true is very disturbing. Because these persons have their heads full of notions which are much determined by wishful thinking rather than reality, we call them idealists. Ideals are pictures of things as one would like to have them, or as one thinks they ought to be; to keep ideals one must have a considerable power to ignore reality. Even in college teaching, one comes into some contact with reality, and this contact is destructive to one's ideals. The idealist usually resents it when his ideals are destroyed and he often turns from positive idealism, the belief that men are angels, to negative idealism, the belief that men are devils. This negative idealism is known as cynicism. The idealist in the college environment usually meets with disillusionment, and when he does his attitudes display a certain characteristic sequence of changes. It is this cynicism of the frustrated idealist which dictates those excessive bitter essays which college teachers sometimes write for the popular magazines. An anonymous article entitled "Confessions of a College Teacher" appeared in *Scribner's Magazine* in 1933. It recounted the soul struggles of a young teacher of English. In analyzing this life-history, one of the authors of this work wrote in part as follows:

The idealist has a life history as exact and determined as the life cycle of a germinating egg, and the English teacher's story is the natural history of the academic idealist.

For the last ten years this man has been engaged in the teaching of literature. He started out full of ideals and began to make fine talk about them. To have ideals and to talk about them eloquently; that was the thing. His students listened to him respectfully, took notes on what they considered important for examination purposes, and did not know what to do with the rest. When the examination came, they made some of the usual boners. One girl informed him that when Juliet heard of Romeo's death she fell prostitute.

The boners made this man angry. It offended his dignity to perceive that he had been so little appreciated. To think that a student who had been in his classes, and listened to his lectures for several weeks, could be so uncomprehending! Enraged and embittered, he did what thousands of other young instructors have done, he decided to get revenge, he decided to make the students work. He "came down on them." He became a stickler for academic standards. He was just as right, in his own mind, in this phase of the process as he had been before. Students fought back, dropped his courses, refused to elect him. He became more harsh on those who could not escape him. There was a long battle, with many amusing incidents. He was sarcastic, and the students retaliated by exaggerating their ignorance to pull his leg; it must have been fun to see the poor fellow tear his hair. Finally the students won. The teacher was instructed to be a little more lenient or else—. Up to this point everything he had done was right, but now he did something that he considered wrong. He gave in. Here lately he doesn't flunk anybody, and gives lots of high grades. He is very popular, but he informs us that he cannot sleep at night.[2]

Our English teacher apparently began his career with a set of ideals rather more vicious than usual, and with a correspondingly grandiose conception of himself. He discoursed at length on man and his dreams and the love of learning and the written dreams of man. Very likely he hadn't the faintest idea what he was talking about, but it sounded nice. He felt that he had a message; he tried to communicate his message and he failed. His students knew perfectly well that they had an examination to pass, and they tried to prepare themselves for it and they failed. The professor did not get his message over because nobody really wanted to hear it and it probably was not a very good message anyhow; when he failed, he became bitter, and then came the long war.

I believe that any sensible man who had failed as signally as this man had might very well have stopped to consider whether he really had anything to say. My own suspicion is that he had not. It strikes me as entirely possible that English literature is not worth

[2]   "Confessions of a College Teacher," Anonymous, *Scribner's Magazine,* October, 1933.—Ed.

teaching in the present undergraduate set up. I do not say this because I do not appreciate the value of literature, but because I believe that it cannot be communicated in the classroom.

Perhaps the literature that our generation learned cannot be passed on to the present generation of students at all. Social philosophy gives us a strong hint that we ought to be prepared to accept this possibility. As the body of culture accumulates, we must constantly pare it down by eliminating all but the most imperatively necessary objects. Humanity must clean out the attic every so often, and the younger generation is going to clean house with ruthless disregard for our sensibilities. We must resign ourselves to whatever damage they may decide to do. There must have been conservatives in the age of bronze who hated to see the fine old art of working stone die out. Stone-working was an old, old art with a great tradition, but it died completely when people ceased to have a use for it. It is beyond the power of the teacher of literature to make students appreciate classic writers who have nothing to say to this generation. Keats and Shelley and Shakespeare, encysted in textbooks for generations, are probably travelling the slow road to oblivion. We can regret their passing, but it will do us no good to exercise ourselves about it.

It is a desolate moment in a professor's life when he grades his first examination papers. His best thoughts come back to him maimed and garbled, and his most eloquent phrases are misspelled. It is a real crisis, and upon the line that one takes thereafter depends the rest of his career. Academic standards only begin to be important to the teacher after the first examination. Devotion to academic standards rests in part upon a spite motivation arising from the teacher's frustrated ego. The first few weeks are an ego-swelling time. For the first time in his life, the young teacher is somebody, an authority. He has a large, eagerly listening audience. He makes some casual comment, and students open their notebooks and write it down; it will be treasured forever. He is great in his little world. With the first examination the new teacher discovers two unfortunate facts, that students have not understood or wanted to understand his message, and that they are powerfully interested in getting a good grade in the course. Then the teacher, frustrated and ashamed, decides to battle for the academic standards. In this, he has the sympathy and backing of all the other disappointed idealists on the faculty. It is regarded as a highly meritorious course of action.

What has really happened is that one has substituted a new self-aggrandizing pose for the old one. Our English teacher began by presenting himself to his students as a lover of learning and an eloquent discourser upon the written dreams of man. His conception of himself collapsed after the first examination. He then decided to become important in the lives of his students in another way, by making them work like the very devil; he would show them! Besides, this would enable him to play a favorable role in faculty society, to be valued among professors in proportion to the amount of red ink on his reports as a soldier is valued among soldiers in proportion to the number of wounds inflicted on the enemy. The sadistic marker, I believe, is frequently the poseur whose pose has failed.

Weekly papers on unnecessary topics, quizzes, examinations, low grades, sarcasm, attacks upon the students' taste, insults to their intelligence—what a way to communicate a love of literature! For apparently this teacher did think that he was still trying to pass on his appreciation of literature. Does it need to be pointed out that the means employed were not adapted to the end? The means were the conventional academic means employed to check up on how much work the student has done. They had nothing to do with passing on the professor's taste for the classics, because dates and facts have nothing to do with literature. The means were fit only for what they actually accomplished, for making students hate literature and the man who taught it.

Literature courses, I believe, almost invariably become perverted in the academic set-up. The teacher tries to communicate attitudes, but is forced to communicate facts. He comes to attach an irrational importance to those facts. The love of learning becomes equivalent to the love of facts about standard authors. Before one can love an author he must be dead and some eminent critic must have written about him in a book.

I do not know anything nor can I imagine anything half so

degrading to the mind as these literary facts that some people pride themselves upon knowing. Does it really matter where Shelley's dog is buried? I confess to the profoundest indifference on the subject. Such learning is perversely futile because it is related to none of the concerns of life. It is the scholarship which consists not of learning things but of learning what people have said about things, and it produces the bloodless scholar who lies at second-hand by quoting something somebody else has said that is not so.

It is a form of perversion constantly produced by the academic situation. Let us say that a certain professor of the humanistic studies knows both literature and life and makes his living by commenting upon them. He realizes that literature is valuable only as a way of understanding life, that the aim of fiction is to communicate true insight by describing false phenomena, and he sees clearly that when literature is so out of touch with life that it does not aid in understanding life, then it is literature and not life that must change. Literature takes its values from the life of man and cannot impose them on it. All this he knows, but he cannot always pass it on to his students, because students have not seen life and cannot therefore know anything about the relation of letters and life. A graduate student comes along; he has a good memory, but he is naïve and inexperienced, and his emotions are set in the pattern of the perennial sophomore; he is a sort of social moron. He regards the professor's performance as a feat of endurance; the professor, for him, is one who earns his living by talking for some forty-five hours on the same subject. The student learns what the professor says, but he is incapable of learning what he is talking about. When this graduate student turns professor, he loves learning for learning's sake, and feels that the world is wrong in not accepting his sophomoric pronouncements. In the academic as nowhere else we need the permanent revolution.

In his last stage the subject of our analysis abandoned altogether the attempt to uphold the academic standards, amused his classes, did not give out so many low grades, but lost his self-respect. He seems to feel that he has done something base, that he has been untrue to his ideals. But this is the wrong time to accuse himself of treason to his ideals; he committed that ten years ago, after the first examination, when he decided not to try any longer to teach literature but to force his students to memorize facts about literature. Of course it is not really the crime against the academic standards that keep him awake at night; it is his inability to assimilate a personal defeat. If, however, he still has any love of literature, he is in a better position to communicate it now than he has ever been before. I feel that for the first time in his career he is acting almost like a sensible man.

He has gone too far. From attempting to cram unwelcome information down the students' throats he went at once to the refusal to try to teach anything at all. Babyish, as ever, in his choices, in his false antitheses, in his overlooking of alternatives. His last stage is just another swing of the pendulum. Just now he has worked up a god-like pity for his students because they come from homes where the arts are so neglected. Tomorrow something else will be seized upon to give him the fleeting illusion of greatness.

If our cynic ever wins back to sanity, it must be by picking up some of these as yet unperceived alternatives. Perhaps after a while he will begin to try to teach his students a little something. If he is tactful about it, begins where he ought to begin, somewhere near the students' present level, does not try to short-circuit the educational process by force of will and executive fiat, but builds up his case point by point and step by step, he may find that students respect him for his efforts. Students expect the professor to struggle with them a little. It spoils the game of getting a degree just as much if he refuses to struggle at all as if he proves an arbitrary and unreasonable opponent. If the professor is just ordinarily fanatic, students will give him a wide break. For whatever we may say of the intelligence of the average college student, he is fundamentally fair and even generous in his attitude toward the professor as a person. If our teacher of English returns patiently to the task which he abandoned after he graded his first set of examination papers, the teaching of literature, he may be able to accomplish a small part of that task. He will be able to salvage a small part of his former favorable opinion of himself, all that he has any right to preserve in a realistic world.

We go on living after we have been defeated in life and we go on forming purposes and we go on fitting our purposes to things we think we can do. Much of our psychic life is merely adjusting ourselves to not getting what we want. In this the professor is one with the rest of humanity. Because his original intentions are more grandiose than those of most others, and his opportunity to fulfill those intentions is certainly not great, it is possible that the professor gets a little less of what he wants than other men. It is not an accident that the academic world abounds with petty distinctions, for praise-hungry men have called these distinctions into being. The first and greatest adjustment of the professor to the forces that defeat him is in his inner acceptance of the academic way of life. The academic pattern of life presents the professor with a realizable ambition, and he knows that if he lives and works by the rules, and lives long enough, he will become a great man. Not all professors are defeated men, for some of them have designed to be just what they have become. There are many others who have come to be something they never wanted to become, who have intended to be more than mere academics, and have tried to be more and have turned out to be professors of the common or garden variety. The process by which these men have substituted the conventional academic dignities for the distinctions of which they one time dreamed is insidious and subtle.

A young professor of sociology conceives of his science as an attempt to understand human life. He attempts to realize this broad conception of his task in his published work; he publishes a book in which he attempts to combine scientific writing and a proper appreciation of the tears of things. It probably is not a very good book. It fails to reach a wide section of the lay public because of its sociological stiffness, and it fails to impress the sociologists because of its popular looseness. The young sociologist is grieved that his literary career should begin so inauspiciously. He rebels for a time, and writes his next book for the academic audience. It is a conventional book and it receives conventional recognition; its author receives conventional promotion and a rise in salary. Before many years have passed he is inclined to be very apologetic about his first book. It was not, he says regretfully, written in academic style.

In many other ways the academic definition of the meaning of life imposes itself upon the young professor. The distinction between knowing things and knowing about things, is an old one. Many a young man in graduate school burns to be a student who knows what people have said about things; he adjust his conception of his role to the status he achieves and perhaps is happy. A young man wishes to write. He commits the deadly error of teaching English for a few years while he perfects his style and learns more about technique. He learns much about technique and style, and does not practice writing. After a few years he is further from his goal than he was when he started. He turns to academic writing and solaces himself with it as he can. Perhaps he is successful in developing a few writers, which is to say that some of his students learn to write for the magazines; the teacher develops the rationalization that he serves the world better by developing great writers than by being one. Perhaps, like our young cynic of a few pages back, he is not a very successful teacher. In that case he turns himself into a battler for the academic standards. As a witty colleague has said, following Bernard Shaw, "If you can't do it, teach it. If you can't teach it, fight like hell for academic standards."

One who is a poor teacher develops to the full negative attitudes toward students, and these attitudes contribute to make his subsequent relations with students unfortunate. The unsuccessful teacher usually manages to rationalize his defeat, and very often he obtains considerable faculty standing as a result of his campaigns against the students, but the trauma of student dislike never fails to have some effect upon his personality. But if it is an unfortunate thing to be a bad teacher it is sometimes no less unfortunate to be a good one. The good teacher is subject to influences which may interfere with his growth as a scientist or scholar, and his adjustment to reality as a man. He is strongly tempted to crystallize in his present pattern; the desire to hold the attention of his student woos him seductively to popularization; and the gratifying esteem of his students tempts him to develop delusions of grandeur. There is a belief among professors that amounts almost to a superstition that when a course is "working" it should not be radically revised. This attitude is strongly in play when a course is popular and attracts many students. The temptation for the professor to fossilize is very marked in such a case; he is like the cheap novelist who early in life finds the formula for writing saleable trash; he usually spends the rest of his life writing trash because he can produce it easily, because he knows he can sell it, and knows that perhaps he cannot sell anything else.

The fact that a professor's lectures are pleasing to students may work upon the professor's organization of life with nearly irresistible force. The ego gratification that one gets from lecturing well to a large audience is direct and tangible, and one who has this gratification offered to him when he is young and unformed is likely to be profoundly affected by it. The knowledge that on Tuesday morning at eight o'clock three hundred faces will be turned toward a certain man may determine the run of attention of even a seasoned lecturer. One cannot help thinking about what he is going to say to them. This sort of social situation dominates phantasy and may define a task for the working of the unconscious mind, so that even undirected phantasy is likely to play upon the problem of what one is going to say to the class. Teaching affects personality by determining the direction of creative phantasy. Some professors are degrading by this mechanism to the intellectual level of the Chautauqua lecturer.

Persons who apparently conform to this type may be seen at the meetings of any learned society. They were brilliant men in their youth, but they have taken up lecturing, and have formed a habit of dodging difficult questions. They are no longer able to realize that problems exist which cannot be explained in terms that are easily and vividly comprehensible by a lazy sophomore with adenoids. For one professor who is definitely degraded by success in teaching, there are many more who fail to develop, who are so pleased by the rewards of short campaigns in the classroom that they neglect over a period of years to make any long campaigns. This is self-defeating, for such men spend themselves and run down like clocks that are not wound, finding in the middle of life that they no longer have anything to say even in the classroom. Imperceptibly their attitude toward their subject matter has been altered by self-consciousness; the classroom organization of consciousness has become so powerful as partially to suppress the subject matter orientation of their minds; they have ended by losing even the minimum command of subject matter which suffices for the needs of the classroom.

13

THE SCHOOL AS A SOCIAL ORGANISM

1932

THE SCHOOL is a unity of interacting personalities. The personalities of all who meet in the school are bound together in an organic relation. The life of the whole is in all its parts, yet the whole could not exist without any of its parts. The school is a social organism;[1] it is this first and most general aspect of the social life of the schools which we propose to deal with. . . . As a social organism the school shows an organismic interdependence of its parts; it is not possible to affect a part of it without affecting the whole. As a social organism the school displays a differentiation of parts and a specialization of function. The organism as an entirety is nourished by the community.

Changing the figure slightly, the school is a closed system of social interaction. Without pedantry, we may point out that this fact is of importance, for if we are to study the school as a social entity, we must be able to distinguish clearly between school and not-school. The school is in fact clearly differentiated from its social milieu. The existence of a school is established by the emergence of a characteristic mode of social interaction. A school exists wherever and whenever teachers and students meet for the purpose

---

Reprinted from *The Sociology of Teaching* (New York: John Wiley and Sons, 1932), chap. 2, with elisions.

[1]   We do not, of course, subscribe to the organismic fallacy, which Ward and others have so ably refuted. We have adopted the analogy here simply as a device of exposition. The school is like an organism; it is not a true organism.

of giving and receiving instruction. The instruction which is given is usually formal classroom instruction, but this need not be true. The giving and receiving of instruction constitutes the nucleus of the school as we now think of it. About this nucleus are clustered a great many less relevant activities.

When we analyze existing schools, we find that they have the following characteristics which enable us to set them apart and study them as social unities:

(1) They have a definite population.
(2) They have a clearly defined political structure, arising from the mode of social interaction characteristic of the school, and influenced by numerous minor processes of interaction.
(3) They represent the nexus of a compact network of social relationships.
(4) They are pervaded by a we-feeling.
(5) They have a culture that is definitely their own. . . .

The school has . . . a definite population, composed of those who are engaged in the giving or receiving of instruction, who "teach" or "are in school." It is a relatively stable population and one whose depletion and replacement occur slowly. Population movements go according to plan and can be predicted and charted in advance. A bimodal age distribution marks off teachers from students. This is the most significant cleavage in the school.

The young in the school population are likely to have been subjected to some sifting and sorting according to the economic status and social classification of their parents. The private schools select out a certain group, and there are specializations within the private schools, some being in fact reformatories for the children of the well-to-do, and some being very exacting as to the character and scholastic qualifications of their students. The public schools of the exclusive residence districts are usually peopled by students of a limited range of social types. Slum schools are for slum children. Country schools serve the children of farmers. In undifferentiated residence districts and in small towns which have but one school the student population is least homogeneous and most representative of the entire community. . . .

The characteristic mode of social interaction of the school, an interaction centered about the giving and receiving of instruction, determines the political order of the school. The instruction which is given consists largely of facts and skills, and of other matter for which the spontaneous interests of students do not usually furnish a sufficient motivation. Yet teachers wish students to attain a certain mastery of these subjects, a much higher degree of mastery than they would attain, it is thought, if they were quite free in their choices. And teachers are responsible to the community for the mastery of these subjects by their students. The political organization of the school, therefore, is one which makes the teacher dominant, and it is the business of the teacher to use his dominance to further the process of teaching and learning which is central in the social interaction of the school.

Typically the school is organized on some variant of the autocratic principle. Details of organization show the greatest diversity. Intra-faculty relations greatly affect the relations between teachers and students. Where there is a favorable rapport between the teachers and the administrative authorities, this autocracy becomes an oligarchy with the teacher group as a solid and well-organized ruling class. It appears that the best practice extends the membership in this oligarchy as much as possible without making it unwieldy or losing control of it. In the most happily conducted institutions all the teachers and some of the leading students feel that they have a very real voice in the conduct of school affairs.

Where there is not a cordial rapport between school executives and teachers, control becomes more autocratic. A despotic system apparently becomes necessary when the teaching staff has increased in size beyond a certain limit. Weakness of the school executive may lead him to become arbitrary, or it may in the extreme case lead some other person to assume his authority. The relationship between students and teachers is in part determined by intra-faculty relationships; the social necessity of subordination as a condition of student achievement, and the general tradition governing the attitudes of students and teachers toward each other, set the limits of variation. But this variation is never sufficient to destroy the fact that the schools are organized on the authority principle, with power theoretically vested in the school superintendent and radiating from him down to the lowest substitute teacher in the system. This authority which pervades the school furnishes the best practical means of distinguishing school from not-school. Where the authority of the faculty and school board extends is the school. If it covers children on the way to and from school, at school parties, and on trips, then those children are in school at such times.

The generalization that the schools have a despotic political structure seems to hold true for nearly all types of schools, and for all about equally, without very much difference in fact to correspond to radical differences in theory. Self-government is rarely real. Usually it is but a mask for the rule of the teacher oligarchy, in its most liberal form the rule of a student oligarchy carefully selected and supervised by the faculty. The experimental school which wishes to do away with authority continually finds that in order to maintain requisite standards of achievement in imparting certain basic skills it has to introduce some variant of the authority principle, or it finds that it must select and employ teachers who can be in fact despotic without seeming to be so. Experimental schools, too, have great difficulty in finding teachers who are quite free from the authoritarian bias of other schools and able to treat children as independent human beings. Military schools, standing apparently at the most rigid pole of authority, may learn to conceal their despotism, or discipline established, may furnish moments of relaxation and intimate association between faculty and students, and they may delegate much power and responsibility to student officers; thus they may be not very much more arbitrary than schools quite differently organized, and sometimes they are very much less arbitrary than schools with a less rigid formal structure.

It is not enough to point out that the school is a despotism. It is a despotism in a state of perilous equilibrium. It is a despotism threatened from within and exposed to regulation and interference from without. It is a despotism capable of being overturned in a moment, exposed to the instant loss of its stability and its prestige. It is a despotism demanded by the community of parents, but specially limited by them as to the techniques which it may use for the maintenance of a stable social order. It is a despotism resting upon children, at once the most tractable and the most unstable members of the community.

There may be some who, seeing the solid brick of school buildings, the rows of nicely regimented children sitting stiff and well-behaved in the classroom or marching briskly through the halls, will doubt that the school is in a state of unstable equilibrium. A school may in fact maintain a high morale through a period of years, so that its record in the eyes of the community is marred by no untoward incident. But how many schools are there with a teaching body of more than—let us say—ten teachers, in which there is not one teacher who is in imminent danger of losing his position because of poor discipline? How many such schools in which no teacher's discipline has broken down within the last three years? How many school executives would dare to plan a great mass meeting of students at which no teachers would be present or easily available in case of disorder?

To understand the political structure of the school we must know that the school is organized on the authority principle and that that authority is constantly threatened. The authority of the school executives and the teachers is in unremitting danger from: (1) The students. (2) Parents. (3) The school board. (4) Each other. (5) Hangers-on and marginal members of the group. (6) Alumni. The members of these groups, since they threaten his authority, are to some extent the natural enemies of the person who represents and lives by authority. The difficulties of the teacher or school executive in maintaining authority are greatly increased by the low social standing of the teaching profession and its general disrepute in the community at large. There is a constant interaction between the elements of the authoritative system; the school is continually threatened because it is autocratic, and it has to be autocratic because it is threatened. The antagonistic forces are balanced in that ever-fickle equilibrium which is discipline. . . .

The political order of the school is characterized by control on three levels. Roughly, these are:

(1) Theoretical. The control of the school by the school board, board of trustees, etc.

(2) Actual. The control of school affairs by school executives as exerted through the teaching force or directly.

(3) Ultimate. The control of school affairs by students, government resting upon the consent, most silent, of the governed.

The school is the meeting-point of a large number of intertangled social relationships. These social relationships are the paths pursued by social interaction, the channels in which social influences run. The crisscrossing and interaction of these groups make the school what it is. The social relationships centering in the school may be analyzed in terms of the interacting groups in the school. The two most important groups are the teacher-group and the pupil-group, each of which has its own moral and ethical code and its customary attitudes toward members of the other groups. There is a marked tendency for these groups to turn into conflict groups. Within the teacher group are divisions according to rank and position, schismatic and conspiral groups, congenial groups, and cliques centering around different personalities. Within the student groups are various divisions representing groups in the larger community, unplanned primary groups stair-stepped according to age, cliques, political organizations, and specialized groups such as teams and gangs. The social influence of the school is a result of the action of such groups upon the individual and of the organization of individual lives out of the materials furnished by such groups. . . .

The school is further marked off from the world that surrounds it by the spirit which pervades it. Feeling makes the school a social unity. The *we*-feeling of the school is in part a spontaneous creation in the minds of those who identify themselves with the school and in part a carefully nurtured and sensitive growth. In this latter aspect it is regarded as more or less the property of the department of athletics. Certainly the spirit of the group reaches its highest point in those ecstatic ceremonials which attend athletic spectacles. The group spirit extends itself also to parents and alumni.

A separate culture, we have indicated, grows up within the school. This is a culture which is in part the creation of children of different age levels, arising from the breakdown of adult culture into simpler configurations or from the survival of an older culture in the play group of children, and in part devised by teachers in order to canalize the activities of children passing through certain ages. The whole complex set of ceremonies centering around the school may be considered a part of the culture indigenous to the school. "Activities," which many youngsters consider by far the most important part of school life, are culture patterns. The specialized culture of the young is very real and satisfying for those who live within it. And this specialized culture is perhaps the agency most effective in binding personalities together to form a school.

14

THE SCHOOL AND THE
COMMUNITY—I

1932

ONE WHO thinks about the relation of the school to the community which supports it will soon come upon questions of public policy which it would take an Einsteinian grasp of the calculus of felicity to answer. Difficulty arises because the aims of the school and the community are often divergent. It is very well to say that the school should serve the community, but it is difficult to decide what opinion should govern when school and community differ. The lights of the school authorities are often better than those of the community in general. School men have given some study to their own problems, and could reasonably be expected to know more about them than outsiders do. Yet the community is often wiser than the school, because the community is whole and the school is fragmentary. The school, as a fragment of the common life, is a prey to institutionalism. Institutionalism causes the school to forget its purpose; it makes the school give education for education and teaching, perhaps for teachers; in short, it makes an end of what is logically only a means to an end. This vice the community escapes because the community is whole, because it is not simply a place where teachers teach and children learn. The community is whole because whole men live in it. And the community is sometimes wise with a knowledge of the complete life that surpasses the knowledge of the schools. It becomes, then, one of the important questions of public policy as to how far the community should

Reprinted from *The Sociology of Teaching* (New York: John Wiley and Sons, 1932), chap. 4, with elisions.

determine the policy of the school and how far the school should be self-determining. We have not yet the formula.

A complication of a different order arises from the fact that communities in general, perhaps especially American communities, have chosen to use the schools as repositories for certain ideals. The ideals which are supposed to have their stronghold in the schools are of several different sorts. The belief is abroad that young people ought to be trained to think the world a little more beautiful and much more just than it is, as they ought to think men are honest and women more virtuous than they are. A high-school student must learn that honesty is always the best policy; perhaps his father secretly believes that he knows better; perhaps the boy himself may be learning something quite different in the world of business, but it does the boy no harm to start with that assumption. We can teach him enough honesty to keep him out of jail all his life; later he can make such amendments to our principles as seem necessary to him. All must learn that the United States is the greatest and best of all the nations of history, unequalled in wealth or virtue since time began. Perhaps it does no harm for students to think that the world is getting better and better, though this is a very dangerous doctrine if one thinks about it very long.

Among these ideals are those moral principles which the majority of adults more or less frankly disavow for themselves but want others to practice; they are ideals for the helpless, ideals for children and for teachers. There are other ideals which are nearly out of print, because people do not believe in them any more. Though most adults have left such ideals behind, they are not willing to discard them finally. The school must keep them alive. The school must serve as a museum of virtue.

We have in our culture a highly developed system of idealism for the young. The young have not yet come into contact with a world that might soil them, and we do what we can to keep the young unsullied. There are certain things that are not for the ears of the young. There are certain facts about human nature that they must not learn. There are certain bits of reality that they must not touch. There are certain facts of history that we think it best not to teach them. There is an idealized world view that it is thought best to pass on to adolescents. The notion that it is not proper to tell the whole truth is often carried over into college teaching, and it affects materially the point of view of many university professors. There is just enough apparent wisdom in the policy of hiding difficult facts from the young to justify it in the popular mind as a general policy. For it is often argued that character training must begin by the inculcation of an impossible virtue, in order that the individual may have a surplus of virtue to trade upon. The world, of course, is thoroughly committed to the policy of not telling the whole truth to youngsters, to the policy of telling them falsehoods which will make the world more attractive or themselves more tractable and virtuous.

The conventional belief, as we have noted, is that the young must be shielded from contact with the unpleasant and amoral aspects of the universe and that they must be kept in an ultra-conservative environment. These ideals may be justified by the fact that they prevent the demoralization of the young; as to that we have preferred to keep an open mind. But it is certain that the necessity of serving as the repository for these ideals limits the larger utility of the school. For if it is the purpose of education to prepare for life in the world, then the school must give its students that world in order that they may get themselves ready for living in it. Actually it cannot give students the world, but only an imitation or a representation of the world; in any case, it should be an accurate imitation or a faithful representation if the training which the student receives in school is to have any validity. The less the discontinuity between the life of the school and the life of the world outside, the better will be the training for life which the school gives to its students. Any ideal which cuts down the ability of the school to reproduce reality interferes with its real function of preparing students for life. The utility of such ideals may even be disputed from the moral point of view; the argument against them is the good one that the individual upon whom we have foisted off a too idealistic world view will be more readily disorganized by contact with a far from perfect world than will an individual who has already had some experience of the world; it is the old principle of inoculation. In almost any case, if a school man believes in the policy of training young persons to be virtuous by not telling them the truth, he sets very definite limits to his own continuing influence upon those who come in contact with him. There is reason for the bitter jest that a school teacher is a man hired to tell lies to little boys.

Our analysis of the relation between the school and the community has so far been very general. The possibilities of such analysis are limited. We may hope to achieve an analysis which will have greater concreteness by basing it upon the connections which are made between the school and the community by the lives of individuals. If we wish an analysis that will bite into reality we must study the roots which persons involved in school life have in the community at large and attempt to discover the interconnection of their lives within and without the school. Each individual represents a reciprocal channel of influence, an influence of the community upon the school and an influence of the school upon the community. Therefore we must study the relation of the school and the community by studying persons and attempting to learn what burdens they carry as they go back and forth between the community and the school. We turn now to an analysis of this sort.

The place of students as the young of a community we have already noted. Toward young persons the community in general has the conventional attitude of the elders, an attitude of protection mingled with regulation. Children live in glass houses. There is the desire to shield the young from all contaminating contact with the world, and this is one reason for the multitudinous restrictions upon the teacher in the community. Every older person tends to take a paternal interest in the young of the community, whether he has progeny or not. The students in a public school thus have a very definite place in the community, and the community conception of this place materially affects the kind of school which the community maintains. . . .

Differences of position in the community determine important differences in the school. The child's status as the son of a particular person affects his status in the school and his attitude toward school. The daughter of an influential man in the community does not expect to be treated in the same way as an ordinary child, and yet it is dangerous for a teacher to make exceptions. . . .

The attitudes of students make very clear the cruel distinction between rich and poor. Many children attain an easy and unhealthy leadership through the use of the economic resources of their parents or merely through their parents' reputations. It is upon the basis of such distinctions that many of the cliques and social clubs of high-school children are formed; the competition is not a healthy one because it is not based upon the merits of the persons competing. Many parents who have the misfortune to be well-to-do or famous have longed to remove their children from this atmosphere. The private school presents a way out of the situation. In Washington it is no distinction to be a Congressman; in a private school it is not usually a distinction to have wealthy parents; competition must therefore ascend to a different plane.

The children of poor and humble parent experience the situation with the opposite emphasis. They are those whom the teachers do not favor; they are the ones excluded from things exclusive. These poorer children frequently drop out of high school because of their inability to sustain themselves in social competition with the children of wealthier parents. Clothes make the student. Teachers sometimes take unusual pains with children who have few cultural advantages and little economic backing at home, and these efforts occasionally have remarkable and heartening results.

Students may likewise stand out as individuals. The high-school athletic hero achieves much distinction in the school, and his prowess is usually bruited about the community as well. Brilliant students may likewise achieve desirable status in the school, with some carry-over into the community at large. The girl who becomes implicated in any scandal is singled out for special attention both in the school and the community. Frequently the attention is an attempt to injure her, and it usually succeeds.

. . . We may state our two most important generalizations concerning the relation of teachers to the community in this form: That the teacher has a special position as a paid agent of cultural diffusion, and that the teacher's position in the community is much affected by the fact that he is supposed to represent those ideals for which the schools serve as repositories.

Teachers are paid agents of cultural diffusion. They are hired to carry light into dark places. To make sure that teachers have some light, standard qualifications for teachers have been evolved. Not only must the teacher know enough to teach the youngsters in the schools competently according to the standards of the community, but he must, usually, be a little beyond his community. From this it follows that the teacher must always be a little discontented with the community he lives in. The teacher is a martyr to cultural diffusion.

It does not matter where a teacher starts, he must always take just enough training to make him a little dissatisfied with any community he is qualified to serve. And it does not matter much how far he goes, for there is, for most of us, no attainable end. A farmer's daughter decides to teach. It seems to her that a rural school would be just right; she is used to country life and it pleases her well. But she must be a high-school graduate before she is qualified to teach in a rural school. When she has finished her training in the nearby village she is no longer enthusiastic about teaching in a rural school. She goes to a normal school, and learns to live in a cultural center of that level. Then she can teach in the high school of a small town. She goes to a state university, which is a first-rate center of learning. What she learns there makes high-school teaching a little dull and life in the smaller community difficult. University teachers and public-school teachers in the large cities are partial exceptions, but for the rest there is rarely an end to the process. The teacher must always know enough to make his subject matter seem commonplace to him, or he does not know enough to teach it. He must always have received teaching a grade higher than he can give. He must always have adjusted his possibilities to a center of learning one size larger than the one he serves. The teacher must take what consolation he can from the fact, made much of by inspirational writers, that he is a carrier of the cultural values.

This nearly universal maladjustment is not without its effect upon the standards of success in the profession. The successful teacher makes progress; that is, he moves occasionally, and always to a larger community. That is one reason why teachers stubbornly go to school. They hope some time to make tastes and opportunities coincide. But the fact that they rarely succeed accounts in part for the fact that teachers rarely take root in a community. They hold themselves forever ready to obey that law of gravitation which pulls them toward an educational center equivalent to the highest center they have had experience of. That is partly why teachers are maladjusted transients rather than citizens. Although the stair steps of primary groups of children no doubt have more to do with it than the attitudes of teachers, this unadjustment of teachers may help to account for the fact that schools of each level ape the schools of the next higher grade, the grade schools imitating the high school, the high schools pretending to be colleges, and colleges trying to become graduate schools.

One may disagree as to the interpretation of the prevalent dissatisfaction of school teachers with the community in which they live, but the fact itself seems indubitable. Over and over again, teachers, asked to tell the story of their experiences in certain communities, relate the same story. Especially keen is the disappointment of the teacher in his first school. The young teacher comes fresh from the training school to his first position. He has accumulated a great fund of idealism during his training; he is enthusiastic over his work and the self-fulfillment it will represent. He is usually elated over the prospect of at last receiving a salary for his services. When he arrives at the scene of his labors, which he has pictured with a certain glitter, as having upon it some of the tinsel of Utopia, he sees that which gives him pause; the community seems barren, sordid, uninspiring; the school itself is uninviting. "The school building displayed that peculiarly drab and unpicturesque deterioration which comes from a generation or so of school children, as if the building, too, were sullen and unhappy because of the unwilling children who entered it. It made me think of a tattered, old-young woman, frowsled and down-at-the-heels, worried from the care of so many children." But the teacher struggles to keep up his courage; he is determined to be pleased. This is a typical situation. A woman teacher phrased it briefly thus: "The two weeks before school opened were not quite so appealing to me as I had hoped. Had I been disillusioned after my visit to the town? I tried to keep up my courage, and say, 'It'll be better than you think.' " But there is no mistaking the fact that disillusionment has already set in. It needs now but a row with the school board, a set-to with a parent, and a wrangle with a colleague, plus perhaps, a few weeks of following the course of study, and the discovery that the community does not approve of his progressive methods of education, to make a discontented professional of the erstwhile enthusiastic amateur. . . .

A truer pathos appears in the struggles of teachers to "keep up." Young teachers fan the little spark burning feebly in their bosoms to keep it alive. Realizing their isolation from the main stream of cultural development, they fall into a sort of intellectual valetudinarianism where reading a good book or a serious magazine acquires a religious significance. The tragedy of those who strain to keep up is that they were never "up." One has more difficulty in sympathizing with those specialists who demand not merely that they shall pass their days in the society of cultured men, but that these men shall have exactly the same kind of learning that they themselves have. Not that the specialist is particularly happy in his relations with those in his own field, for rivalries sever him from them. The college professor criticizes one half of his colleagues, as a witty friend suggests, because they have written books, and the other half because they have written none. The cultural isolation of the new teacher is further complicated by the breaking of personal ties in transplantation, by a conflict of urban and rural behavior norms, and by the teacher's status as a newcomer.

Our second major generalization is that the teacher is supposed to represent certain ideals in the community. These ideals differ somewhat from one community to another, but there is an underlying similarity. The entire set of ideals in their most inclusive form is clearly stated in the contract which teachers in the public schools of a certain southern community are asked to sign. The contract follows:

I promise to take a vital interest in all phases of Sunday-school work, donating of my time, service, and money without stint for the uplift and benefit of the community.

I promise to abstain from all dancing, immodest dressing, and any other conduct unbecoming a teacher and a lady.

I promise not to go out with any young men except in so far as it may be necessary to stimulate Sunday-school work.

I promise not to fall in love, to become engaged or secretly married.

I promise not to encourage or tolerate the least familiarity on the part of any of my boy pupils.

I promise to sleep at least eight hours a night, to eat carefully, and to take every precaution to keep in the best of health and spirits, in order that I may be better able to render efficient service to my pupils.

I promise to remember that I owe a duty to the townspeople who are paying me my wages, that I owe respect to the school board and the superintendent that hired me, and that I shall consider myself at all times the willing servant of the school board and the townspeople.[1]

The contract quoted above is so extreme that it will seem incredible to persons who are not familiar with the moral qualifications which teachers in general are supposed to fulfill. Those a little closer to the facts will be willing to credit its literal truth. In any case, the contract itself is so explicit that comment upon it is unnecessary.

The demands made by the smaller community upon time and money of the teacher are unremitting. The teacher must be available for church functions, lodge functions, public occasions, lecture courses, and edifying spectacles of all sorts. Not infrequently he is expected to identify himself closely with some particular religious group and to become active in "church work." School executives occupy an even more exposed position than do underlings. Yet some unbelieving superintendents in very small communities have been able to work out compromises that satisfied the community and yet involved no sacrifice of their own convictions. One tactful agnostic declined to attend any church services at any time, but made it a point to be present at all church suppers, "sociables," and other non-religious ceremonies. Such a policy would need to be coupled with a great deal of skill in evasion and putting off if it were to work successfully; the teacher must not only avoid the issue and wear out those who urge church attendance upon him, but he must do it without giving offence or getting himself classed as an adherent of the devil. The teacher is also under considerable

---

[1]   Quoted by T. Minehan, "The Teacher Goes Job-Hunting," *The Nation*, 1927, Vol. 124, p. 606.

pressure to contribute to good causes. The difficulty is that he is not always permitted to judge of the goodness or badness of a cause. Quite aside from any such factor of judgment, the very multiplicity of the good causes to which the teacher is expected to contribute may make them a heavy drain upon his resources.

These demands are often resented, and with reason. But an interesting dilemma presents itself in this connection. A part of the solution of the problems of the teaching profession depends upon the assimilation of teachers to the community. Is not this conscription of teachers for edifying occasions a step in that direction? Where the participation of the teacher is quite unforced, as it sometimes is, it would seem that such demands work out favorably. Yet such participation will never really assimilate the teacher to the community, because it is not the right kind of participation. The teacher participates as a teacher, always formally and *ex officio*, too often unwillingly and by force. What is needed is participation by the teacher as an individual in community groups in which he is interested. If the teacher is ever really to belong, he must join in local groups as John Jones and not as the superintendent of schools.

The moral requirements that go with school teaching are extremely important. A colleague sometimes says, half in jest, that the schools of America are primarily agencies for moral and religious instruction. If anyone accepts the challenge laid down by that proposition, he points out the fact that the most complete ineffectiveness as a teacher does not always constitute a valid ground for dismissing a teacher from his position, whereas detection in any moral dereliction causes a teacher's contract to be broken at once. Undoubtedly the fact that teachers must be models of whatever sort of morality is accepted as orthodox in the community imposes upon the teacher many disqualifications. With regard to sex, the community is often very brutal indeed. It is part of the American credo that school teachers reproduce by budding. In no other walk of life is it regarded as even faintly reprehensible that a young bachelor should look about for a wife, but there are indications that courtship is not exactly good form in the male teacher. The community prefers its male teachers married, but if they are unmarried, it forbids them to go about marrying. With regard to the conduct of women teachers, some communities are unbelievably strict. Youth and beauty are disadvantages. Husband-hunting is the unpardonable sin. The absurdity of this customary attitude, as well as its complete social unsoundness, should be apparent from its mere statement; it becomes all the more significant that, in presenting the subject of sex prejudice against school teachers, one must usually go on to point out that this is a situation almost without parallel in modern life. Women teachers are our Vestal Virgins.

15

THE SCHOOL AND THE
COMMUNITY—II

1932

In THEORY, the ultimate authority of the school system is
vested in the school board, a group of local citizens elected by the
community to oversee the schools. In fact, the most important function of the school board is usually to see to the hiring of a superintendent. Once the superintendent, a specially trained teacher
vested with authority over other teachers and titular headship of
the schools, has been employed, a sharp struggle usually ensues
between him and the outstanding members of the school board over
the right actually to determine the policies of the school. The advantage is with the superintendent so far as this issue is concerned,
for he is a specialist, and can claim the specialist's right to carry
his point over those who have not had equal or equivalent training;
he is in fact the titular head of the schools, and bears the responsibility before the community if anything goes wrong; he is on the
scene constantly, and must deal with many minor matters without
consulting the board except, perhaps, for routine ratification afterwards, and he usually carries on dealings with teachers and students single-handed, from which he acquires a considerable
amount of prestige with both bodies.

By mediating to the school executive the sense of the community concerning the administration of the school, the school board
may perform a legitimate function and one that in no way interferes with the initiative or the efficiency of the school administra-

Reprinted from *The Sociology of Teaching* (New York: John Wiley and
Sons, 1932), chap. 8, with elisions.

tor in his specialized field. It is part of the superintendent's technique so to define the situation as regards himself and the school
board as to make an extended and bitter struggle over the control
of the school system seem unnecessary and fruitless; he should
accept the principle that he should have sufficient authority to deal
adequately with all school situations and that he should not be interfered with in the legitimate performance of these functions, and
he should take his authority so much for granted that others will be
disposed to grant it as legitimate and in the scheme of things. The
technique of avoiding major conflicts with a school board is apparently similar to the technique which the teacher uses in avoiding
such trials of strength with his students; it consists in settling minor
details so swiftly and with such assurance that no question ever
arises as to one's competency or right to deal with the greater. This
is the question of dominance and subordination, and it is settled in
most cases, or it may be settled, without an actual trial of strength
by the assurance and completeness of detail in the alternative plans
of action presented by the persons involved in the situation. In this
matter, as in many others, there appears to be a great difference in
personalities. Some superintendents have their way with their
school boards over many years, and no one arises to contest their
claims; in fact, authority is genially taken and genially granted.
Other superintendents are always in difficulty with the board, and
we must conclude that it is a difference in their personal techniques
which accounts for this difference of results; this is what we are
attempting to analyze. (It may be suggested, too, that the ability to
dominate a school board pleasantly is a greater factor in determining personal advancement in this walk of life than the ability to
administer a school system of students and teachers.) A judicious
superintendent will be able, by devices subtle and hard to recognize, to avoid any conflict over policy, taking that matter and
others very largely into his own hands. He will then be able to make
his board see that running a school is a cooperative enterprise, and
to direct them into various lines of cooperative endeavor with him,
thereby not only avoiding conflict, but actually making use of the
collective intelligence and community connections of the board,
and letting the members feel that they are being of use. But between

this and a policy of asking advice which will lead to conflict, or permitting interference which in the end can only handicap the executive, is another line that is not easy to draw. The line is there, and many persons know how to draw it, but it will require acute powers of observation and much tact to draw it in the individual instance.

Some board members are captious, and some superintendents let relations with the board get out of hand; there is, besides, in many communities a tradition of interference which effectively precludes any school executive from ever obtaining a quite free hand. Superintendents caught in such situations have evolved many interesting devices whereby they get their own way and yet preserve their position with the board relatively undamaged. In discussing some mistake which he was alleged to have made, one young and inexperienced "principal" remarked to his school board, "Why, I thought that would be all right, so I went ahead and did it." A member of the board, anxious to preserve the right of the board to dictate all policies, came out upon him roundly, "We didn't hire you to think. We hired you to be the principal of this school. Hereafter you leave the thinking to us. We'll do all the thinking for you." Thereafter he adopted a policy of making a great show of consulting his board members on all minor matters, and of pushing essential matters so far before consulting the board that only one decision was possible. His position was then something like that of the president, who can involve the country in war, but cannot declare war.

Another policy which has many converts is that of pitting one faction of the board against another. It frequently happens that bitter personal enemies and business rivals are asked to serve together on the school board; it is then possible for an adroit manager to play many tunes upon these personal oppositions and antagonisms. Often enough it is one man who controls the board; the superintendent's problem is then to maintain some sort of hold upon this one man. For this, many hundreds of devices have been evolved by harassed superintendents. These devices cover almost the whole gamut of human possibilities, ranging from identifying one's self with the leading member's church to buying supplies

from his store or failing to pay a note. One small-town superintendent invariably selected a leading grocer from among the members
of the school board, and patronized him with the intention of
maintaining a hold upon him; it was a device which did not, because of the personality of the superintendent, have by any means
unfailing success; this man might have done better, it would seem,
to have kept the upper hand of this grocer, as of any other, by the
threat of removing patronage, or at least to have kept the grocer
from coming to believe that he was cleverer than the superintendent. A less obvious policy was that of a small-town superintendent
who kept a hold upon the president of the board, a banker, by refusing to pay a note at the bank. Though the banker hated this
teacher, as he had almost from the first, he wanted to keep him
in the community, until he had paid his note; since this man was
the most influential member of the board, the superintendent retained his position as long as the note was unpaid. A more general sort of policy is that adopted by many executives of showing
a great deal of interest in the scholastic and personal welfare of
the children of influential members of the community.

It is a difficult thing to succeed a man who has been popular in
the community, and this is a fact which often affects the fortunes
of individuals who fill prominent positions in the schools, such as
the position of superintendent, high-school principal, coach, etc.
One's friends do not at once forget him, and often they think to
benefit him by making things hard for his successor. A lax superintendent is a hard man to follow, for he has allowed the school
machine to disintegrate. He has allowed authority to escape from
his hands, and his successor will always have a difficult time in restoring the school system both internally and externally. Added to
this is the fact that such lax superintendents have usually made a
number of friends in the community who, though perhaps not
numerous or powerful or devoted enough to prevent his dismissal,
are still ready and able to raise the cry that he has been dismissed
unfairly and to work a reprisal for the injustice upon the man employed to take his place. Since this new man comes from the outside, he is usually, of all the persons involved in the situation, the
most innocent of wrong. This mechanism is most noticeable within

the faculty, and the carryover of old loyalties is one of the most difficult things which the new executive has to face. Sometimes the teachers who still preserve the memory of the former super-intendent band themselves together in order to handicap the new executive; such fights are usually carried over into the community at large, and they often become very bitter. . . .

The opposite situation . . . is that of the person succeeding a man who has left many enemies in the community. The enemies of the former superintendent, especially if they are members of the board or otherwise prominent in the community, attach them-selves at once to the new superintendent, as if determined to prove that they are not trouble-makers, that it is possible for this new man to get along with them, and that it therefore should have been pos-sible for his predecessor to do so. This type of situation is often found when an executive of some vigor and aggressiveness has just been at the head of the schools. Such a man pushes the program of the school energetically, he fights for needed supplies, equip-ment, and salaries, and he insists upon centralization of authority in his own hands. He integrates the school machine at the expense of the independence of some of its parts. But such an energetic man makes enemies. Sooner or later his enemies oust him. His suc-cessor finds a well-organized and smoothly functioning school sys-tem, and a community ready to receive him cordially. This mech-anism comes out particularly in smaller communities where there has been a fight for a new school building. The superintendent, let us say, becomes convinced that there is need of a new building, or for extensive improvements upon the old one. He argues the case strongly. He enters into the fight for the new building. He wins, but in the process he makes many enemies. These enemies oust him from the school system. Then he goes to a new commu-nity and repeats the process. It is significant that in teaching and in the ministry certain individuals early acquire a reputation as "builders."

It is a fact that has sometimes been remarked upon that cer-tain communities change the chief executive of their school sys-tem very frequently, perhaps every two or three years. (Sometimes other members of the faculty are involved in these changes, and

leave for the same reasons, though this is not necessarily true.)
This tendency of the community to oust a man when he is just beginning to know his way around in the community has often been
inveighed against, but its reasons and its causes have not been
analyzed. It seems worthwhile to point out that this insecurity of
the school executive inheres in the nature of his relationship to the
community. The relation of the superintendent to the community
which he serves is one in which alienation is always implicit, and
the alienation begins to work at once when he appears in the community, but it reaches its culminating point two or three years later.

We may say that the superintendent has a typical life history
in the community. This typical life history repeats itself again
and again in the life of one executive, and in the community with
different executives. The life history seems to be about as follows:
When the new executive takes charge of the school system, he has
the support of nearly the entire community (except in such a
situation as the one described above, where the outgoing executive
has left behind him a considerable and well-organized opposition
to the new one). The board is usually with him to a man. This un-
divided support is his until some incident occurs which brings him
into conflict with an individual or an organized group in the community. It is not long before such an incident occurs; the executive
metes out some disciplinary measure with which individual parents
disagree, or supports a teacher who becomes similarly embroiled
(or refuses to support her), or he refuses to cooperate with some
group in the community in the program they are promoting, or he
launches some school policy which proves to be unpopular with students or teachers. The essential weakness of his position is that it
gives him an opportunity to make many more enemies than friends.
Opportunities for becoming unpopular, to the point, almost, of
infamy, are numerous, but opportunities for gaining friends are
few.

The life of a superintendent is from spring to spring. At the end
of his first year the superintendent has made some enemies, but the
majority of the community, let us say, is still satisfied with the manner in which he is conducting the school. He has made some bitter
enemies, as, apparently, he unavoidably must. Those enemies are

criticizing him severely. But as yet they are not powerful enough to dislodge him from his position. During the second year of his incumbency, the superintendent continues to be harassed by these same enemies, who become increasingly bitter. Perhaps he becomes embroiled in something of a feud with them; in any case the opposition group becomes increasingly compact and well organized. The superintendent has by now acquired certain enemies on the school board and they serve in the community as further radiant points of antagonism toward him. But the important fact, and the inexorable tragedy of the superintendent's life is that in the second year he usually makes a few more enemies, but he rarely has an opportunity to restore the balance by making friends of those who have previously been inimical to him. At the end of the second year, the opposition is sufficiently powerful to "make a fight on the superintendent." Making a fight on the superintendent usually implies an open attempt to elect persons to the school board who will vote against his reelection; it implies a great deal of gossip and poisonous whispering, and, usually, conspiracies to discredit him in the eyes of the community. Not infrequently teachers become involved in these conspiracies. Let us say that the superintendent has given the community a satisfactory school and that he is able at the end of the second year to win the fight. Sometimes he is not, and the process, for him and the community, can begin again. But if he does win at the end of the second year, he stands a greater chance of losing at the end of the third, for his position is continuously weakened. He makes more enemies than friends. And he makes decided enemies, if not bitter enemies, and only lukewarm friends.

In the larger communities, the mass of the community is large enough to absorb without damage those individuals who have come into conflict with the superintendent over personal matters incidental to school administration or concerns of general school policy, so that his enemies will have less hope of removing him, and therefore less motivation to organize an opposition to him. (His enemies are likely also to be scattered and without acquaintance with each other, which would make organization difficult.) Greater security of tenure is also assured in the larger communities by the very unwieldiness of the political machinery, which is so cumbrous that it is rarely set in motion for trivial reasons. Further, if the school executive manages to remain in a smaller community for as long as, let us say, five years, he becomes pretty stable in his position, for he is then accepted as a member of the community and there is as little thought of discharging him because of disagreements concerning school policies as there is of running a farmer off his land because of his politics; he is a member of the local in-group, and he is something of a fixture; he has had time to develop firm and enthusiastic friends, and is not easily to be removed. We may, however, allow for all these exceptions without destroying the truth of our generalization, that the relationship of the school executive to the community has within it the elements of its own destruction. And as long as the traditional conception of the school, and the conception of school administration which goes with it, persists, and as long as the school continues to be controlled by the local community, the school systems of the smaller communities are doomed to frequent changes of head.

16

TEACHING AS INSTITUTIONALIZED LEADERSHIP

1932

LEADERSHIP is the control of one individual over the behavior of others. Every social situation tends to polarize itself in the relationship of leader and led.

Some persons lead because they cannot help it. They lead spontaneously, and perhaps they lead without any awareness of the fact that they are leading. Park has noted that leadership depends upon a psychic set-up of expectancy, upon a certain eager attentiveness focussed upon the leader, and upon a willingness to take a cue from him. Such leadership arises inevitably from the association of unlike persons; it has its roots in the relative mental complexity of the leader which renders him unpredictable to those he leads. The leader must be a little readier to act than his followers, a little more determined to have his own way, a little more ruthless in carrying his projects through; the led must have some faith in the competence of the leader. These are the elementary conditions of personal leadership.

Other persons lead because they have to. A social situation has been set up and its pattern has been determined. The pattern is one which calls for a leader. The pattern governs also what the leader shall do with the led. This is institutional leadership.

Personal leadership arises from the interaction of personalities. It is an effect of personal gradients among the parts of a social whole. Personal interchange is at its height in personal leadership;

Reprinted from *The Sociology of Teaching* (New York: John Wiley and Sons, 1932), chap. 14, pp. 189–98, with elisions.

there are no barriers shutting off one person from communion with another. In institutional leadership, personalities must be strained through the sieve of the social pattern before they can come into contact with each other.

In personal leadership, the properties of the interacting personalities determine the pattern of social interaction. In institutional leadership, personalities are forced to conform to the preexisting pattern; they are pumped up or deflated to make them fit their station. This is not to say that there is no pattern in personal leadership, but that the choice of the pattern and the place of each person in it are determined by the interplay of human forces in the situation.

The relationship of personal leadership arises when the group waits to see what some one person is going to do, feeling that what he does will be something very much to the point, and that it will be such a thing as the others would never think of. Superordination and subordination of this kind is determined by the relative range of personality and the complexity of mental organization of those involved in the situation. The extreme form of such leadership is found in the religious sect with an inspired leader, for then God is the leader, than whom no leader could possibly be more inscrutable or unpredictable.

In institutional leadership the leader has been established by another process, and he steps into a situation already prepared for him. Some sort of formal organization intervenes between the leader and the led. The extreme form of institutional leadership is probably that provided by the hereditary kingship. The king steps into the station made for him by his predecessors. His subjects wait to see what he will do, but, then, he must do what is expected of him, too. The school teacher is another kind of institutional leader.

In personal leadership, social patterns are always more or less in the way; that is why the dynamic leader breaks precedents. Personal leadership is borne more or less gladly, because it conforms to the realities of the situation; if conventionalized fictions come between the leader and the perception of the actual situation, he is an institutional leader. There is a need in human nature for personal leadership.

Institutionalized leadership gains by a clear demarcation of boundary lines and by rigid adherence to them. Personal influence must always be strained through the sieve of formality. Institutional leadership cannot remain institutional save by an insistence upon the lines of demarcation, for there is always a tendency for the human interaction in the situation to transcend those boundary lines. Where the pattern of leadership is predetermined, there must be a continual struggle to keep a more spontaneous kind of leadership, with the same or a different leader, from arising.

Institutional leadership persists because it satisfies a human need for dependence; it makes all a man's difficult decisions for him, and carries him along in a "moral automobile." But institutional leadership, no less than personal leadership, is ever destroyed and ever created anew; it seems likely, too, that because of its more rigid character, leading to a certain amount of inadaptation to the dynamics of present situations, and because of the conflict between institutional and personal leadership, the institutional kind arouses a greater amount of hostility.

But personal factors exist in both kinds of leadership, and patterns exist in both. In personal leadership, the social patterns are carried in personalities. In institutional leadership, the personalities are contained in the pattern—sometimes hampered by it as by a straight-jacket, sometimes expanded and ennobled to fit it.

All leadership proceeds from a mode of defining the situation. Institutional leadership sets up a ready-prepared definition of the situation and adheres to it rigidly. Non-institutionalized leadership defines the situation in terms of policies to be elaborated later, in terms of measures to be improvised according to the demands of the situation. Institutionalized leadership tends to break down under conditions of peculiar strain, and personal leadership, with its continual modification of measures, steps in to take its place. The peace-time army can afford to be rigid, but under battle conditions it must improvise, and every subaltern in it must improvise, in order to adapt to the rapidly changing situation. Personal leadership tends to become institutionalized when time has made its forms explicit and usual, and when the mantle of the prophet descends upon his successor.

Some prestige is necessary for all leadership. In personal leadership the prestige attaches to the person. In institutional leadership, the prestige attaches to the office (and is more likely to be associated with a rebellion against the officer as a person).

Prestige depends upon idealization. In personal leadership, the elements of the person are selected out and made to fit into some prestige-carrying pattern. In institutional leadership the pattern is already present, and the individual must be assimilated to that pattern or to none. Social distance is necessary in both kinds of leadership, for prestige is usually an illusion produced by the partial perception of a personality and the fitting into the picture of qualities not incongruous with those perceived. But in institutional leadership the necessity for social distance is greater, since the pattern is more definite, and the chance of the leader's failing to categorize favorably if all his qualities are known is immeasurably increased.

Personal authority is the principle of personal leadership. The authority of the office is the principle of leadership that is relevant to the institution. Personal authority, because it is gladly borne and always in point, is arbitrary but does not seem so. Institutional authority, being subject to strict rules and a long tradition, seems arbitrary but is not. It seems arbitrary because it does not grow out of the situation directly but is imposed from without. It is really the leader that makes the difference; where the leader is determined by social interaction in the situation, his power is not arbitrary. But where the leader is determined otherwise, his power seems arbitrary. In the non-institutional situation the power of the individual depends upon the fact of leadership. In the institution, power goes with a certain official capacity and makes the leader.

The school depends almost entirely upon institutional leadership. Our discussion will be relevant to the kind of institutional leadership found in the school. We shall attempt to describe in detail and to analyze as minutely as possible the personal aspects of this process. . . .

Underlying our discussion of dominance and subordination in the school is the notion of the school as an institution. There is a certain routinization of the behavior of students and teachers.

There is a pattern determining the situation; there is a set of inter-locking definitions of the situation. We are discussing the inter-action of personalities within that conventionalized situation. . . .

We may generalize a bit further concerning the characteristic features of institutionalized dominance and subordination. Simmel has endeavored to show how subordination is possible as a social arrangement between human beings. The gist of his discussion seems to be that subordination is possible because the relationship is meaningful to the dominant person, and, relatively, not meaning-ful to the subordinate one. Thus the dominant personality enters into such relationships with his whole personality or with a rela-tively large segment of it, whereas the subordinate gives but a small part of himself. One man may be ruler over millions, be-cause the one man gives his entire self to the relationship; the mil-lions participate in it but slightly. So by a psychic arrangement within the subordinated and the dominant personalities the perma-nence of a social structure is made possible.[1]

A certain conflict of interest must always exist between the person who rules and the person who is ruled. And there seems al-ways to be a certain amount of friction between the persons playing those rôles as long as the relationship continues. But it is possible for the relationship to persist; subordinates do not always hate their masters, and inferiors do not always rebel, and this is because the flow of self-feeling in the subordinate is away from the relation-ship. Subordination is bearable because it is meaningless. The self expands in a pleasant situation, and contracts in an unpleasant one. The self grows into a pleasant relationship, and moves away from

---

[1]   We are conscious of some oversimplification. All of Simmel's three types of subordination are found in the school. Subordination to the teacher is subordination to a person. There appears also subordination to the group. Many teachers attempt to establish subordination to a prin-ciple; that is the meaning of "justice" in the school situation. We are dis-cussing principally subordination to a person. The student should consult N. J. Spykman, *The Social Theory of Georg Simmel*, pp. 97–108; Dawson and Geddes, *Introduction to Sociology*, pp. 462–472; Park and Burgess, *Introduction to the Science of Sociology*, pp. 688–703; and Georg Simmel, *Soziologie*, pp. 141–186. The last, in a translation by Small, appeared in the *American Journal of Sociology*, Vol. 2, pp. 172–186.

a relationship in which one feels inferior or thwarted. Subordination in the institution is possible because institutional and non-institutional selves are split off from each other. The whole social order may be seen as a tangle of interlocking social selves. Every man must have some pride, and he must have some relationship in which he really lives. Defeated on one surface of the tetrahedron, he grows into another. When a thousand men come together, each striving to establish an equilibrium of superiority and inferiority in a multitude of activities, each continually altering his participation in those activities and revising from moment to moment the psychic weighting of that participation, each striving to obtain for himself a favorable balance of trade in that coin with which social debts are mostly paid, namely, praise, and each disturbing the equilibrium which every other has worked out, when a thousand men live together, then each man lives a thousand lives.

In terms of this psychic adjustment to the institutional situation, the struggle between master and subordinate goes into a new phase; the same mechanisms seem to operate in all kinds of institutions, in armies, churches, schools, and penitentiaries. The dominant personality strives not only to maintain the relationship, but to maintain and if possible to increase, its meaning. He lives in the relationship, and he expands into it. The subordinate, on the other hand, strives to achieve a psychic reorganization which will reduce the meaning of the relationship to nothing. The subordinate does not live in that relationship, and therefore superiors are not important as persons. This is a process which has many complications. It is important from the standpoint of sociology to remark that groups of superiors and inferiors commonly develop into in-groups. Each of these in-groups has its own life, which tends to be rich and full of meaning, and each has its own standards and its own morality. It is the problem of administration to prevent these in-groups from becoming conflict groups. The system of personal relationships is complicated by the entry of various mechanisms of abnormal psychology which are brought into play by the personal disunity which the complex situation engenders. Thus the subordinate commonly refuses to remain conscious of the actual meaning of the subordinate relationship, and compensates by an unreal phantasy life. The superior, too, must often repress certain elements of his personality, usually tendencies to social responsiveness directed toward his inferiors which might damage his standing in the relationship.

Formality is a compromise, an accommodation, which enables institutional leadership to survive. Formalities, a complicated social ritual and a body of rules and regulations, define once and for all the rights and privileges of all persons involved in the situation. Formality prevents friction by preventing the contact of personalities. Politeness is a device enabling us to get along with persons whom we do not like, more accurately, a device enabling us to get along with persons whether we like them or not.[2] Formality usually relates, on the surface, to the formulae of respect and consideration owed by the inferior to the superior; perhaps a return is exacted, such as the salute, but it may not be, as in the case of the "Sir" which army officers "rate." But formality is not wholly one-sided, for it confers an equal benefit upon the subordinate. It allows him, if he conforms to all external forms, to reduce the psychic weighting of these formulae of respect to nothing if he wishes, to mechanize the ritual of respect as he will, and to live his inner life on another level. We salute the uniform and not the man. And formality protects the inferior from arbitrary exactions of the superior. The social ritual of the Japanese under the Samurai prescribed how many teeth the peasant should show when he smiled in the presence of a noble; it was his privilege, then, to give of himself neither more nor less. It is a failing of the recently elevated to demand too much; this, formality prevents. The art of command is the adjustment of personality to the rôles that are most in conformity with one's station. Authority carries with it both privilege and inhibition; new authority is often irksome to all concerned, but old authority is as proper a thing as an old hat.

The teacher-pupil relationship is a form of institutionalized dominance and subordination. Teacher and pupil confront each other in the school with an original conflict of desires, and how-

[2]   G. H. Mead speaks of good manners as a "means of keeping possible bores at a distance," in "National-Mindedness and International-Mindedness," *International Journal of Ethics*, vol. 39, 1929, p. 393.

ever much that conflict may be reduced in amount, or however much it may be hidden, it still remains. The teacher represents the adult group, ever the enemy of the spontaneous life of groups of children. The teacher represents the formal curriculum, and his interest is in imposing that curriculum upon the children in the form of tasks; pupils are much more interested in life in their own world than in the desiccated bits of adult life which teachers have to offer. The teacher represents the established social order in the school, and his interest is in maintaining that order, whereas pupils have only a negative interest in that feudal superstructure. Teacher and pupil confront each other with attitudes from which the underlying hostility can never be altogether removed. Pupils are the material in which teachers are supposed to produce results. Pupils are human beings striving to realize themselves in their own spontaneous manner, striving to produce their own results in their own way. Each of these hostile parties stands in the way of the other; in so far as the aims of either are realized, it is at the sacrifice of the aims of the other.

Authority is on the side of the teacher. The teacher nearly always wins. In fact, he must win, or he cannot remain a teacher. Children, after all, are usually docile, and they certainly are defenceless against the machinery with which the adult world is able to enforce its decisions; the result of the battle is foreordained. Conflict between teachers and students therefore passes to the second level. All the externals of conflict and of authority having been settled, the matter chiefly at issue is the meaning of those externals. Whatever the rules that the teacher lays down, the tendency of the pupils is to empty them of meaning. By mechanization of conformity, by "laughing off" the teacher or hating him out of all existence as a person, by taking refuge in self-initiated activities that are always just beyond the teacher's reach, students attempt to neutralize teacher control. The teacher, however, is striving to read meaning into the rules and regulations, to make standards really standards, to force students really to conform. This is a battle which is not unequal. The power of the teacher to pass rules is not limited, but his power to enforce rules is, and so is his power to control attitudes toward rules.

Rules may be emasculated by attrition through setting up exceptions which at first seem harmless to the established order but when translated into precedent are found to destroy some parts of it altogether. One value of experience in teaching is that it gives the teacher an understanding of precedents. A trivial favor to Johnny Jones becomes a ruinous social principle when it is made a precedent. Or students defeat a rule by taking refuge in some activity just beyond its reach; what the rule secures, then, is not conformity but a different kind of non-conformity. Both teachers and pupils know well what hinges on these struggles over rules and evasions of rules. Johnny goes to the blackboard but he shuffles his feet; he is made to walk briskly but he walks too briskly; he is forced to walk correctly but there is a sullen expression on his face. Many teachers learn to cut through the rules to deal with the mental fact of rebellion; this is a negation of institutionalized leadership and requires a personality strong enough to stand without institutional props.

Most important in making conformity to external rules harmless are habitual adjustments to the inconveniences which teachers can impose upon students. A certain boy is in rebellion against the school authorities; he violates many rules and he devises new offences which are not covered by rules. Penalties do not stop him from breaking rules, for he is used to penalties, used to "walking the bull ring" or staying in after hours, and toughened to beatings. New penalties, likewise, do not stop him long, for he soon becomes accustomed to them as thoroughly as to the old. Likewise, it does little good to devise rules to cover a wider range of contingencies, for the new laws, the new risks, and the new penalties are soon a part of life. A social machine, however finely worked out, can never make a human being go its way rather than his own, and no one can ever be controlled entirely from without.

Dominance and subordination in the schools are usually discussed as "discipline." On the objective side, discipline is a social arrangement whereby one person is able consistently to exert control over the actions of others. Subjectively, discipline is the morale obtaining under institutionalized leadership. It is observable in the social interaction of the persons concerned, and it rests upon psychic arrangements in the minds of those persons. "Discipline" is often used as a value term to denote something regarded as constructive and healthful for the student or something of which the teacher approves.

In the bad old schools, partly as a result of the school curriculum and partly as an outgrowth of a stern ideal of character, an almost Spartan ideal of discipline was in vogue. Children had to do things they did not like because they did not like to do them. This rule had its correlate, of course, in that philosophy of the adult world, a philosophy not, to be just, altogether unproductive, that we should do every day something difficult simply because it was difficult, "to give the will a little gratuitous exercise." When such a philosophy ruled the schools, it was a mere incident of academic routine that if children were forced to do certain things because they did not like to do them, they did not like doing them because they were made to do them. The subtler personal effects of this sort of discipline were not considered. Education consisted of learning things one did not want to know because he did not want to know them. Whatever seemed bad was therefore good and what seemed good was bad. The best rule of school management was to find out what the children were doing and tell them to stop it. This disciplinary ideal must be classified with those other superstitions in our folklore, the belief that medicine is good if it tastes bad and that asafoetida keeps away the evil spirits. There is in fact more to be said for these primitive medical beliefs than for their educational parallels, for bad medicine may work because we think it will and a bag of asafoetida around the neck undoubtedly reduces contagion by eliminating contact. But education that is not in some sense pleasant is not education.

Discipline is partly personal influence and partly the social standing of an office. It is the resultant from the filtering of the teacher's personality through the porous framework of the institution. The larger the pores in the framework, the more personalities come into contact through it, and the more profound and permanent are the effects of social interaction. The more evident the social pattern in the schools, the less are personalities involved.

Discipline is a phenomenon of group life. It depends upon a

collective opinion which superiors cause inferiors to form of superiors and of the tasks imposed by superiors. Essentially it depends upon prestige, which is largely a fiction, upon the ability of leaders to capture and hold attention (and by shifting objectives, to maintain the tonus of the relationship), upon formality setting the stage for social interaction, upon social distance which keeps primary group attitudes from eating away at formal relations, upon the reenforcement of respect for superiors by the respect of superiors for each other and upon the reenforcement of the inferior's respect for the superior by the respect which other inferiors pay him. (The maintenance of discipline may depend also, in the long run, upon the establishment of channels for the hostility of subordinates to superiors.) Discipline shows itself, in the group, as a one-way suggestibility. . . .

WHAT TEACHING DOES
TO TEACHERS

1932

TEACHING makes the teacher. Teaching is a boomerang that never fails to come back to the hand that threw it. Of teaching, too, it is true, perhaps, that it is more blessed to give than to receive, and it also has more effect. Between good teaching and bad there is a great difference where students are concerned, but none in this, that its most pronounced effect is upon the teacher. Teaching does something to those who teach. Introspective teachers know of changes that have taken place in themselves. Objectively minded persons have observed the relentless march of growing teacherishness in others. This is our problem.

It is necessary to see this inquiry in its true perspective. The question: What does teaching do to teachers? is only a part of the greater problem: What does any occupation do to the human being who follows it? Now that differences of caste and rank have become inconspicuous, and differences that go with the locale are fading, it is the occupation that most marks the man. The understanding of the effects upon the inner man of the impact of the occupation is thus an important task of social science. It is a problem almost untouched. We know that some occupations markedly distort the personalities of those who practice them, that there are occupational patterns to which one conforms his personality as to a Procrustean bed by lopping off superfluous members. Teaching is by no means the only occupation which whittles its followers to convenient size

Reprinted from *The Sociology of Teaching* (New York: John Wiley and Sons, 1932), chap. 22, pp. 375–401, with elisions.

and seasons them to suit its taste. The lawyer and the chorus girl soon come to be recognizable social types. One can tell a politician when one meets him on the street. Henry Adams has expanded upon the unfitness of senators for being anything but senators; occupational molding, then, affects the statesman as much as lesser men. The doctor is always the doctor, and never quite can quit his rôle. The salesman lives in a world of selling configurations. And what preaching most accomplishes is upon the preacher himself. Perhaps no occupation that is followed long fails to leave its stamp upon the person. Certainly teaching leaves no plainer mark than some other vocations, though it is, perhaps, a mark which a larger number of people can recognize. It is our present task to determine, as objectively as may be and as completely as possible, the effect of teaching upon the person.

Before we can understand the occupational type to which the members of any profession belong, we must take account of the operation of four sorts of factors: (1) selective influences affecting the composition of the profession, (2) the set of rôles and attitudes which the member of the profession must play consistently, (3) the effect upon individuals of the opinion which the community has of the profession, and (4) traumatic learning within the occupation.

1. Following out the operation of the first of these factors, we find that one reason for the similarity of doctors to each other is that there is a type of personality which is especially attracted to medicine. Likewise a certain type is attracted more than others to law, another type to engineering, another to the ministry, etc. There is in no case complete consistency, but there is a sufficiently heavy aggregation of one sort of personality type in a given profession to justify the assumption of a selectivity affecting the composition of the professional population.

2. Those who follow certain occupations are continually thrown into certain kinds of social situations. These social situations call for, or are best met by, a certain kind of reaction on the part of the professional. The individual thus plays certain rôles and shows certain attitudes habitually, and there is a tendency for him to distort other social situations until they conform to a pattern

which can be met by his habitual rôles and attitudes. (This is the transfer joke, the mainstay of overworked humorists.) Training an individual for the practice of such a profession often consists in teaching him what he is expected to do or say upon certain occasions, as when the minister offers the consolations of religion to a bereaved family, a teacher assigns a lesson, a doctor enters a sick room, or a lawyer threatens suit. Long practice in the social techniques enjoined upon one in a profession makes those the deepest grooves, and at length they grow so deep that there is no getting out of them.

3. From community experience of persons playing certain kinds of rôles in the practice of certain callings, worked over and somewhat distorted by the conscious and unconscious attitudes of the community toward that profession, arise certain subjective patterns, or stereotypes, which embody the community idea of the individual belonging to a certain occupational group. The stereotype helps to determine the true occupational type, for it affects the selectivity of the occupation, and it limits and canalizes the social experience of the member of the occupation. The attempt of the individual to escape from the stereotype may itself become as in teaching and the ministry one of the important determinants of the occupational type proper.

4. The social situation surrounding the practice of any occupation is set to inflict upon the individual whose occupational behavior is eccentric certain shocks, or trauma. From the viewpoint of social organization, these shocks or penalties are means of enforcing conformity to social codes. Upon persons they produce special effects due to psychological shock. Though not easily differentiable from situational molding, these effects seem to deserve special discussion.

The selective influences determining the type of person who elects to follow a given occupation are always a little obscure, and to determine them even for a single occupation would require extended research. We must at once confess our inability to map out the set of social influences which lead certain individuals to take up teaching and discourage others from entering the profession. We may attempt an answer in the most general terms by noting briefly some of the conditions which determine the selectivity of any occupation. The economic standing of a vocation is one of the most important factors determining its selective pattern. In this are included the matter of financial return, immediate and future, the opportunity for advancement (more or less graded into steps to constitute a career), and economic security. Economic considerations do not solely determine the power of an occupation to attract desirable individuals, but they are an important part of the general configuration in which the occupation makes its appearance in the minds of individuals, for some callings have a "personality wage," and others have not. The social standing of the occupation is also important. Under this, it needs to be considered what social circles those in the occupation move in, and what stereotyped ideas the community has concerning the profession; for women, the question of marriage opportunities is not a slight one. The nature of the work is another condition of its attractiveness or unattractiveness to particular individuals. Some persons take naturally to routine; others are satisfied only with an occupation which presents a series of crises to be met and conquered. For some, obscurity is no hardship, but for others it is necessary always to be in range of the spotlight. There are yet other persons in whose minds the opportunities which an occupation yields for self-expression outweigh all other factors. The amount and kind of special training required for entry into the ranks of a given occupation are further considerations which select out some few of the many called. This will affect the psychic composition of the profession. It is certain, for instance, that those who come into the medical profession in these days of long and expensive training will always have plenty of patience. . . .

When the mills have ground which supply to each profession its accustomed human material, the teaching profession receives each year a large number of plastic and unformed minds. These new recruits have whatever qualities they may have, and upon the basis of their present personalities their life in the teaching profession will build a different structure. They do not know how to teach, although they may know everything that is in innumerable books telling them how to teach. They will not know how to teach until they have got the knack of certain personal adjustments which adapt them to their profession, and the period of learning may be either long or short. These recruits who face teaching as a life work are ready to learn to teach, and they are ready, though they know it not, to be formed by teaching. When teaching has formed them, what shape will it give them? Their daily work will write upon them; what will it write?

What teaching does to teachers it does partly by furnishing them those rôles which habit ties to the inner frame of personality and use makes one with the self. Our method in this discussion will be to describe those social situations which the teacher most often encounters, and to analyze them to discover how the qualities considered to be characteristic of the teacher are produced in them. We must admit that this is a method of empirical analysis, and that it has its first and most important basis in what the writer has seen and thought and done. The only test of such analysis and of the generalizations which come from it is the judgment of other writers who have had equal opportunity to observe. Although this method is vague and is little subject to control, it is the only method available at the present time for pursuing an inquiry of this sort, and we shall endeavor to apply it in as fair-minded a way as possible. Where there seem to be two sides, we shall state both and leave the reader to choose for himself.

Aside from a scattering company of panegyrists, most of those who have presumed to comment on the teacher as an occupational type have done so in an unfriendly manner. This is perhaps regrettable, but certainly significant, for most of those who have passed unfavorable judgments upon teachers have been teachers themselves; from pondering this, one gets a little insight into the conditions of stress and strain in the teacher mind. Unfriendly commentators upon the manners of teachers are able to compile a long list of unpleasant qualities which, they say, are engendered in the teacher's personality by teaching experience. There is first that certain inflexibility or unbendingness of personality which is thought to mark the person who has taught. That stiff and formal manner into which the young teacher compresses himself every morning when he puts on his collar becomes, they say, a plaster cast which at length he cannot loosen. One has noticed, too, that in his personal relationships the teacher is marked by reserve, an incomplete personal participation in the dynamic social situation and a lack of spontaneity, in psychological terms, by an inhibition of his total responses in favor of a restricted segment of them. As if this reserve were not in itself enough to discourage ill-considered advances, it is supplemented, when one has become very much the teacher, by certain outward barriers which prevent all and sundry from coming into contact with the man behind the mask and discovering those inhibited and hidden possibilities of reaction. Along with this goes dignity, the dignity of the teacher which is not natural dignity like that of the American Indian, but another kind of dignity that consists of an abnormal concern over a restricted rôle and the restricted but well-defined status that goes with it. One who has taught long enough may wax unenthusiastic on any subject under the sun; this, too, is part of the picture painted by unfriendly critics. The didactic manner, the authoritative manner, the flat, assured tones of voice that go with them, are bred in the teacher by his dealings in the school room, where he rules over the petty concerns of children as a Jehovah none too sure of himself, and it is said that these traits are carried over by the teacher into his personal relations. It is said, and it would be difficult to deny it, that the teacher's mind is not creative. Even the teacher's dress is affected by his occupational attitudes; the rule is that the teacher must be conservative, if not prim, in manner, speech, and dress. There are other traits which some observers have mentioned: a set of the lips, a look of strain, a certain kind of smile, a studied mediocrity, a glib mastery of platitude. Some observers have remarked that a certain way of standing about, the way of a person who has had to spend much of his time waiting for something to happen and has had to be very dignified about it, is characteristic of the teacher. Sometimes only small and uncertain indications betray the profession. Sometimes, as a cynical novelist has remarked of one of his characters, one cannot see the man for the school master. If these traits, or those essential ones which make up the major outlines of the picture, are found among the generality of teachers, it is because these traits have survival value in the schools of today. If one does not have them when he joins the faculty, he must develop them or die the academic death. Opinions might differ as to how widely these characteristic traits are found among the members of the profession and as to how deeply they are ingrained, as to whether the ordinary man might see them, or only one with the curse of satire. But Henry Adams has said that no man can be a school master for ten years and remain fit for anything else, and his statement has given many a teacher something to worry about.

There is enough plausibility in the above description to make us teachers ponder about the future, if not the present, of ourselves and our friends. But there is another side, and we may well pause to look at it before going on with our analysis. Teaching brings out pleasant qualities in some persons, and for them it is the most gratifying vocation in the world. The teacher enjoys the most pleasant associations in his work; he lives surrounded by the respect of the community and the homage of his students. Teaching affords a splendid opportunity for a self-sacrificing person (how many of these are there?) to realize his destiny vicariously; in any case the teacher is less soiled by life than those who follow more vigorous professions. It may well be questioned, too, whether there is any occupational conscience more strict than that of the teacher. Teaching breeds patience in some teachers, patience and fairness and a reserve that is only gentlemanly and never frosty. There are some persons whom teaching liberates, and these sense during their first few months of teaching a rapid growth and expansion of personality. While we are stating this side of the case, we must record the pointed observation of one person on the constructive side of the argument that those very teachers who are bitterest in the denunciation of teaching would not for a moment consider doing anything else, and that even the most discontented teachers can rarely bring themselves to leave the profession. These considerations should be enough to convince us that there are two sides to everything that can be said about the teacher, perhaps that teaching produces radically different effects upon different types of persons. But whatever the classification of the qualities which are produced in the teacher by teaching, they all mark the occupational type.

Our theoretical problem should now be clear; it is to account for the genesis of the character traits belonging to the teacher by showing how they flow out of the action of his life situation upon his personality, if possible, to show how different effects are produced upon different basic personality types.

The weightiest social relationship of the teacher is his relationship to his students; it is this relationship which is teaching. It is around this relationship that the teacher's personality tends to be organized, and it is in adaptation to the needs of this relationship that the qualities of character which mark the teacher are produced. The teacher-pupil relationship is a special form of dominance and subordination, a very unstable relationship and in quivering equilibrium, not much supported by sanction and the strong arm of authority, but depending largely upon purely personal ascendency. Every teacher is a taskmaster and every taskmaster is a hard man; if he is naturally kindly, he is hard from duty, but if he is naturally unkind, he is hard because he loves it. It is an unfortunate rôle, that of Simon Legree, and has corrupted the best of men. Conflict is in the rôle, for the wishes of the teacher and the student are necessarily divergent, and more conflict because the teacher must protect himself from the possible destruction of his authority that might arise from this divergence of motives. Subordination is possible only because the subordinated one is a subordinate with a mere fragment of his personality, while the dominant one participates completely. The subject is a subject only part of the time and with a part of himself, but the king is all king. In schools, too, subordinated ones attempt to protect themselves by withdrawing from the relationship, to suck the juice from the orange of conformity before rendering it to the teacher. But the teacher is doomed to strive against the mechanization of his rule and of obedience to it. It is the part of the teacher to enforce a real obedience. The teacher must be aggressive in his domination, and this is very unfortunate, because domination is tolerable only when it stays within set bounds. From this necessary and indispensable aggressiveness of the teacher arises an answering hostility on the part of the student which imperils the very existence of any intercourse between them. The teacher takes upon himself most of the burden of the far-reaching psychic adjustments which make the continuance of the relationship possible. . . .

A clever friend has perhaps summed up the matter by saying, "The successful teacher is one who knows how to get on and off his high-horse rapidly." (As it happened, the author of this remark did not himself possess this skill, and failed in teaching, as so many other clever men have done, for want of dignity.) Thus one says, "I am your teacher," in a certain unemotional tone of voice. This begets discipline, perhaps some sullenness, certainly emotional and personal frustration on the part of both student and teacher. Before this reaction has been carried through to completion, one says, "But I am a human being and I try to be a good fellow. And you are all fine people and we have some good times together, don't we?" This is rôle number two, and if taken at its face value it begets a desirable cheerfulness and a dangerous friendliness. If he tarries too long upon this grace note, the teacher loses his authority by becoming a member of the group. He must revert to rôle number one, and say, with just a hint of warning and an implication of adult dignity in his voice, "But I am the teacher." All this occurs a hundred times a day in every school room, and it marks the rhythm of the teacher's movements of advancement and retreat with reference to his students, the alternate expansion and contraction of his personality. It does not occur, of course, in so obvious a form as this; it is perhaps only the very unskillful teacher who needs to put such things into words. This pulsation of the teacher's personality, with its answering change of posture on the part of students, is usually reduced to a mere conversation of gestures. This conversation, for all that habit has stripped it so bare of identifying characteristics and drained it so dry of emotion, is the most significant social process of the classroom. It is also a very important determinant of the teacher's personality, and one of the points on which transfer is said to be made most easily. After all, it need cause us no amazement if one who has learned to get his way in the school by alternate applications of hot and cold water should fall into that technique of control in his more intimate relationships. In the life of every teacher there is a significant long-term change in the psychic weight of these rôles, a not unusual result being that rôle number one, the authority rôle, eats up the friendly rôle, or absorbs so much of the personality that nothing is left for friendliness to fatten upon.

The authority rôle becomes very much formalized, both because of the psychological law that performances lose their meaningfulness by frequent repetition and because there is an advantage in having it so. Army men speak of a voice of command, a flat, impersonal, unquestionable, non-controversial tone of voice in which commands are best given. It is a tone of voice without overtones, representing only a segment of the officer's personality and demanding obedience from only a segment of the subordinate. School teachers learn by trial and error, by imitation and practice, to formalize their commands. They develop, too, the voice of exposition, which is a voice perfectly dry and as mechanical as a dictaphone, a voice adapted to the expounding of matter that has long since lost what interest it may have had for the expounder. Lack of enthusiasm has survival value. Hence the paradox that sometimes the best teachers are those least interested in their work, and that others do their best work when least concerned. But all these things contribute to the final flatness and dullness of the teacher who falls a prey to them. . . .

One is puzzled to explain that peculiar blight which affects the teacher mind, which creeps over it gradually, and, possessing it bit by bit, devours its creative resources. Some there are who escape this disease endemic in the profession, but the wonder is they are so few. That the plague is real, and that it strikes many teachers, the kindest critic cannot deny. Those who have known young teachers well, and have observed the course of their personal development as they became set in the teaching pattern, have often been grieved by the progressive deterioration in their general adaptability. And hardly a college teacher who has taught a class in summer school has failed to lament that lack of supple comprehension and willingness to follow the ball of discussion which characterizes the teacher in class. Teachers make a sad and serious business of learning, and they stand mournfully in contrast with students of the winter session, in whom a reasonable degree of willingness to judge every question on its own merits is much more frequent.[1]

Some of the gradual deadening of the intellect which the observer remarks in the teacher as he grows into his profession may no doubt be explained as an effect of age. Perhaps age does dull some persons, and certainly experience disciplines the creative impulse out of many. But if all the deterioration in the teacher is due to age, there must be a special type of short-blooming mind that is attracted to teaching; if this is so, we are thrown back upon the unanswered question of occupational selection. Another type of explanation could be based upon the tendency inculcated upon one practicing any profession to respond to recurring social situations in stereotyped ways. The deepening of some grooves of social expression is apparently inevitable in any occupation, and this emphasis of the part must involve deterioration of the whole. The mental structure of the unspecialized person is necessarily plastic; by specializing and developing particular proficiency along some one line, one nearly always loses some of his general adaptability. Perhaps that was why the elder James regarded so many of the established pursuits as "narrowing." The extent to which a profession stereotypes and narrows the social expression of the individual depends upon the range of variation in the social situations which the practice of the profession presents. The situations which the teacher faces are somewhat more stereotyped than those which the lawyer and the doctor must confront. Perhaps teaching is only a little more rigid in the social patterning which it imposes upon its devotees, but it is a very important little. The over-attention of teachers to tool subjects must certainly be called in to help explain

---

[1]   The witticism of a clever colleague is perhaps worth recording. It is one of many current in the profession concerning the peculiarities of summer-school students. He said: "The difference between students in the winter term and students in the summer session is this: When I go into my classroom in the winter I look at the class and say, 'Good Morning,' but the students are all making so much noise they don't hear me. When I go into a summer-school class I say, 'Good Morning,' and they all take out their note-books and write it down."

the smallness and unimportance of the contributions which teachers have made to the arts and sciences. The teacher, from the very nature of his work, must spend most of his time in the classroom in drilling his students upon those subjects which may later open to them the doors that lead to wisdom. Other men, when they have reached maturity, may themselves use those tools to unlock the doors of the palace and enter within. But the teacher, unfortunately, must always sit upon the front steps and talk about the means of opening the door; he must instruct others in the technique of door-opening, and usually he finds when he has finished his task that he has no energy left for explorations of his own. All this is incidental to the fact that the teacher must deal with persons living in a world of childish attitudes and values, and comes himself to live in it part way. This is what one teacher called "the drag of the immature mind."

The routine situations which the teacher confronts give rise to routine habits of social expression adapted to meet them. This we have mentioned. What we have not dealt with is the influence of these routinized reactions upon the selective pattern of experience which the teacher builds up within himself. Actually the teacher faces a narrow but complex and dynamic social situation, one from which he might well receive a liberal education in adaptability, but from this complex network of human attitudes and activities he is forced to select mainly those which affect his discipline. He may peer into the book of human life, a various volume which has many obscure and devious passages, but he is privileged to read in it only the insults to himself. As to subject matter, the teacher's possibilities of reaction are equally limited. Not confutation, nor understanding, nor yet the notation of the heart must be his aim as he reads, but merely the answering of the most obvious questions and the prevention of the most stupid errors. The selectivity which the teacher builds up must be one which will give him a maximum of discipline and a minimum of subject matter. We have noted the partial paralysis of the teacher's personality through a fear of possible consequences if he allows himself freedom in his social life; this is a sort of self-frustration produced by the elaborate system of defence reactions which the teacher builds about himself. We

ersonality traits are in most cases exaggerated rather than
ed by traumatic experiences; these are unsually distressing
ences, and they fall precisely upon the persons least capable
milating them. The lunatic fringe of teaching, every year
ed off and every year renewed, is made up of personalities
by many traumas.

ninor sort of traumatic learning results from the effect of
upon the system of values. Points in one's scheme of life
must be sharply defended come to assume a disproportionate
ance. Recurrent crises in the teacher's life, such as inter-
nen squabbles, constellate a temporary organization of
lity ound the values then to be defended from attack.
mporary organization leaves traces in the nervous system,
a result of the traces this fighting organization is more easily
nto play the next time; the traces may indeed grow so great
t the tone of the personality. That for which men must often
dear to them. This mechanism is very important in the life
school teacher. The experienced teacher fights harder for
ne than does the novice, and he begins to fight a great deal
adily. The head of the department fights for the privileges
epartment much more valiantly than instructors, and has a
nose for sniffing out conspiracies. In all this the person who
lied the social psychology of conflict groups will find noth-
ling or new.

have mentioned, too, a certain tenseness as characterizing the
teacher, a tenseness which arises out of the conflict implicit in the
inhibition of the major part of his potentialities of response in
favor of a few necessary but personally unsatisfactory responses.
This tenseness prevents the wholesome fulfillment of creative
process. Creation requires motivation with control; the teacher
has an excess of motivation with an even greater excess of inhibition. . . .

We have spoken of certain situational necessities which mold
the teacher, of the rôles which these situational imperatives impose
upon him, and of the enduring effect of these rôles upon personality. It remains to consider in a connected way traumatic learning
as a determinant of the occupational type, the effect of shock upon
the teacher personality. What we have in mind is that learning
which takes place under terrific penalties, and in which the learner
is subject to shock if he makes the wrong choices. The pathological
effects of shock have been investigated frequently, but these effects
have rarely been discussed as learning, nor have they ever been
treated in their proper relation to the social organization. Yet, in
that learning which involves modification of personality, shock
often plays a dominant rôle, and the giving of shocks is one of the
principal means by which the social group tailors persons to its
specifications. Traumatic learning is therefore important in both
sociology and psychology.

This kind of learning is not easily separable from other sorts
of learning, and still it has characteristics which seem to justify a
distinction. Traumatic learning is continuous with habit formation,
being, perhaps, a special instance of the law of effect; the use of
slight penalties is also a common incident of laboratory procedure.
Traumatic learning is continuous with the normal molding of personality by social conditioning, and we have already discussed
minor shocks which mold the teacher's personality. Traumatic
learning is continuous with the modification of personality in crisis
situations, but represents the reaction of personality to the most
sudden and extreme crises. We are justified in regarding traumatic
learning as different from ordinary learning because radical differences appear between reactions to slight shocks and reactions

to severe shocks. The psychological and psychopathological effects of shock have indeed been investigated, but their meaning in terms of personality and social organization has perhaps not been sufficiently pointed out.

For the teacher, traumatic experiences usually concern the loss of his position, especially the sudden and unforeseen loss of his position. The loss of control over a class may be traumatic in its effect, and so may a quarrel with a colleague. Various minor shocks arise, and we shall need to reconsider all that we have said concerning the molding of personality by the teaching situation in the light of the new insight furnished by the concept of traumatic learning. Individuals, of course, differ greatly in their ability to assimilate shocks without damage to their personalities.

These shocks which teachers experience may induce light dissociation, more pronounced in persons of hysteric constitution, and associated with a tendency to repeat the traumatic experience in a manner akin to that of the war neuroses. The dissociation very likely prolongs and exacerbates the conflict, since it prevents the individual from facing it and reacting to it, but allows the conflict to produce effects indirectly. Whatever the ultimate adjustment, the mind dwells upon such crises a long time, relives them incessantly for months and even years, elaborates reactions to them without end. Usually, a curiously bifurcated adjustment appears. On the one hand, the individual refuses to accept the responsibility for the shocking event and that part of his behavior which led up to it. He multiplies rationalizations to the same end: "It wasn't my fault," "The circumstances were most unusual," "I was the goat," etc. This is often attended by a conscious or unconscious refusal to evaluate the situation correctly, the face-saving rationalizations demanding that the realization of responsibility be shut from consciousness. On the other hand, the individual behaves as if he accepted responsibility completely, something which he does not find at all inconsistent with his conscious insistence that it was not his fault. He multiplies precautions to prevent the recurrence of the unfortunate event, taking an almost obsessive interest in the protection of that which previously was threatened. This, of course, represents the reaction to the other side of the ambivalence. Like-

wise, an individual may insist that in a cer[...] world he has lost no status, the while he i[...] havior which can only be interpreted as co[...] of status. Much of the ruthlessness of teacl[...] the nature of compensation for fears tra[...] cipline experiences.

As a result of shocks, too, there appea[...] to the specific conditioning of the behav[...] nisms which are very little dependent u[...] contexts and which therefore tend to be se[...] circumstances if the specific stimulus is pr[...] certain positive behavior patterns which[...] the stimulus sound is heard. Teachers co[...] lently to specific stimuli. A teacher once[...] from his principal asking him to call at th[...] He called at the office, and was summarily[...] experienced acute fear whenever he rec[...] the office of a school superior, and this[...] suffer attrition in spite of the fact that th[...] expose him to attack.

Conversion, as a sudden change of th[...] attitudes in personality, may result from[...] ence. Traumatic experiences redefine situ[...] it is probably correct to speak of it as a cl[...] titude; it is likely to take the form of[...] sides of an ambivalence. Trauma may res[...] of moral codes or in radical change of p[...] is common among teachers who suffer sl[...] kind to students. Conversion usually inv[...] allegiance.

Most likely to be subject to the crude[...] ing are ego-centric persons, and other m[...] ing type. These persons either fail to obs[...] feel capable of overriding them, and the[...] Some persons are completely demoralize[...] and if those consequences are so severe[...] the social world, they usually have most[...]

18

A PRINCIPAL REASON WHY

INSTITUTIONS DO NOT

FUNCTION

1932

A FRIEND who is a minister is fond of the following story:
"I was walking down the street one morning not long ago. A
fine-looking man came alongside and kept pace with me.

" 'I am the devil,' he announced.

" 'Well,' I said, 'I have always been very curious about you
and I'm glad to see you at last. And what are you doing this morning?'

" 'Oh, my usual business. I am going about corrupting the
works of man.'

"We chatted pleasantly, for I have never been a devil-hater,
and kept company for some distance. I was surprised to find the
devil such a pleasant and well-spoken gentleman. After a time, we
noticed a man in front of us who gave all outward indications of
having been struck by a good idea. He stopped suddenly still, his
face lighted up, he struck his hand to his head in joy, and rapidly
walked away to execute his idea. Thinking that this gave me at
least a temporary advantage, I said, 'Now there's a man who has an
idea, and I venture to say that it is a good idea. That's a point
against you. What are you going to do about that?'

" 'Nothing easier,' said the devil, 'I'll organize it.' "

Something happens to ideas when they get themselves organized into social systems. The ethical ideas of Christ, flexible and
universal, have nevertheless been smothered by churches. A social

---

Reprinted from *The Sociology of Teaching* (New York: John Wiley and
Sons, 1932), chap. 24.

principle degenerates into a dogma when an institution is built about it. Yet an idea must be organized before it can be made into fact, and an idea wholly unorganized rarely lives long. Without mechanism it dies, but mechanism perverts it. This is part of the natural flow and recession—the life principle in society.

Institutions have their informal beginnings in the mores; they are "formal trends in the mores." In Sumner's classic words, "An institution consists of a concept and a structure." The structure is defined as "a number of functionaries set to cooperate in prescribed ways at certain conjunctures." Where the structure has become too intricate, or too rigid, or the idea of function has faded from the minds of functionaries, we speak of the institution as suffering from formalism. This clinical entity which we have called formalism is variously designated in sociological literature; Cooley mentions six names for it: institutionalism, formalism, traditionalism, conventionalism, ritualism, and bureaucracy. As Cooley has said, it is difficult to tell when mechanism is in excess; the best rule that can be formulated is perhaps that of Cooley, that mechanism is in excess when it interferes with growth and adaptation.

The school must always function as an organization of personalities bound together in a dynamic relation; this is true whether the school be a live organism or dead matter. But in a living bit of social tissue, persons transcend offices; they embody offices but they engulf them; they are persons first and offices afterwards. But in dead tissue offices transcend persons. In live tissue, the man is always too large for the job, and he is forever bursting his uniform at the elbows and shoulders. In dead tissue the man rattles about in the office like a seed in a gourd. When officers are more concerned with the perquisites of their offices than with the human values of their job, that is formalism.

Every social structure and every system of thought must grow old in time, and every one of them must die. And each of these, in its senescence, grows formal. One aspect of age in the social organism is a disorder of communication, an "excess of the organ of language" attended by a lack of real communication, a growth of verbiage and a failure of that inner contact upon which communication depends. This may occur, and often does, within the life cycle of individuals, and it then keeps pace with the mental ossification of men. But this breakdown of communication is most clearly visible when one generation is succeeded by another. It is easy to communicate duties, and it is easy to find men to do duties, but it is difficult to communicate a mission. So that it often happens that what is passed on to the newer generation is not a living insight into function, but dead information about duties.

A fading of the distinction between means and ends is one of the things that marks formalism. The general tendency in human process is for ends to turn into means, and this probably favors a healthy growth of personality and of society. Our achievements range themselves on different levels, and we readjust our standards as we pass from one level to another. But there is an opposite tendency which transforms means into ends; means are at first subwholes in greater wholes, but the greater whole fades out and leaves nothing but the part. Then the part is the whole. Man is a stupid child that can understand all the parts of his lesson but cannot understand the whole. This happens in teaching whenever a teacher overemphasizes the intrinsic value of his subject. It happens when learning is for school. It happens when learning is dry and dissected into facts. It happens when children are means and knowledge is an end.

Formalism, as Cooley has noted, is psychically cheap, and that is why an overburdened teacher turns to it. The necessities of the teaching situation may compel even the teacher who has a higher conception of education to turn to routine methods of instruction. The teacher must do something in the classroom, and routine teaching is the easiest thing to do. He must, ordinarily, teach something definite, and from this comes the tendency of the teacher to build up courses from definite but probably unimportant facts. And the teacher must have some standards, in any system, and it is therefore not difficult for him to magnify to the size of the whole that part of his job which consists of keeping lazy students from getting credits too easily. When this easiest way has been transmuted into a self-justifying moral order, formalism has taken possession of the school.

A different kind of social degeneration, characterized also by a maladaptation of mechanism and function, arises as a result of primary group attitudes among the functionaries of a social system. The institutional group becomes a more or less self-sufficient in-group, and conducts the institution for its own benefit rather than its social function. It is very difficult to tell when this kind of institutionalism becomes a vice, for in some of its forms it may be very useful in that it furnishes morale for the discharge of social functions. The *esprit de corps* of the Canadian Mounted Police must in part arise from the fact that the members of the force are bound together by ties of personal acquaintance. But a bureaucracy that has no crises to meet does not find the acquaintance of its members with each other an unmixed profit, and there is a point beyond which it is clear loss.

The typical large school is overridden with this sort of institutionalism. The members of the faculty think of themselves as forming a closed group whose interests are sacrosanct; students must take just what the faculty chooses to give them and ask for nothing more; all members of the faculty unite in condemning any attempt to subject the school to control or regulation from the outside. A different institutionalism grows up among the lesser sort of help, who develop in-group attitudes and a group consciousness from which both faculty and students are excluded. An incident illustrating the bureaucratic attitudes that spring up among the hired help of a university was furnished by a professor in a midwestern university.

I was in the periodical room of the university library. A woman approached the attendant with a special request.

"I'd like to take this back number of *Harper's* with me for a while," she stated.

"I am very sorry," said the attendant, "but that is not permitted."

There was some discussion. Finally the attendant asked the woman her official status in the university. It developed that she was a clerk in a nearby administrative office.

"Oh, take the magazine along. We let the people in the administrative offices have whatever they want. But I thought for a while you were some faculty member!"

It is difficult to believe that the purpose of the university was better served by giving the clerical help free access to such material than it would have been by making it easily available to the faculty.

Institutionalism of this sort in the school is analogous to graft in politics. It springs from the same root. The official, whom society and the law supposes to be actuated by considerations of public service and official duty (secondary group norms), is actually governed by considerations arising from his own little group of friends and acquaintances. Friendship flourishes while official duty suffers. That is why the grafting politician is so hard to oust, for he really is a good fellow, as the saying goes, "if you know him." The institutionalized teacher is in exactly the same situation. The morality of his own primary group takes precedence over that of the secondary group which his group is supposed to serve. The difference between the teacher and the politician is in the nature of the public trust which they handle. The politician handles money. The teacher handles children. The politician steals money. The teacher steals personality values.

This kind of institutionalism is also very common in the schools; these cancerous primary groups flourish in dead tissue where an understanding of function no longer exists. The school is especially liable to institutionalism of this sort because of the presence of a large element of dominance and subordination in the relation of teacher and student. The fact of domination shuts both teacher and student off from real communication with each other. Students as well as teachers have put up walls, as many a teacher has learned who has tried to form a real and vital contact with his students. If the teacher cannot establish contact with his students on a common human level, or if he does not dare, because of the enmity between students and teachers in general, then the teacher is thrown back upon formalism in his classroom and upon the primary groups of the teaching profession for friendship and sanction for his own attitudes and behavior. The isolation of teachers in the community also throws teachers upon each other for society, and this also makes for teaching for teachers.

It does not seem unreasonable to conclude, on the basis of the evidence which has been presented throughout this study, that the schools are a barren ground for the cultivation of personality.

Some personal interchange there is in the schools, but it is of a limited sort and is largely vitiated by the limitations placed upon it. For the ordinary student in the ordinary school, and for any but the most exceptional teacher in the ordinary school, there is lacking any opportunity for that full, unforced, and unfettered self-expression from which personal development proceeds. It is necessary to consider the personalities of all who are involved in the social situations of the school, for it is not possible to develop the personalities of students favorably without giving like opportunities to teachers, and it is not possible to liberate students from present inhibitions without also liberating teachers.

We have stated . . . that the school is a social organism, that it is an artificial social order built on the despotic principle and is in a state of perilous equilibrium. In the light of our study of formalism these statements take on a new interrelation. The school is an organism some of whose tissues are dead; it is this dead tissue which we sense as artificial; it is the deadness of the tissue which makes necessary despotic government within the dead parts. It is this deadness of certain relationships, this artificiality of the conventional order and the despotism that goes with it—it is this which constantly creates the rebellion which the teacher must forever put down. The formal, artificial social order of the school does not furnish a proper milieu for the development of normal personality; that is why students are rebellious: they want to live. Cooley has written, "In the same way a school whose discipline is merely formal, not engaging the interest and good-will of the scholar, is pretty certain to turn out unruly boys and girls, because whatever is most personal and vital to them becomes accustomed to assert itself in opposition to the system."

All this is very far from the discipline of personal leadership. Real leadership is unconscious and informal; it is deeply personal in that it flows out of the man rather than the office. It is domination which the dominant one himself cannot prevent, which he quite possibly did not plan, domination that arises from a mind more complex than the minds of the followers and a hand readier and bolder than theirs. This is a kind of disciplined cooperation into which both leader and follower can enter fully; it is that which is lacking in the schools. Formal leadership, the leadership of the person who must be a leader because of the position he holds, and who, because of his position, is forced to be a purely formal leader, takes the place in the schools of natural leadership.

There is need for a natural social order in the schools. That does not mean a chaotic social order, or an uncontrolled social order, but rather a social order which students and teachers work out for themselves in the developing situation, an order which is intrinsic in the personalities of those involved, a social order resulting from the spontaneous, inevitable, and whole-hearted interaction of personalities. It is the function of the schools to help the individual organize his life out of the social materials which are presented to him. This process is now dominated by groups outside the school and is but little influenced by the school. If the school is to become really important in the lives of its students, it must allow them to be as free in school as they are outside it.

19

NOTES ON HIGHER EDUCATION

Diffusion of Intellectual and Professional Culture

CERTAIN VERY complicated processes of diffusion take place within the academic universe, that is, in the world of professors. Diffusion takes place from certain culturally dominant universities to the rest of the academic world. These universities are centers of academic invention and have extraordinary facilities for graduate training. Cultural processes in the academic universe are made apparent by the movements of persons and ideas from these central universities to minor sub-centers. The leading or central schools are those in which the invention of culture is most important and cultural diffusion and transmission are least important. As one goes from leading schools to schools further from the center, the relative importance of invention as measured by faculty productivity, support of research, etc., diminishes and the importance of diffusion and transmission increases. In minor institutions invention disappears altogether and in institutions which are furthest removed from the central or leading schools diffusion has very little importance while transmission becomes the major function. A valve-like arrangement apparently governs the movements of men and ideas within the academic universe. Ideas run easily from the center to the periphery of this universe and run backward only with very great difficulty. When an idea originates on the periphery it is able to establish itself in the academic universe usually only through a process of rediffusion from a large center or a sub-center.

Previously unpublished.

Likewise, college teachers rarely occupy positions in universities which are more central than those in which they took their training. A person who took his Ph.D. at the University of Nebraska can get a job in a normal school in Colorado, but it is extremely unlikely that he will be offered a position at Columbia University. Those who manage to swim up the rapids are exceedingly few. Because of this fact it happens that persons with doctor's degrees from leading universities who hold positions in less important schools are often persons of very slight ability; on the extreme edge of the distribution appearances are all against the central universities, but this is fallacious and merely shows that only the worst of those who took their doctor's degrees in the best schools are relegated to positions on the academic frontier. Within the central universities themselves this generalization concerning direction of movement may not hold good, yet it seems to be true that these universities have a very high index of inbreeding and that they frequently import foreign scholars in order to escape the necessity of having to hire a teacher who was trained in a lesser school.

Many people who have observed the colleges closely confirm that such a distribution as we have outlined exists. Among the publication houses a distinction is made between manuscript schools and adoption schools. Quite different tactics are employed in dealing with faculty members of these two different kinds of schools and occasionally different representative of the same company will call upon faculty members at schools which are close together geographically but of which one is a manuscript school and the other an adoption school. Further evidence is furnished by the cultural inferiority complex which persons have who are located in schools which are relatively far from the center. The college teacher, like the high school teacher, is a martyr to cultural diffusion. A person who has taken his doctorate at one of the leading graduate schools, if he spends his life thereafter in teaching in a third-rate university or a small college, will usually develop some interesting defense reactions and compensatory mechanisms which bespeak a considerable underlying feeling of inferiority. In one third-rate university there is a great deal of cheerful talk in a certain group of men who had just passed the age at which it seemed likely that they would receive a call to a school a little nearer the center of things. And yet this cheerful talk was sometimes interrupted by discussions of the good luck of others who had been called to other schools and these persons never quite managed, in talking of these others, to keep a tone of envy from creeping into their voices. The fact seems to be that all the ambitious men who are teaching at the University of Nebraska or the University of Oklahoma really wish to get away but have put this desire out of their minds because it makes them unhappy to be forced to face it constantly. They have developed a façade of forced cheerfulness. Now a person who criticizes their institution attacks their system of repressions and reveals their own dissatisfaction with the world and their place in it. The emotions which are then released are centered upon the individual who released them. They are no longer recognized as coming out of their own dissatisfaction with their place in the world, but are thought to arise from the unpleasant characteristics of the destructive critic. This explains the hatred that faculty members of second-rate universities have for soreheads. It explains in part why one has to like it at a school that is not very good but may be as critical as he wishes at a good school.

The diffusion of academic subjects follows our outline to a certain extent. Within any field of specialization new subjects are likely to be established first at schools which have already built up a position of dominance in those subjects. They are diffused from these schools because the persons who go out to teach these new subjects have been trained in the school where the subjects were first established. Some exceptions appear, however. The new subject of sociology was very early introduced into the curriculum of Chicago and Columbia. It diffused, however, over a great field of minor schools before it was formally recognized by Harvard University and some other leading eastern institutions. Furthermore, subjects which have long been in the curriculum and which have begun to decline in importance may persist longer in minor schools than in central schools. It is said, for instance, that the leading authorities in medieval history are now located in minor universities.

Textbooks are likewise diffused from the center to the periphery though the majority are written at secondary universities. In central universities it is considered not quite appropriate to depend upon textbooks to any degree and text writing is not ordinarily looked upon as a worthy intellectual exercise. The leading scholars in any field are likely to guard themselves against degrading their minds to the textbook level of expression. Textbooks, therefore, are mostly written in secondary universities and are diffused from them as centers. Texts which have become archaic are likely to have a certain sale for many years in outlying schools. An abridged version of William James's text on psychology was still being taught in a few schools in 1930. In sociology some of the older texts have persisted in minor colleges for a surprisingly long time. It seems to have been unusually true that the textbooks which have the largest adoption list are these very old books.

Particular schools dominate particular areas. There is an ecological organization within the academic universe as truly as in the great city. There are a number of cultural areas characterized by the domination of certain academic institutions and these are as separate and distinct as were in other days the areas occupied by the Indians who followed the buffalo and those who caught salmon. There are certain leading universities which apparently dominate the eastern part of the United States, there is one which occupies a dominate position in the middle west, there are two or three leading institutions on the west coast and one or two in the south. Each one of these has a well-recognized area of dominance. In the south this condition is complicated by the fact that presidents and trustees of southern colleges prefer, other things being equal, to employ a man who is a southerner by birth rather than to take a northerner. A condition of closed competition is thus produced in the south.

These generalizations which we have attempted to put forward have many exceptions. It should be understood that a university may be a leading school in engineering or agriculture and be very backward in psychology or history. Further, particular departments may be so strong in one school that they are able to dominate a wide area while other departments are unrecognized and unknown the world over. It is also true that particular professors may occupy a dominant position while remaining at minor universities. All these exceptions should be carefully noted.

Faculty Mobility and Intellectual Contexts: The Major Schools

There are manifest advantages for the young scholar in taking his training at one of the central universities. He will have an opportunity to familiarize himself with the latest work in his field and even if he does not keep up his scholarly pursuits very earnestly after obtaining his degree, he has at least enough knowledge in his little bucket to enable him to quench the thirst of students for a few years. Further, the young scholar who comes into close contact with the leading thinkers of his field secures contacts which are enormously valuable to him. He has an opportunity to imitate the mental processes of really great men, and unless he is very dull, he can not help catching some of their spirit. By cooperating with great scholars he comes to know better than he could otherwise how scholarly works are produced. Great scholars in these central universities are not always too careful to give their students credit for the work they have done. It very often happens that a volume which is compiled by a number of graduate students is published under the teacher's signature and the names of the students who produced it are merely mentioned in the preface. There are many who feel that even this is not too great a price to pay for the privilege of studying under really great men. By working for some years without gaining any right in their own product they acquire recognition and at length attain to a position which permits them to exploit oncoming generations of students.

The fact that a man trained in a central university acquires an inside knowledge of the workings of the academic world and contacts which will be very valuable to him in after years seems undeniable. Another benefit is the enormous confidence which one gains by taking his graduate work in a leading university. One who has taken his work in such a school has come in close contact with really leading men and he has very possibly come to the conclusion that his mind is not much different from theirs. He has seen these great men in error and perplexity. He has faith in his own competence which a man who has trained in a secondary university usually lacks. There is as great a difference between the man trained in the central university and the man trained in the secondary university as between the college man and the non-college man, and it is exactly the same kind of difference. A great part of the advantage of the college man over the non-college man inheres in the attitude of the non-college man who thinks that the college man has got something that he has missed.

If it is an advantage to a young scholar to take his training in a central university, it is an even greater advantage to teach in one. Here again we see strikingly illustrated the old adage that nothing succeeds like success. Small original differences between A and B may be greatly accentuated in the course of ten years if A is fortunate enough to be chosen for the faculty of a really great university and B is not and the two of them continue to compete with one another for academic prestige. A, who is chosen for the great university, has an opportunity to serve an extended apprenticeship under great masters. There is as much difference between a man who has taken a degree and served an apprenticeship as there is between the average doctor of philosophy and the average master of arts. If A continues to be a member of a leading faculty after completing his apprenticeship, he has a number of stimulating contacts and the persons around him contribute notably to the continuance of his education, making it possible for him to form ideas which differ from the accepted ones in the field.

A great university is a great sounding board, and a small college is a wall of felt. Because Mr. A has met a large number of the persons who are likely to review his books he has an excellent chance of obtaining generous reviews, for it is always possible that the books of the reviewers may later fall into his hands. Further, Mr. A will have to deal only with a highly selected group of students; it will not be necessary for him to develop schoolmaster traits in order to do his job with them, and it is very likely that they will do a certain amount of work which he will be able to use in his own publication. It is not surprising that what was once a small gap between Mr. A and Mr. B becomes in a few years a very wide gap. Since the administrators of the central universities are not all-wise it sometimes happens that they choose the man of lesser intelligence and allow the more brilliant one to go elsewhere. Unless the original nature of the difference is very great the advantage is still with the man at the central university.

And yet the central universities are not exactly paradise. It often happens that a great scholar prefers to build around him a very mediocre department in order that he may seem the more brilliant by contrast with their dullness. Such a department is frequently lock-stepped and regimented in a way that does not conform to the best academic ethics. We should make mention, also, of the plight of those persons of lesser intellect who have contrived by some means to get connected with a great university. They are unable to produce worthwhile things, and they spend their lives in trying to understand and in trying to hide the painfully obvious fact that they lack intelligence. Many of them become bewildered intellects and hammer themselves senseless against the stone wall of what for them is the Unknowable.

Faculty Mobility and Intellectual Contexts: The Minor Schools

The minor universities are trial grounds for younger men. A young man who takes his Ph.D. at one of the leading universities, having perhaps served as an instructor or teaching fellow there for a few years, obtains a position at a minor university with the rank of assistant professor. After a certain length of time he establishes a reputation and perhaps secures an offer from a university of higher rank. These offers are selective in that they take the most promising young men from the faculties of the minor universities. It is, therefore, usually true that the younger professors at minor universities are of a higher order of capacity than the older men.

The work of men at the minor schools is often characterized by tangentiality. Usually, of course, the intellectual product of the professor at the minor university is not very much of an innovation; it is usually a textbook or a piece of hack-writing of some other sort which assembles between two covers material not otherwise available. Occasionally a book or an article is produced which strikes off from the beaten path markedly but not in a direction in which the intellectual life of the time is likely to follow. Innovation which is important is innovation which goes down the middle of the road and anticipates the work of future generations. The scholar at the minor university strikes off on a path which is introdden before and which no man will ever tread again. It is tangential as regards the main subject matter of a body of knowledge.

The reasons for this tangentiality of the able professors at the minor university are quite numerous. Many of these men are persons who have high ability but are not quite geniuses and who have the mental conflicts that go with the certain possession of high ability and the uncertain possession of real genius. Such persons, if they could find their vein or work within their limitations, could produce excellent academic contributions, but in trying to be more profound than they can they succeed only in becoming unintelligible.

One must also take into consideration the lack of stimulating contacts for the able man in the minor university. If he were connected with a school near the center, he would have constant criticism and his ideas would be brought back to contact with reality before they had departed very far from it. There would be that in his environment which would stimulate and encourage him to make innovations which would be acceptable to the majority of his colleagues. In the minor university these conditions are not fulfilled. The man of high ability is almost completely isolated. His colleagues are unable to criticize his ideas, and he soon falls out of the habit of discussing serious matters with them. Nor do his colleagues relay to him and digest for him ideas which are floating around in the academic universe, and thereby stimulate him to make sound inventions. If there is in him any tendency to get out of touch with reality, his isolation in a minor university accentuates it. Further, the awe with which mediocre colleagues regard such a man is probably not a healthy environment for him. All of these conditions contribute to make the able person in a minor university go off on tangents, to make his contributions less sound than they would be if his intellectual and social environment were different. It also happens that he is very often anticipated in his results. Minor universities are full of men who once started to write good books with sound ideas in them but who were anticipated by the publication of some other book which expressed exactly the same ideas.

As one goes from the center to the periphery one finds that moral considerations increase in importance and efficiency considerations decrease in importance. Professors in central universities have considerable freedom in their personal lives. Professors in universities and colleges on the periphery are watched narrowly for any symptom of moral turpitude and are sometimes spied upon systematically. Both extremes of attitude could be illustrated by a number of incidents. A committee of busy-bodies is said to have called upon a certain very famous president of a central university to protest against the immorality of one of the leading professors. He was, it seems, living in sin with some woman to whom he was not married. After the story had been told, the busy-bodies asked the president what he intended to do about it. The president said that he intended to do nothing at all. They asked, "Just what would a man have to do to get fired from this institution?" He replied, "Well, if he raped one of the coeds in class. . . ."

At the other extreme one should consider the cases in which instructors at minor schools have been dismissed for such small offences as smoking on the street or where they have been spied upon by private detectives paid by the college administration. This dominance of moral over efficiency considerations introduces irrelevant competition so that teachers are valued and retained not so much for what they can do as for what they do not do; unquestionably this mechanism contributes to the continued failure of the minor schools to produce valuable intellectual products.

Similar generalizations may be drawn with regard to the lives of students. It seems to be generally true that the larger universities are willing to limit themselves to the education of the mind and are quite unwilling to intrude unnecessarily into the private lives of students. Perhaps the best measuring stick of any university is its set of regulations for women students. In the extremely peripheral schools there is a strong tendency to treat women students as *jeunes filles,* to regard them as treasures who must be protected from any marauders and be handed on intact to future husbands, who, of course, attach no little importance to the fact that they still possess their pristine purity. In the larger universities there is a growing tendency to accord women students just about the same privileges that are granted to men. The attitudes of parents, however, constitute a constant check upon the granting of new privileges to women students, for parents who are not at all strict with their daughter in hand at home apparently prefer to feel that they are very closely guarded when they are away from home.

A similar generalization may be made concerning schoolmasterishness. In the central universities it is relatively little in evidence, but its importance gradually increases as one goes to schools which are further from the center. Schoolmasterishness is very easy to recognize and to identify, but somewhat difficult to define; it shows itself in the tendency of the person who teaches school to be mainly occupied with things that have to do with his job as a teacher. The man who is much the schoolmaster gives little thought to anything other than that which goes on in the classroom. He talks about what happens in the classroom when he meets with friends, discusses students, relates incidents and perhaps boasts of the stand that he has taken on some matter of classroom discipline. It seems very clear that the mind of the professor in the central university is turned upon invention, upon creation, and that the extent to which he devotes his attention to this aspect of his job precludes any undue preoccupation with merely schoolteacher matters or with things which have to do only with institutional politics. A friend who is taking work in two large institutions contrasts them as follows:

"When I go to the University of Chicago I meet my friends and they ask me 'What are you doing?' By this they mean 'What are you writing, or what research are you doing?' I tell them and they are satisfied. When I visit the University of Pennsylvania the same question is asked. I start to tell what research I am doing and they interrupt, 'Oh no, I mean what courses are you teaching?'

They force me to tell the name and to define the content of every course that I am teaching, to tell what textbook I am using in every course and to defend my choice. Now my friends at the University of Chicago know as well as these others that I make my living by teaching, but they prefer not to wound me by too obvious reference to this vulgar fact. Besides, they are not interested."

Faculty Mobility and Intellectual Contexts: The Small College

Whether leading small colleges or minor universities stand nearer to the center of the academic universe is a matter legitimately in dispute. If the decision is left to the faculty of the minor universities, it will be rendered without hesitation in favor of the university, however low its standards, as against the small college, however good it may be. Faculty members who are attached to the larger schools try to think as charitably as they can of these lesser breeds who are not so privileged. Without giving the matter very much consideration, they believe that men at even the leading small colleges are somewhat inferior to professors in state universities. In the group of academic specialists, persons who teach at the smaller schools rarely count for very much. Those who are identified with the larger schools constitute a small, rigidly limited primary group which has a rather high degree of solidarity. Naturally the members of this group do not believe that those who do not belong to it are of any considerable importance. Yet is seems very likely that faculty members of a leading small college are of a higher average capacity than those of the minor university. The professors at the best small colleges are a highly selected group, whereas the professors at large universities are an exceedingly ill-selected group, and even those who have attained to some position may have demonstrated their ability to live through a period of starvation rather than their productive capacity. As to the average student of the small college as contrasted with the state university, the comparison is again altogether in favor of the smaller colleges. Smaller colleges can sometimes afford to select their students quite rigidly, whereas state universities are prevented by the pressure of the public from exercising any considerable degree of selection.

It is usually true, however, that the faculty member of even a good small school fails to make much of a mark in his field. For one thing he lacks those stimulating contacts which are supposed to be one of the chief advantages of a larger school. The person who teaches in a leading small college may associate with fellow faculty members who are men of very high ability, but since they have no proficiency in his field, they serve rather to polish him as a human being rather than to stimulate him as a thinker, or to lead him to outstanding achievements as a scholar. Further, the faculty member of a small school is not under any very strong pressure to publish. Although this pressure to publish often leads to the publication of a great deal of ill-digested stuff, it is still true that it also leads many able men to record their ideas which might not, otherwise, ever reach any degree of clarity or precision. Again, the specialist who is teaching in a school which has a student body of five hundred can not specialize. He can not spend most of his time in studying or in cultivating such a field as public finance or criminology. He probably gains as a human being, but being forced to spread himself thinly over several fields he must fail to attain a creative mastery of any of these fields.

Most all of the professors at the small colleges suffer. In a large university there are usually several persons who are closely associated in one subject matter department; these persons are able to discuss one another's work intelligently and probably they manage to stimulate one another in research. These contacts are entirely lacking in the small college, and it seems likely that professors in the small college turn to discussing schoolmaster shop because their position as schoolmasters is the only thing that they have in common. Two men who know the same field may talk over many things which have to do with the field, but two professors who have cultivated different fields may have little in common with one another except the fact that they are professors. Put them together and they reinforce one another in schoolmasterish preoccupations. Nor should any aspiring professor who is trying to make a choice between the opportunities offered him by a minor university and those presented by a good small college ever forget that the man who teaches in a small college suffers from low visibility. The name of a college which has ten thousand students is frequently in the news and it therefore often happens that some specialist in paleontology reading of a football victory in Pennsylvania State College turns to some other person who is interested in his field and asks: "Who is the professor of paleontology up at Pennsylvania State College?" It does not so often happen that such a question is asked and answered about the smaller college.

There are certain advantages, however, which are very clearly on the side of the professor in the high-grade small college. Relatively less of his time must be devoted to the Chautauqua lecture type of course which is presented to a large number of students, and since his time is not spent upon this sort of thing, he does not experience the degrading effect upon the mind of popularization. Further, a great deal of a professor's time in a large state institution is often spent in various political activities which are thought to contribute to his security or to help him to attain advancement; this type of thing must be relatively less important in the smaller institution. For a man who has well developed esthetic principles which govern his attitude toward his work, a man who would like to keep his contribution within his own breast until it is ripe, the small college has a further very pronounced advantage: a professor in a small college is not usually under any immediate necessity to publish or lose his job.

V. On War

20

WAR AND THE MORES

1940

PERHAPS THE MOST useful of all sociological concepts is that of the *mores*. The word *mores* is a Latin importation of plural form possessing no singular in English. William Graham Sumner introduced the term into the vocabulary of sociology and used it to designate the customs which regulate the standards of right and wrong, and indeed all the standards of value, of a people. It is a sociological truism that the mores can make anything right and prevent condemnation of anything, a view which Sumner developed with inexhaustible fertility of argument and example in his book, *Folkways*. Sumner distinguished two classes of customs: the folkways, which are simple customs, and the mores, which are regarded as necessary for group welfare and are supported by strong sanctions.

Our conceptions of right and wrong are in fact almost altogether dependent upon the customs of the group to which we belong. In some cultures unwanted children are strangled or exposed with no thought of wrong. In others the old are abandoned or killed as a matter of duty and affection. The sexual exclusiveness of marriage varies widely over the face of the earth, as does also the value attached to premarital chastity. The values of property, of human rights, and of life itself seem to be fixed almost arbitrarily by the custom of the group. These basic standards, the mores, are the sacred customs which it is wrong to violate and right to follow.

Reprinted from *War in the Twentieth Century* (New York: The Dryden Press, 1940), pp. 485–92.

Their observance is regarded as somehow necessary for group welfare. Every group has such customs, but they vary widely from group to group. There is no absolute right or wrong anywhere in the world; everything is relative; there are only acts which are right or wrong in accordance with the code of some particular group.

All social institutions may be thought of as founded upon the mores. Institutions represent formal trends in the mores. An institution consists of a concept and a structure. The concept is the basic idea of the institution; the structure is a body of functionaries prepared to act in a certain way in a prescribed conjuncture of circumstances. Institutions derive their existence from the mores, and are at all times dependent upon them. The law, for example, cannot successfully depart very far from the moral sense of the people. Many of the difficulties of wartime social change arise from the attempt to create institutions for which the existing mores furnish no basis.

We may therefore estimate the effect of war upon society by analyzing the effect of war upon the mores. War changes the mores in a number of ways. Ordinarily the mores change rather slowly; they adapt to the changing situation and perhaps it may be said that they evolve, but ordinarily they do not go through striking or sudden metamorphoses. Because they are the basic standards of many people, because they are interwoven with the habits of many people which are in turn interwoven with one another, the mores present a stubborn resistance to any attempt at a sudden change.

War produces confusion and decay of the mores. It is beyond human nature for a group to change its mores suddenly, and yet the driving necessities of war demand that the group should suddenly change its mode of living. And it does change it, as needs it must when the devil drives, but it retains its old moral ideas. Gradually new, wartime mores arise to cover novel situations; also adaptations of the old mores. There are many violations of the prewar mores, some of which are condoned by the mores of war time. Still the former mores persist and one cannot violate them even under the urge of imperative necessity without paying some penalty. In time this confusion of the mores may give way to a new moral consensus, but that is a matter of many years, and wars do not usually last that long. After the war, there is a process, but not an equal and opposite process, of readjustment of the mores to the conditions of peace.

A social philosopher who was sufficiently bold might attempt to describe the effect of war upon the mores in a single formula. The formula might possibly be something like this: In war time there is a decay of all the established moralities, which tend to be replaced by hedonistic life adjustments on a short-term basis. In a word, the mores decline, and vices spread and become respectable. This formula does not, of course, describe the nascent new codes of war time.

If we study the impact of war upon the mores more soberly and in more detail, we discover a long series of moral dislocations comparable to the dislocations of economic life which war entails. The most obvious change in the mores is the reversion to the tribal morality which commands solidarity within the group and enmity toward those outside. This moral distinction between the in-group and the out-group is not, of course, a real change in the mores, although it looks like one, because the mores allow for certain exceptions in case of war. There is a codicil to the commandment, "Thou shalt not kill," to the effect that killing is permissible in war. Nothing is said about this codicil, but nearly everyone accepts it. It is significant that only a few sects take the commandment against killing literally and become conscientious objectors. Revision to tribal morality not only relaxes the taboo against homicide, but renders various kinds of deception entirely legitimate when perpetrated upon the enemy. In-group morality also imposes great obligations of solidarity and mutual aid within the group; it is understood that there must be social peace within the group when an enemy threatens. In the first World War, France had her *union sacrée*, Germany her *Burgfrieden;* in other countries also there was a truce to inner struggles. Kirkpatrick has called attention to the way in which modern methods of communication reinforce this feeling of intimacy within the group. Propaganda, the radio, and the movies make the leaders of the nation members of every intimate group. They are almost literally members of every family. It is noteworthy that Germany had obviously made the transition to the tribal morality by the time Hitler came to power. The tribal morality of the in-group and the out-group is contained in the mores of every military power. Reversion to this morality is a necessary precondition of war.

War creates a great number of new social situations and forms of human association which are not regulated by any pre-existing custom. People of all social classes are thrown together in the air-raid shelters. This is precisely the sort of situation which calls for the development of new folkways which may in time harden into mores. The great concentrations of population in the armies are regulated as to the most important ways of life by military rules, but there are many interstices in such a social order, and customs soon arise which furnish a sort of guidance. War sometimes creates entirely new communities or expands existing ones to several times their size. In such cases new mores must emerge. When some hundreds of young women, for example, are brought together in a new or greatly expanded community for the manufacture of munitions, they soon come to live by a greatly changed morality. On a smaller scale are the adjustments of life to the ever-present gas mask, the "little brown box" which Britons have celebrated in song and feminine ingenuity has adorned.

War interrupts the routines of life corresponding to every major social institution and in time affects the mores upon which these institutions are founded. The basic conditions of family life are changed; men are taken out of the family by the army, and women by the new tasks of war; many children are sent to refuges in the country. Death breaks up many families; other families lose their physical basis when their members become refugees. Under such circumstances the mores supporting the family must inevitably give way. The same kind of situation changes the mores of private property. Under war conditions, the control of the individual over his property is weakened; the whole attitude toward private property changes.

The school must also give up its sacred routines. Teachers must forget some of the fine points of their art and do the best job they can under difficult circumstances. Even the church must change the nature of its message. In general, it seems to be the task of the church to rationalize the moral *volte-face* involved in the reversion to tribal morality; the church must explain that the commandment "Thou shalt not kill" does not mean "Thou shalt not kill," but that under certain circumstances, such as a holy war, it really means "Thou shalt kill the enemies of thy country without mercy and by every means in thy power." . . .

A perplexing phase of the change of mores in time of war is the great apparent gain in the mores of humanitarianism. It is not barbarism alone which grows under war conditions, for there is a great effulgence of humanitarianism and idealism. For the most part, this phenomenon is a phase of the reversion to the tribal morality of the in-group and the out-group. The direction of hostility toward the enemy leaves the in-group at peace. There is a rapid growth of organizations for the care of the wounded, the widowed, and other victims of the hazards of war. Members of different social strata draw closer together in the common cause. Members of the group now have a common purpose, and realize at length that they are necessary to one another. Revelling in their new-found solidarity, sustained by a sense of their righteous cause, people vie with one aonther in service and sacrifice. There is often a "great spiritual awakening," or some movement of opinion so described by optimistic divines. In modern wars, where the economic strain is so important, sacrifice is often as valuable as service. A movement of the mores toward asceticism is therefore functionally appropriate. Chambers describes such a phenomenon in Germany in the early years of the first World War:

A wave of asceticism swept the country. Meetings and exhibitions were held to propagate the virtues of frugality. *Wanderredner* instructed eager audiences in the homely science of mastication. Schoolmasters and clergymen joined in the campaign for the plain and simple living. Civilized man has a complicated diet, and he is the most wasteful of feeders. The natural foods of his animal ancestry had much to recommend them, and the necessities of war indeed might restore a simpler, healthier life to the people at large.[1]

[1]   Frank P. Chambers, *The War behind the War*, Harcourt, Brace, 1939, p. 158.

Similar phenomena were observable in the United States, where the campaign against waste took on an aura of holiness.

The reversion to tribal morality is not quite sufficient to account for the growth of the humanitarian spirit during a war. In various ways a war emancipates people from their routines of habit and makes them see the social order in an unaccustomed light. There emerges a determination to make the nation over into a better and juster pattern when once the war has been settled; but first the war must be won. Liberal leaders acquiesce in this compromise, and frequently attain considerable recognition. The sacrifices which war asks of peoples demand constant redefinitions of war aims; in such oratorical interludes of war many vague and unenforceable promises of reform are made. It is probable, too, that the mass misery of war has considerable effect. Humanitarian efforts flourish in neutral as well as belligerent countries. Great campaigns for war relief were started in the United States almost immediately after the commencement of hostilities in 1939. . . .

The end of a war finds the mores in confusion. The mores of the pre-war period are still powerful and despite their losses, they are still the most important code governing behavior. There is certain to be a strong tendency to return to the former moral consensus, a tendency which Warren G. Harding expressed in his "back to normalcy" slogan. But situations have inevitably changed, and the old mores are no longer adapted to life conditions. In addition, new mores have arisen which contest the field with the older codes. Further, war leaves a great many people who are emancipated from nearly all codes; they have lost their old moorings but found no new ones. Culture conflict and personal shocks have combined to put them outside the influence of the ordinary controls of society. The soldier especially has come to live by a code which conflicts sharply with that of civilian life, and it is hard for him to find the road back. The humanitarianism of war is in eclipse in the post-war period, if not actually in disgrace, but there are many who still feel its influence. These frustrated idealists become the cynics and futilitarians of the post-war period. Naturally, when the mores are confused, it is the young who feel it most. Older persons somehow work out the necessary compromise, but the young tend to be thoroughly disorganized.

of the army has taken shape through some thousands of years of evolution in which new techniques have been slowly evolved and less effective techniques eliminated.

The army achieves its result of activating a million men with a single will by effectively annihilating the individual will of the soldier. It overrides the individual will; it refuses to recognize that the individual will exists and acts as if it did not exist. The soldier must obey. Orders come all the way down from the top. Everyone obeys someone. Everyone is responsible to someone. But no one is responsible to his subordinates or may be questioned by them. The flow of commands, of will, is in one direction only.

When a man becomes a soldier, he surrenders to his duly constituted superiors his right to think and act as an individual. He makes a voluntary sacrifice of his private will, his last voluntary act until the military machine at length disgorges him; and if he is conscripted, one might argue about the voluntary nature of this surrender. In any case, the army must start with some sort of consent on the part of the soldier: he must somehow want to do his bit. The army instills in the man the habits of the soldier, and it has its own techniques for this, but it must always build upon pre-existing habits and attitudes. Men can become soldiers because their previous life has so conditioned them that the military way of life is possible.

When a man has made the sacrifice of his own private will, it remains for the army to instill in him those habits of obedience which make him the perfect instrument of the will of his superiors. The army begins to teach him to obey orders. There are a great many orders to obey, for one reason, because the living together and working together of great masses of men demand regulation of the minutiae of existence, for another, because it is thought good to give the private soldier plenty of practice in obeying orders. Orders are multiplied. The emphasis is upon precision, upon snappiness in executing commands, upon the synchroniza-

---

structure here described. For a description of the army system of the U.S.S.R., see Albert Rhys Williams, *The Soviets*, Harcourt Brace, 1937, pp. 499–507.

Why War Changes the Mores

At the risk of some repetition, it seems desirable to describe somewhat more specifically the ways in which war changes the mores of a people.

The mores change because the situation changes in such a manner that the mores are no longer adapted to it. When husband and wife live apart for long periods, the mores of monogamy give way; so with other family mores. Furthermore, war breeds widespread poverty, and hunger is a universal solvent of institutions: no moral code is proof against starvation. Nor can patriotism or military discipline or fear of the secret police hold the people in line when hunger really begins to get in its work. It is, of course, the aim of economic warfare to break the enemy's will to resist by means of hunger.

The mores change because the normal process of transmitting the mores to the younger generation is interrupted. The family institution suffers greatly in war, and the family is a great conservative force as regards the mores. When members are removed from the family, the moral equilibrium inevitably changes.

The family and the intimate groupings of the community normally keep their members under surveillance and prevent behavior contrary to the mores. *In war human beings are emancipated from these groups and are free to behave in the manner which strikes their fancy.*

War produces a great number of ruined persons; individuals who no longer have a stake in the moral order and are therefore beyond the ordinary standards of good and evil. Some have lost their occupations or careers, some their families, some their homes and their families; some suffer from incurable injuries or diseases. All such persons are a threat to the moral order. They are often widely diffused through the nation. They carry confusion wherever they go.

War stimulates internal migrations and thus produces conflict of cultures. In the warring nations hordes of refugees tramp back and forth in accordance with the progress of the war. Millions move about as a result of economic changes. Even in neutral nations the unsettlement is felt. The migration of Negroes to northern cities of the United States during the first World War was an enormous movement involving at least 400,000 migrants in a brief period. It unsettled the rural South as well as the urban areas of the North. In the War of 1939 the attempt to evacuate the larger cities created stupendous movements of population. The effects of such mass migrations are certain to be incalculably great.

Wartime propaganda inevitably disturbs the equilibrium of the mores. The mobilization of the national effort necessarily involves the fracture of some of the settled habits of the group, and often propaganda is employed for this purpose. When some of the mores are attacked, the authority of the others is weakened.

The morality of the soldier exerts a disturbing influence upon the rest of the population. The soldier's moral code is much simpler than that of the civilian. He must be brave and obedient, as clean as possible, and loyal to his own small in-group. Sexual license, "scrounging," and pilfering, and the cultivation of various vices are permitted to the soldier. Outside the purely military sphere the soldier is not held repsonsible.

In war time there is an immense extension of social control of the military sort, which favors a decline of moral responsibility. Moral responsibility presupposes autonomy, which is lacking when one is under orders. This facilitates further decline of social norms. The vices flourish in war time. The inability of anyone to make plans, both because the future is uncertain and because it depends upon the will of others, is another factor in the decline of moral responsibility. Both soldiers and civilians must spend a great deal of time waiting: waiting for supplies, for orders, waiting for something to happen, waiting for news of what has already happened. And this is very demoralizing.

21

THE ARMY AS A SOCIAL INSTITUTION

1940

The Army as a Social Institution

EVERY CIVILIZED nation has its army and its milita[ry es]tablishment. In the piping times of peace, and in the demo[cratic] nations, the military organization occupies a subordinate [place.] Soldiers must take orders from civilians. When the prosp[ect of] peace seems favorable, the army may suffer sharp losses of p[erson]nel and be forced to economize rigidly. When war come[s the] situation changes. The army fights the battles; it will win th[em,] therefore its needs come first. There is either an actual m[ilitary] dictatorship or something closely approaching it. The army [insti]tution dominates all others. Family, school, church, the eco[nomic] system, the ordinary processes of government, must all be [sacri]ficed to the imperious demands of the military machine. Th[e war] pervades the whole of life. It is therefore important to try to [under]stand the nature of the army institution.

The army is a social machine by which a million men a[re en]abled to act with a single will. In order to meet a crisis, men [neces]sarily adopt a military form of organization; this is the [raison] *d'être* of military organization and discipline.[1] The organi[zation]

Reprinted from *War in the Twentieth Century* (New York: The Dr[yden] Press, 1940), pp. 514–26.

1   The material that follows is for the most part based upon [a descrip]tion of the American army. More democratic forms of army orga[nization] have sometimes been attempted, for example, at various times [in the] American armies and in the new Russian army. It is the opinio[n of the] writer that all armies would tend to reproduce, sooner or later, mos[t...]

tion of the movements of masses. Close order drill and the manual of arms are well adapted to this sort of training. There is also a multitude of petty regulations in any army. They are and must be enforced in an utterly humorless manner, and they involve much ordering about.

There is great emphasis upon appearance. It is thought that a man cannot possibly be a good soldier unless he holds himself erect, salutes in a crisp manner, and keeps his uniform spotless. One might suppose, with all this emphasis upon appearance, that uniforms would be so designed that it would be easy to keep them presentable; but if one supposed this he would be utterly wrong. Uniforms, except a special few adapted to execptional conditions (destroyers are called the "dungaree navy") are very hard to keep clean and presentable. Private soldiers suspect that buttons are put on the uniforms just because they are hard to shine! Certainly the emphasis upon appearance plays a real part in the making of the soldier. This emphasis is based upon a sound psychology, at least in part, because there is a close relationship between morale and appearance. And it is often true that the less time the private soldiers have for themselves the better it is for their morale.

The social system of the army involves a caste-like division between commissioned officers and enlisted men, originally derived from actual caste differences between the two groups. The officer is a gentleman; the enlisted man is the instrument which he uses in his profession. In all respects the officer is set off from the enlisted man. He wears a uniform of superior quality and bears glittering insignia of rank. He lives better than the men; draws more pay; stays at better hotels; smokes a different brand of cigarettes. The officer cannot gamble with enlisted men. He cannot carry a package. If he were, with the most honorable intentions, to court a sergeant's daughter, he might be relieved of his commission. In the presence of enlisted men, the officer must always behave with gentlemanly reserve, exacting the last ounce of respect due him and his rank.

A considerable amount of army training consists of learning the ritual of respect toward commissioned officers, a subject known as military courtesy. The private salutes when he meets an officer;

he salutes first and holds the salute until recognized. Between the officer and the man there is an immense social distance. In the old Austrian army, it is said, the enlisted man was supposed to keep an actual physical distance of five paces from the officer. The private is supposed to ask the permission of his immediate superior, the noncom, before speaking to the commissioned officer. When he speaks to the officer, he refers to himself in the third person.

In some measure, the social distance between the officer and the man is functionally appropriate. It helps to make subordination bearable by preventing any real clash of personalities. In the army, ceremony not merely regulates the relationship between officer and man; often it *is* the relationship. The wise officer does not overstep his ceremonial limits; he avoids a clash of wills by restraining himself to the exercise of his generally accepted institutional prerogatives. The army has even evolved a "voice of command," a flat, emotionless but vibrant tone which gives the command with complete impersonality. By staying within his own sphere, by rigidly observing the decorum proper to his rank, by making his domination an impersonal thing, the officer makes it possible for the men to say, "We salute the uniform and not the man."

Subordination to the commissioned officer is also possible because he has prestige. Prestige is a quality with which the leader is endowed in the imagination of those he leads, whether rightly or wrongly we need not say. The leader, such as the officer or the teacher, shows only a small and resplendent portion of his personality to the persons he leads, and they immediately fill out the total picture of the man in the same shining pattern. The social distance which we have described is a necessary condition of the officer's prestige, and therefore of the smooth working of the army system. It is often said that familiarity breeds contempt. In the army, carefully regulated unfamiliarity breeds respect.

This ritual of respect, however, is nearly all a one-way respect. The officer must return the private's salute. If he is wise, he will studiously avoid overstepping the ritualized limits, and he will as studiously demand the fulfillment of all that is legally due him. But it is contrary to the idea of the army for the superior to make any direct concessions to the will of the subordinate. In civilian life we surround ourselves with certain rituals of respect to others. We say *please* and *thank you*. One of the first things we teach children is to say *please;* all our lives we keep on saying it and hearing it, unless we join the army. All this is a concession to the autonomy of the other person. It is precisely these concessions that the army cannot make. The officer cannot say *please* because the private is not supposed to have any will of his own. That is the nature of the army system. The wise officer, and most of them are quite wise in such matters, avoids all situations where the private might do something for him of his own free will. That way lies sycophancy.

So rigid is the military system of annihilating the individual will that it accepts very few excuses of non-performance of duty. Freud has pointed out that the excuse, "I forgot," will be accepted in many places, but there are two persons who will never permit it to stand: one's sweetheart and one's drill sergeant. Every forgetting, every omission, every neglect, every sub-standard performance, is treated as an instance of the surgence of the private will of the soldier and is sternly penalized. Only so can the army maintain discipline.

Like the commissioned officer, the non-commissioned officer must maintain discipline. He cannot, however, employ the same methods. He cannot employ any great amount of social distance. He must live with the men; he is one of them. His office may be taken away from him for any small misdeed and he may revert to the ranks. He must meet the men on their own level, answering their force with his own force and employing the harsh persuasions of army penalties. It is here that the struggle between the army system and the buck private's private will is carried out. It is the sergeant whom the men hate. The non-com must be something of a natural leader or his cause is lost. The development of a staff of efficient non-coms is one of the most difficult parts of organizing and training an army.

The army has a culture which differs sharply from that of the larger group. It has its own traditions, its own mores, its own culturally transmitted attitudes. It has also, as we shall see, its own moral code by which soldiers live and die. The songs, the tall tales, the rumors, sagas, and meaningless catchwords developed by the American Expeditionary Force would fill volumes. Linton has made an excellent case for an interpretation of certain phenomena as forms of spontaneously generated totemism.[2] The process of adjustment to army life involves as one of its aspects the assimilation of the army culture.

When an army system is functioning properly, we say that the soldiers display *morale* or *esprit de corps*. In order to display these qualities, an army must not only be well drilled; it must also be activated by a sense of pride in army membership, and a sense of army solidarity. Patriotism helps, but is perhaps not altogether necessary; Caesar's Tenth Legion had *esprit de corps*, but one may question whether it was patriotic in the modern sense. In order to have a good army, most of the soldiers must have real faith in their fellows and in their commanders. *Esprit de corps* is perhaps commoner and easier to obtain than *morale*. Any outfit that is well dressed, well equipped, and well drilled would be likely to have *esprit de corps*. Troops may be said to have *morale* when they show their ability to fight and to hold on against odds. The English rearguard action at the beginning of the first World War and the French defense of Verdun rank as great exhibitions of *morale*. Neither *esprit de corps* nor *morale* is in any way inconsistent with a great deal of grumbling and apparent internal friction in the army system. All soldiers grumble, at least according to tradition. Quite possibly it makes them better soldiers.

Roucek has described the transition from civilian to military life in the following vivid passage:

The soldier finds out that the military life is a hard one. It involves a renunciation of the comforts and securities of a normal domestic existence. The denial of the body, the deprivation of the senses, the suppression of spontaneous impulses, the forced drills, the exhaustion of the marrow, the neglect of cleanliness—all these conditions of active service leave no place for the normal decencies of

[2]   Ralph Linton, "Totemism and the A. E. F.," *American Anthropologist*, Vol. 26, pp. 296 ff.

existence. In the place of the average life is offered iron-bound discipline, a development of the sense of duty, a worship of obedience to authority, a new clothing, a regular and planned existence, a lack of informality in social usages, the absence of womankind, relatives, friends. The soldier is swallowed up in this current without any regard to his previous background, his previous attitudes, or his intellectual capacity. . . . All individuality and initiative are suppressed. . . .

The most important events in men's lives in such days are passed to and fro in letters. All the emotions are poured out in written script, disguised or declared, adorned with all the phrases of sentiment. Letters give an outlet to the emotions, and they are read and reread with great pleasure because they recall all the pleasant aspects of civilian life. Little traits of behavior are recalled, even though they once seemed commonplace and tedious.[3]

Of all this we question only the phrase "the neglect of cleanliness," at least in respect to the American forces. Nor does it seem likely that cleanliness is neglected in any modern army. Under front-line conditions, of course, cleanliness becomes almost impossible, which may justify the phrase.

The army toughens men. It must toughen them so that they can endure hardship, so that they can kill or be killed. When civilians are being recruited and trained, the army must accept men who faint at the sight of a hypodermic needle, and turn them into heroes who can face death without flinching. It is a hard job, but it can be done. This is the rationale of much of the army regimen and a great deal of the army culture. This is the reason for the long marches completed on aching feet, for the interrupted sleep, the chilly barracks, the hard-boiled non-coms, the unpleasantness of taking orders, the lack of holidays, the parades on any and all occasions, the boxing matches, and all the things which revolt the occasional sensitive soul which is subjected to the regimen. There develops in the army a cult of toughness for the sake of toughness: it is a good thing to be tough and the toughest man is the best man. The soldiers fight with one another because it is the thing to do. Each one wants

[3]   Joseph S. Roucek, "Social Attitudes of the Soldier in War Time," *The Journal of Abnormal and Social Psychology*, 1935–1936, Vol. XXX, pp. 164–174.

to be able to say, "I can take it and I can dish it out." They cultivate vulgarity and obscenity and the stronger forms of profanity
because it is virile to do so; they swear and threaten one another
constantly in order to show how tough they are. Refinement, of
course, is taboo; coarseness is the thing sought after. In comrade
relations, or in time of danger, it is one for all and all for one; in all
other matters it is dog eat dog. Aggressiveness is a necessity for
survival in such a group. The character ideal of the army is that of
the hard-boiled non-com made famous by certain recent movies.
There seems no possibility of doubting that the toughening process
really works.

Some of the toughening process is art and some of it nature.
The military tradition has evolved through some centuries. No one
person planned it but many persons have improved upon it, and
the tradition is wiser than any of its practitioners. We may explain
how such machines work without implying that anyone has planned
them to work in this way and no other. It is clear, for example, that
one thing which makes men willing to die is the fact that the army
has interrupted all their life plans and their life-long habits and
prevented them from making any plans of their own thereafter.
They are willing to die because there is now less to tie them to life.
It is doubtful whether anyone planned army institutions with this
end in view, but that is the way they work.

The ultimate aim of all this, it should be said, is to weld the men
together into a social machine which will not disintegrate in a crisis
situation. The parts of the machine must fit together perfectly; the
parts must be interchangeable, and the succession to authority must
be clear and undisputed. Every man must be so trained that he performs his job mechanically. It is interesting to note that any less
well-organized group experiences a considerable period of confusion and delay when it meets a severe crisis. Now this confusion
and delay would be fatal in the face of an enemy army; therefore
one man is made responsible and is trained, as far as possible, to
meet all crises that are expected to arise.

The army achieves its results, but at a terrific cost. It is not
really possible to annihilate the will of the individual soldier; it is
merely possible to force that private will to express itself in some

other form, which is often a vicious one. The army technique breeds its own forms of resistance. The attempt to annihilate the individual engenders a particularly vicious form of individualism. The one-way flow of will from the superior to the inferior generates a counter-will which resists authority in all its forms. The soldier traditionally shirks his duty; he "soldiers" on the job. The use in common speech of the words "soldiering" and "regimenting" is eloquent of popular recognition of these military vices. And "passing the buck" (*non est mea culpa*) is widely known as the "old army game." This shirking of duty may become quite extreme. The writer has seen a work detail of fifty or more men start off with two men to watch them and arrive at its destination with no more than half of those who started. After a time, the soldier spends his mental energy in figuring out ways to shirk his duty; it is as natural that he should do so as that a prisoner should try to escape from prison. Apparently the military form of organization cannot remain efficient for any length of time. An army is almost certain to be inefficient just because it is an army.

A few officers of rare ability manage to build up in the soldiers a personal loyalty strong enough to overcome in large part this resistance of the soldier against domination. For such leaders of men, the soldiers give that last ounce of exertion which, as it has been said, can never be commanded but must always be offered up freely. Robert E. Lee was such a man; so, probably, was Stonewall Jackson, and many stories tell of the devotion which Napoleon inspired. General Pershing was not of the breed of which we speak. It should be noted that such officers are more than institutional figureheads and they are more than efficient managers and commanders; they manage somehow to become real as persons. They do much to overcome the institutional handicaps of the army.

The conditions of the soldier's life change from generation to generation, but there is a characteristic soldier mentality which seems to have been about the same in all ages and places. The soldiers who threw dice for the garments of Christ have much in common with the men in the front lines in the twentieth century. The military mentality is in part a result of the actual conditions of war, and in part a product of the army as a social environment.

The soldier is constantly subordinated, and he is subjected to a rigorous routine; therefore he has great need of a life of his own which is not subjected to army regulations. This he finds in barracks life, in amusements, often vicious, or in phantasy. The soldier is subject to an alien will. Usually he does not even know the meaning of the operations in which he takes part; he can make no plans of his own because he is under orders. Therefore the soldier is irresponsible; he does not know what the plans of the high command are, neither is he greatly interested in them. (This same disinterest is said to be observable in Fascist nations. It obviously stems from some of the same roots.) Because he can make no plans, because he is deprived of many of the comforts of life, because a great deal of his time is spent in just waiting and those empty hours must be filled somehow, because life itself is uncertain, the soldier adopts a philosophy of life on a short-term hedonistic basis—hence his vices.

He develops his own characteristic morality. He must be obedient; he must do his duty in a fashion, that is, he must not shirk in the hour of danger. His morality permits, however, an endless amount of trickery against constituted authority. He must be loyal to his own in-group, but that is not difficult because it is a very small in-group. He stands by his comrades. That is just about the sum total of the soldier's moral code on the positive side. The military machine has him; it regulates him; he has no longer much need of morality. Rather, he has need of escape. He achieves a moral code which facilitates escape.

The soldier's morality condones a great many things which are not permitted in civil life. The soldier despises civilians; he believes that they hate him (soldiers and dogs keep off the grass). Almost any trick upon a civilian is legitimate. The soldier also hates men in different branches of the service. The sailor hates the marines; the infantry hates the cavalry; everybody hates the military police. Probably he also hates his own officers and even the well-intentioned Y.M.C.A. All these hates found expression in 1918 in the bitter question, "Who won the war?"

As to sex morality, anything is permitted except homosexuality. Naturally the soldier does not expect to keep promises made to women. The soldier's life does not permit either privacy or fastidiousness in the sexual life; therefore he can visit a prostitute and afterwards stand in line with a hundred others while waiting for a prophylactic.

The sense of property is completely metamorphosed in the army. Partly this is a matter of the want of goods and the lack of money. Anyone who has observed the complicated financial operations by which a private soldier sometimes raises a dollar will understand this. Partly it is a matter of a changed morality. The soldier has little respect for the property of others. He "scrounges," to use a euphemism of the first World War, and his morality justifies him in scrounging.

Of course there is no taboo upon such ordinary vices as drinking and gambling in the army. Of course one gambles with his pay, and gets drunk if he wins. The compulsion is all in favor of such indulgence rather than against it.

Obviously there are compensations in the soldier's way of life. Moral irresponsibility is a great privilege for some. For others, the sense of social security in the army system is worth all its sacrifices, even the dangers of war. The easy comradeship and tribal solidarity of the barracks life also gives many otherwise frustrated persons a sense of belonging. In the actual combat situation, which even in war is rare, there are, of course, yet other compensations. If anyone doubts that army life has its compensations, let him attend a convention of the American Legion. It is perfectly clear that for many of the veterans, their war experiences mean about the same thing as his college does to the old grad at the reunion.

In the officer ranks, the penalties of the military form of organization are scarcely less. It is apparently not possible to paralyze the will of the subordinate without also paralyzing his intelligence. Officers are under orders; they, too, are taught to believe that the man giving the commands is always right. There is little or no flow of ideas from the bottom to the top of the officer ranks, and, since one can come to the upper ranks only after long service in the lower, there is little creativeness on any level. In war time, the officer ranks are enriched by a great number of able persons trained in other professions and not accustomed to thinking in the military grooves. These men must go through a period of apprenticeship, but, after they learn the rules of the game, they probably contribute heavily to the improvement of traditional army methods.

The entire routine of army existence in the officer ranks contributes to the sclerosis of the army as a social system. The routinization of life, the emphasis upon ceremony and upon appearance, upon externals, the personal disorganization of the army officer in time of peace, the hierarchical system, the seniority system of promotion, the maddening slowness of promotion, lack of encouragement for originality and initiative, the freedom of military thought from vitalizing influences from the outside, emphasis upon past rather than future wars, the prejudices of caste and class unmodified by knowledge of or contact with the larger society and the changing world but rather enforced and rigidified by the narrow routine of the army post, contempt for the ideas of civilians—all these things conspire to make the army officer unduly conservative. This, in brief, is why armies are inefficient just because they are armies. Anyone who doubts that these things do in fact have an effect upon the military mind has only to read the works of Liddell Hart, in which the stupidities of the first World War are exposed with brutal realism. Probably Hart is somewhat unfair to the generals, but his comments are in the right direction. He is the army's best friend because its severest critic.

The army officer does, however, learn certain things extremely well. His training is narrow but it is thorough. An intelligent officer —and there are few who are not intelligent, however antediluvian their social and political opinions—is often one of the keenest practical psychologists in the world. He understands the art of command, which he has perfected by long practice, by trial and error, and by observation of others. The officer is often a wonderful administrator; he has drive and ability to get things done, and he knows men. The trouble is that the officer, because of the world he lives in, has a short-blooming mind. Since there is no way to eliminate those who have gone to seed, there are likely to be men in high office in almost any army who could not successfully organize and conduct a Sunday School picnic. The matter of efficient army organization calls for our best thought.

In sum, we may say that the social system of the army is one of dominance and subordination made bearable by social distance. Like any other social system, it has its own inherent strength and weakness. Its strength is its adaptation to crisis situations. Its weakness arises from the crushing of the more desirable manifestations of individuality. In time any army tends to become stagnant; it must be constantly revitalized if it is to function properly.

The process of levying and training a large civilian army puts great strain upon the army system. There is a shortage of officers in both commissioned and non-commissioned ranks. The army's caste system comes dangerously close to breaking down. In the peacetime army, the caste system works fairly well because there is in fact a great social gap between officers and men. Under war conditions, this tends to be less true. The conscripted soldiers are from all walks of life, and there are some who serve out the war as privates in spite of blue blood and social-register backgrounds. Among the new officers many utterly lack any of the hallmarks of gentility. Many are ill-trained, having neither the necessary technical knowledge nor any familiarity with the art of command. Many of us remember with amusement some of the "shavetails," and "ninety-day wonders" who exercised command in the first World War. Their impersonations of the army officer were sometimes rather weird. The men resent domination by such men, and rediscover all the soldier's ancient techniques of expressing this resentment. There is a great shortage of efficient non-coms. When one considers the inherent difficulties of the task, the achievements of England and America in training civilian armies in the 1914-1918 war seem little short of miraculous.

When the actual fighting begins, the ritual of the army undergoes rapid simplification. No longer does the private ask the permission of the non-com before speaking to the captain. Salutes are often overlooked; the salute becomes a real mark of respect to officers whom the men admire. They salute the man and not the uniform, which is a horrible departure from military tradition. Natural leaders appear among the men, and the men are apt to pay as much attention to them as to their officers. Once the men have tasted blood, it is not easy to get them into the training-camp and parade-ground state of mind again. There is more than humor in the statement that war certainly plays hell with an army.

22

THE VETERAN COMES HOME

1944

MANY FEATURES of army life contribute to a certain moral irresponsibility on the part of the soldier. The soldier is isolated from the family that nourished him and kept him in tutelage until he entered military service. He is more or less out of contact with the young women of his own age who would ordinarily be his eligible mates; ordinarily he cannot marry and if he does marry he cannot live with his wife in the normal manner. The church with which he was formerly associated can reach him no more; in its place stands the army chaplain who, hardworking as he probably is, can hardly hope to control his flock of young men. The local community with its thousands of Mr. and Mrs. Grundys and its small groups of people whose opinion matters cannot any longer keep watch on the boy now in uniform and regulate his behavior by gossip. In a word, the soldier is emancipated from most, if not all, the controls of civilian life.

Economically, the soldier does not need to strive. Financial incentive is, for all practical purposes, non-existent. Food, shelter, clothing, and medical care are free goods, all made available to him without his asking. No planning or management on his part is likely to enable the soldier to obtain more than these elementary necessities plus a few equally elementary luxuries. He must do his military duty, and the army will take care of his needs.

Reprinted from *The Veteran Comes Back* (New York: The Dryden Press, 1944), pp. 56–62. By permission of Josephine Bouchard. © 1944 by Willard Waller.

Money does not and cannot mean to the soldier what it means to the civilian. It does not stand between him and starvation, guarantee his future, or purchase social position. It may therefore be spent recklessly or gambled with, and gambling is in fact a sort of fighting play that grows out of sadistic-aggressive tendencies cultivated by the army. While money has no real value for the soldier, simple luxuries are often extremely rare under war conditions; if he wants them badly enough he will not hesitate to pay fantastic prices—and, in fact, he has paid as much as three dollars for a lemon, five dollars for a bottle of 3.2 beer, fifty dollars for a bottle of whiskey. From the civilian's point of view, this is irrational behavior. In the soldier's world, it makes sense, because money has little value. In the case of the officer, long trips and sudden changes of residence make it expedient for him to keep large sums of cash in his pocket, which similarly produces an attitude toward money utterly alien to the civilian.

Because the soldier's life is not under his own control, he is freed from the sense of personal responsibility. He cannot plan, because he has no control over his future. His task is to play the part that the military machine assigns to him and to await the decisions of an inscrutable destiny. Even his time is not his to budget and to organize; it is all but useless for him to keep a date book or a schedule of engagements. Time is not money to the soldier and not a dimension of self-initiated designs. It is merely something that belongs to the army and that passes. Death is always possible, and it may be just around the corner. Any day, any hour may be the last. Small wonder that the soldier snatches eagerly whatever satisfactions his life affords without weighing the implications of his behavior with too great a degree of moral nicety.

The solidarity of soldier society gives plenary indulgence to those sins that soldiers are most likely to commit. Everyone else commits them, or so it seems, and therefore one's own behavior has social justification. The army attitude toward sex behavior traditionally permits a certain license. The rest of the world expects the soldier to behave with some freedom in such matters. Similarly, prescriptions and taboos concerning property change their nature when one goes from a civilian life to the army. Property may not only be appropriated and used by persons other than its legal owner, but it may also be put to many uses for which it was never intended, and it may be wantonly destroyed. Where masses of men are concerned, it does not seem to matter very much whether they are a group of chaplains or recruits for the regular army; both groups are highly destructive except when military discipline brings this tendency under control. However, the soldier's morality combined with his feelings of brotherhood in war demands the sharing of property to a degree unknown in civilian life. It is reported that Marines on Tarawa shared their last cigarettes, carefully fluffing up the package to hide the fact that it was the last. Such incidents have been reported many times in the annals of war. This is morality, and a high morality, although it is opposed to the customary practices of our society.

And it may come about that the soldier's morality demands the sacrifice of life itself. . . . Lieutenant Robert Craig, . . . on July 11, 1943, at Favoratta, Sicily, charged a group of a hundred Germans in order to draw their fire away from his men—a feat from which there was no possibility of personal survival. Lieutenant Craig received the Congressional Medal of Honor posthumously. Such instances are recorded in the annals of almost every nation. Apparently such things have always been, and men have always admired them.

He "Takes the Cash and Lets the Credit Go"

Almost inevitably, the soldier falls into a short-term hedonism. In the place of the accepted morality of civilian society, the soldier regulates his life by individualistic, hedonistic adjustments on a short-term basis. Morality is a matter of the long pull; it involves long-term rewards and punishments. The college boy studies now, content in the belief that he will collect his greatest rewards thirty years from now. He is continent, because he intends one day to marry; honest, not only because he has been taught to be honest but because, in the long run, it is much the best policy. But if the soldier has no future, as all too often he has not, morality cannot have much appeal. The soldier "takes the cash and lets the credit go," hoping to "live a little while before he dies forever." Giving up hope of the first-rate and despairing of the worth-while, he grasps eagerly at the cheap and quick and tawdry. When he returns to civilian life, it is difficult for him to adjust his life to long-term planning once again. It is harder for him to work for the distant future than it can ever be for the man who has never known war and the luxury of living entirely for the present.

The . . . novel *Shore Leave* tells of the reckless hedonism of the front-line fighters of the present war.[1] The novel, recounting certain episodes in the life of four young naval aviators, centers around one Crewson, a fabulous character who has a hectic love affair with a gorgeous creature named Gwynneth. These young men pride themselves on having seen the worst of war and braved its deadliest perils; only fighters count in their universe. They prefer their gold-braid tarnished and their uniforms almost in tatters, preferences that cause much grief to the shore-bound admirals and the special police. Civilians—male civilians—are vague creatures who mean little in the combat pilot's world. The chatter of civilians is so much hog-wash. Men of battle and of the sky need not even trouble to tell the truth to civilians; it is useless to try to communicate anything to them anyhow, and better to spin out some fantastic yarn. When a civilian explains that he would like to do his part, but what can he do with a wife, three children, and a mortgage, the young aviators become slightly nauseated. They joke, as did the soldiers of World War I, about what they are doing to maintain the morale of civilians. War aims are not for such men. They are for civilians; they are big sloppy words and combinations of words such as civilians like. The Four Freedoms? Big, sloppy words. Why do these men fight? Says Crewson, "You fight to win, period." One forgets so easily the end of war when he is actively engaged in the war process.

Like many other men who have a rendezvous with death, these young aviators have the morals of alley-cats. "All I ever see of a town any more are the bars, the hotels, and the women," as Crewson puts it. Crewson has a wife, but she is far away, and he may

---

[1]   Frederic Wakeman, *Shore Leave*. Farrar and Rinehart, 1944.

never have another shore leave, and the others have wives also, but such things do not matter in war. Crewson's wife is no more to him than a nasty reminder to call Operator Six at Great Neck. No property rights mean anything any more; money does not mean anything; nothing counts but liquor, women, and fighting. Like Hemingway's characters, the young men of Wakeman's novels philosophize sometimes and strike off crisp cynicisms when they are not too drunk. At least from the surface of their minds they exclude the thought of the morrow.

Courage and Valor Are the Highest Virtues

That the soldier develops compensatory virtues should go without saying. His job is to fight, to die if need be with antique courage. The pages of history are full of the names of brave soldiers who did their duty unto death, and literature abounds in eloquent tributes to such men. One of the best of such eulogies is Carlyle's little oration concerning the Swiss Guards at the Tuileries. It illustrates our point well.

Oh ye stanch Swiss, ye gallant gentlemen in black, for what a cause are ye to spend and be spent! Look out from the western windows, ye may see King Louis placidly hold on his way; the poor little prince royal "sportfully kicking the fallen leaves" . . . And ye? Left standing there, amid the yawning abysses, and earthquake of insurrection; without course, without command; if ye perish, it must be as more than martyrs, as martyrs who are now without a cause! The black courtiers disappear mostly; through such issues as they can. The poor Swiss know not how to act; one duty only is clear to them, that of standing by their post; and they will perform that . . .

Surely few things in the history of carnage are painfuler. What ineffaceable red streak, flickering so sad in the memory, is that, of this poor column of red Swiss, "breaking itself in the confusion of opinions"; dispersing, into blackness and death. Honor to you, brave men; honorable pity, through long times. Not martyrs were ye; and yet almost more. He was no king of yours, this Louis; and he forsook you like a king of shreds and patches; ye were but sold to him for some poor sixpence a day; yet would ye work for your wages, keep your plighted word. The work now was to die, and ye did it. Honor to you, Oh Kinsmen; and may the old Deutsch *Beiderkeit* and *Tapfer-keit*, and valor which is *worth* and *truth*, be they Swiss, be they Saxon, fail in no age! Not bastards; trueborn were these men; sons of the men of Semback, of Murten, who knelt but not to thee, Oh Burgundy! Let the traveler, as he passes through Lucerne, turn aside to look a little at their monumental lion; not for Thorwaldsen's sake alone. Hewn out of living rock, the figure rests there, by the still lake waters, in lullaby of distant-tinkling *ranz des vaches*, the granite mountains dumbly keeping watch all round; and though inanimate, speaks.[2]

All sorts and conditions of men have contributed to these armies, great and small, that died for duty and for honor—white, black, red, and yellow men, slaves and freeborn, criminals and law-abiders, infidels and God-fearers, all have been martyrs with or without causes. Often they were mercenaries who died so; sometimes they were poor "pressed men" forced all unwilling into service. They may have been evil men whose only goal was booty; possibly they were patriots enamored of a cause. It does not seem to have mattered very much: they were soldiers. Men will die just as readily—and as heroically—in a bad cause as in a good one. Housman tells of the army of mercenaries who "took their wages and are dead;" they "saved the sum of things for pay," but they might just as well have "died in defence of a chicken-brained harlot." They could equally well have been patriots who offered up their lives in a glorious cause. Their valor was their justification whether they died in good causes or bad. That is the implicit creed of the soldier. Valor is the great virtue—courage, steadfastness in duty, bravery.

So urgent is this virtue in the mind of the soldier that Christian civilian society accepts it unquestioningly, even though the implications are strongly pagan. The very Christian Robert E. Lee remarked after the Battle of Gettysburg: "The conduct of the troops was all that I could desire or expect, and they deserved success in so far as it can be deserved by heroic valor and fortitude."[3] The

2   Thomas Carlyle, *The French Revolution*, Vol. II, Chap. VII.

3   Douglas Southall Freeman, *R. E. Lee*. Scribner, 1934, Vol. III, p. 155.

major premise is clearly that success is deserved by courage and not by the merits of one's cause. How far is this from the "might is right" slogan that America uttered with such scorn when Kaiser Wilhelm proclaimed it in the 1914-1918 years? Not only is Lee's premise amoral in terms of Christian civilization; it is also the soldier's philosophy implicit.

Lincoln subscribed to the same credo in speaking of the same battle. In his Gettysburg Address he expressed sentiments utterly non-Christian in nature but marked by a high religious tone. "But in a larger sense, we cannot dedicate, we cannot consecrate, we cannot hallow this ground. The brave men, living and dead, who struggled here have consecrated it far above our poor power to add or detract." Religious, certainly; but certainly non-Christian; for Christianity, custodian of absolute truth, cannot grant that two opposed ideals can both be true—can both be virtuous. The consecration, therefore, that Lincoln pays tribute to, is one that arises from courage—great, valorous courage of men dedicated to *an* ideal. By implication the ideal itself—content of the cause—cannot matter because any army dedicated to an ideal and valorous in behalf of an ideal must be virtuous and capable of consecrating the battlefield. The content of the ideal (the end) is secondary; the valorous act of striving (the means) is primary.

It is interesting in this connection to examine our word "virtue." Its Latin root *virtus* is best translated as "valor." The roots of the pagan cult of bravery are in fact very deep in our culture. We cannot believe that any man who is brave can be wholly bad. The most abandoned criminal, the cruelest outlaw, if he dies bravely, wins a portion of our admiration and so softens somewhat our condemnation of his acts. For his courage has "consecrated the act" in our eyes—our still somewhat pagan eyes!

This central virtue of the soldier—like the other virtues that constitute his new morality—is far from useful in peacetime society. A man does not have much chance to be brave in civilian life. In fact, physical bravery does not matter greatly either by its presence or absence once the war is over. If a man is a coward, that rarely interferes with his business or profession; if he is brave, he rarely receives any credit for it. So with the other virtues of the soldier; they are often irrelevant to competitive peacetime living. If a man is loyal to his friends, very good, provided he does not carry the matter to extremes, but if he is too loyal, so that he sacrifices himself for others, then the more fool he.

By and large, virtue in the soldier inheres in just one kind of thing for which there are many names—adherence to duty, loyalty, steadfastness, bravery, call it what you will—and this one intensive and solidary virtue matters to the civilian hardly at all.

23

THE VETERAN'S ATTITUDES

1945

SOME FACTORS determining the peculiar attitudes of the veteran are the following:

Use as a means. The veteran has been used as a means, as an instrument of war, and has often suffered some damage in the process. All our Occidental religions and systems of ethics teach that we must treat people as ends and never use them as means; but the soldier is only a means and not an end at all, and, what is more, he is an expendable means. Few people recognize this contradiction consciously or can state it clearly, but many people react to it. The reaction to this dimly recognized contradiction produces the civilian's feeling of guilt toward the veteran, and contributes to his ultimate neglect of this man whom he has sacrificed to the national purpose. The veteran's realization of the manner in which he has been used accounts for much of his bitterness and for his all too frequent feeling that the world owes him a living. In some region of his mind the veteran, particularly if he has been injured, knows that no matter how successful a war may have been in attaining its political objectives, it can never be worth as much to himself as he has lost in fighting it.

Setback in competition. Closely allied to the above is the fact that the veteran has been set back in the process of competition.

Reprinted from the *Annals of the American Academy of Political and Social Science* 238 (March 1945) : 174–79.

The social arrangements of modern America are such as to guarantee that we cannot wage war without inflicting the maximum of injustice upon the soldier. Ours is a competitive society. Every man is supposed to take care of himself. It is the part of virtue, and almost the whole of virtue, for a man to try to get ahead in the world. The essential American idea is that it is possible for a man to rise to high position through industriousness, that the status which a man attains in society adequately reflects his ability and conscientiousness. All we ask of the young man is that he work and make the most of his own abilities. He is brought up to believe that that is his full social duty. In ordinary times, military service is no part of what one owes to the world. . . .

When war comes, we take these young men trained for peace and send them off to fight. Having conditioned our young men to compete and to look to their own interests, we compel them to sacrifice their personal good and their personal lives to the collective good. They could hardly have been worse prepared for the experience of war. We remove them from the competitive society for which they have been trained, and demand of them services and sacrifices that can really be justified only in a communal society in which each person lives for others. Then, with a pat on the back and some hypocritical words of praise, we return them to competitive society, where, for a time at least, they compete at a considerable disadvantage. . . .

While the man selected for military service is giving his time to the collective effort, others forge ahead in the competitive race of civilian life. . . . While we were away, as Vera Brittain put it, "others stayed behind and just got on—got on the better since we were away."[1]

Group solidarity. The veteran has had the almost mystical experience of solidarity with his fellows. This solidarity, or comradeship, characteristic of soldiers since time immemorial, is one of the few rewards of military life. When the man who has tasted this loyalty which is stronger than the love of life returns to the dog-eat-dog existence of civilians, he finds it unsatisfying. Therefore the veteran is often the victim of extreme disillusionment or else he spends himself in the vain effort to find in civilian life a solidarity which does not exist. This fruitless attempt to recapture his van-

[1]   Willard Waller, *The Veteran Comes Back* (New York: Dryden Press, 1944), pp. 106–7.

ished comradeship and the resentment of the fact that it cannot be found explain much of the veteran's behavior.

Various factors. In yet other ways the veteran has been conditioned by military life and possibly by combat in such a manner that he is no longer adapted to civilian living. He has been subjected to iron regimentation by a social machine in which his individual will counted for nothing and his very life was secondary to the purposes of the machine. From this come dependence, a need of direction, and at the same time rebellion against it. The veteran has learned a new code of morals in which courage and devotion to duty are the paramount virtues. He has changed his concept of the sanctity of private property and of the uses to which it may be put. He has acquired a new language and partly lost his facility with the old; he has grown familiar with fear, horror, and guilt and become a connoisseur of boredom in all its forms. Accustomed to ordering and being commanded, he has lost, or never gained, a mastery of those phases of life where everything depends upon consent. In all these ways the veteran has been alienated from civilian society.

Changes in homeland. The veteran's maladjustment is enhanced by the changes which occur in his homeland while he is away. In time of war, communities become disorganized, sex and family morality decays, the relations of classes are profound altered, usually becoming embittered, living standards deteriorate, strange new political creeds and practices arise, a curiously problematic generation of neglected youth grows to maturity. The soldier observes few of these changes, and suffers their full impact all at once when he becomes a veteran and returns to civilian society.

Some Problematic Attitudes of Veterans

The great majority of veterans ultimately adjust to civilian life and become useful citizens. All must, however, go through a period of some maladjustment before they can settle down and adapt their personalities to "the savage wars of peace." Some never adjust, but retain their typical veteran attitudes throughout life.

These attitudes profoundly affect the veteran's adjustment to industry.

Some problematic attitudes of veterans are the following:

Bitterness toward civilians. The veteran is often bitter, because he is the one singled out to fight and die and experience horrors, because he gives so much and others so little, because civilians see the glamour of war and he sees the dirt and the dead men, because of his comrades who have been killed or wounded and perhaps allowed to starve when the fighting is over—because he has been used as a means. This bitterness is closely related to the veteran's tendency toward explosive aggression, which is most common among those who have broken mentally or nervously, though by no means confined to that group.

This characteristic, understandable bitterness of the veteran sometimes complicates his adjustment to industry when he comes back and finds that he must work under the supervision of civilians for whom as a class he has acquired a certain contempt. Perhaps he must try to submit himself to the orders of a man of his own age, who is, in his mind, not merely a "soft civilian," but a "draft-dodger," or "4-F-er."

Dependence. The tendency of veterans to become dependent is traditional. Partly it results from objective factors, from wounds or disabilities which have not been overcome or from lack of adequate employment or from pauperizing charity in the postwar years. But there are also attitudes engendered by military service which predispose to dependency. The veteran knows very well that when we use a man to fight a war we owe him something; history has given many examples of this attitude. Then, too, the soldier becomes institutionalized and thus to some extent unfitted for civilian life. One does not need to strive in the Army, or to plan or foresee; one needs only to give himself over to the great machine which takes care of everything and asks nothing in return save unflinching devotion. As a result of such things, the veteran often feels that society owes him a living; and until he gets over this attitude he cannot make a satisfactory adjustment to our kind of economic society.

We may suppose that many of our present soldiers will find it easy to become dependent. Many are depression children, accustomed from infancy to look to the Government for support. Many had no employment record before joining the Army. Many had known unemployment or employment in blind-alley jobs. Even before the war, a large percentage of them considered economic security their most urgent personal problem.[2] Bossard has pointed out that more than half the families of those inducted into military service in eastern urban areas are known to the social service exchanges in their areas.[3] One of the least pleasant aspects of the situation is that the soldiers are now being fed a lot of buncombe concerning the probable utility of army skills in civilian life.

Impatience with talk. For various reasons, but particularly because army life does not permit discussion of orders, the soldier comes to value action and to be impatient with talk. The veteran retains this trait, which is an extremely dangerous one, because we can arrive at certain kinds of decisions only through discussion, and the man who disbelieves in discussion is the ready tool of the demagogue who talks against talk and promises direct action. If labor trouble arises, some veterans may be inclined to go to extremes. Other important effects of this impatience with talk arise in the political sphere.

Distorted family attitudes. Military experience has deprived a whole generation of young men of some years of informal education in family life, and has in addition twisted attitudes toward sex and the family into strange patterns. We must therefore expect a period of widespread confusion and trouble in family relations.

[2]   See Howard M. Bell, *Youth Tell Their Story: A Study of the Conditions and Attitudes of Young People in Maryland between the Ages of 16 and 24,* Washington: American Council on Education, 1938.
[3]   James H. S. Bossard, "Family Problems in Wartime," *Psychiatry, Journal of the Biology and Pathology of Interpersonal Relations,* Feb. 1944.

The Bibliography of Willard Waller

1928   Review of Edgar M. Foltin, *Die chronisch erhöht Gefährlichen mit besonderer Berücksichtigung ihrer Behandlung im englischen Recht,* in *Journal of Criminal Law and Criminology,* 18, no. 4 (February) : 626.

Review of Gerhard Daniel, *Gefährlichkeit und Strafmass im Sinne der positiven Kriminalistenschule,* in *Journal of Criminal Law and Crimonology,* 18, no. 4 (February) : 626.

Review of André Touleman, *Le Progrès des Institutions Pénales,* in *Journal of Criminal Law and Criminology,* 19, no. 2, pt. I (August) : 286.

1929   "A Deterministic View of Criminal Responsibility," *Journal of Criminal Law and Criminology,* 20: 88–101.

Review of Robert Michels, *Sittlichkeit in Ziffern?* in *Journal of Criminal Law and Criminology,* 20, no. 1 (May) : 156–57.

Waller, Willard, and Rice, Stuart N., "Stereotypes," in *Personality and the Social Order,* Ernest W. Burgess, ed. (Chicago: University of Chicago Press), pp. 192–97.

1930   *The Old Love and the New: Divorce and Readjustment* (Philadelphia: H. Liveright).

1931   Review of Sophonisba R. Breckinridge, *Marriage and the Civil Rights of Women: Separate Domicile and Independent Citizenship,* in *American Journal of Sociology,* 37, no. 1 (July) : 147–48.

We have included only published material in this bibliography.

1932   *The Sociology of Teaching* (New York: John Wiley and Sons).

1933   "Personality Changes in Practice Teachers," *Publications of the American Sociological Society*, 27: 148–49.

"The Professor Looks at Students," *The Old Main Bell*, May, pp. 9–10, 34.

1934   "Insight and Scientific Method," *American Journal of Sociology*, 40, no. 3 (November) : 285–97.

Review of Gladys Hipple Watson, *Success and Failure in the Teaching Profession*, in *American Journal of Sociology*, 39, no. 5 (March) : 723.

1935   Cowley, W. H. and Waller, Willard, "A Study of Student Life," *Journal of Higher Education*, 6, no. 3 (March) : 132–42.

"Personality Changes in Practice Teachers," *Journal of Educational Sociology*, 9, no. 2 (October) : 556–64.

1936   Hawkins, Edward Russell and Waller, Willard, "Critical Notes on the Cost of Crime," *Journal of Criminal Law and Criminology*, 26 (January) : 679–94.

"Discussion" of George A. Lundberg, "Quantitative Methods in Social Psychology," *American Sociological Review*, 1, no. 1 (February) : 54–59.

"Social Problems and the Mores," *American Sociological Review*, 1, no. 6 (December) : 922–33.

Review of David Snedden, *An Introductory Sociology for Teachers*, in *American Journal of Sociology*, 42, no. 2 (September) : 282.

1937   "The Rating and Dating Complex," *American Sociological Review*, 2, no. 3 (October) : 727–34.

Review of Thomas Henry Clark, *The Sociological Theories of William Torrey Harris*, in *American Sociological Review*, 2, no. 3 (June) : 447–48.

Review of Frank J. Lowth, *Everyday Problems of the Country Teacher*, in *American Sociological Review*, 2, no. 3 (June) : 453.

Review of Mary L. Ely, ed., *Adult Education in Action;* Dorothy Rowden, ed., *Handbook of Adult Education in the United States, 1936*, in *American Sociological Review*, 2, no. 4 (August) : 571.

Review of S. Howard Patterson, Ernest A. Choate and Edmund deS. Brunner, *The School in American Society*, in *American Sociological Review*, 2, no. 4 (August) : 570–71.

1938   *The Family: A Dynamic Interpretation* (New York: The Cordon Company).

"Contributions to Education of Scientific Knowledge about the Organization of Society and Social Pathology," National Society, for the Study of Education, *37th Year Book*, pt. 2: 445–60.

Review of Howard K. Beale, *Are American Teachers Free?* in *American Sociological Review*, 3, no. 1 (February): 117:18.

Review of Carter V. Good, and others, *The Methodology of Educational Research*; William A. Wattenberg, *On the Educational Front: The Reactions of Teachers Associations in New York and Chicago*, in *American Sociological Review*, 3, no. 2 (April): 832–33.

Review of Le Mon Clark, *Emotional Adjustment in Marriage*; Margaret C. Banning, *The Case for Chastity*, in *American Sociological Review*, 3, no. 4 (August): 604–5.

Review of Lloyd Allen Cook, *Community Backgrounds of Education*; H. B. Alberty and Boyd H. Bode, eds., *Educational Freedom and Democracy*; Samuel Everett, ed., *The Community School*; Dorothy Hewett and Kirtley F. Mather, *Adult Education*; Lyman Judson and Ellen Judson, *Modern Group Discussion*; Edgar E. Robinson, *Independent Study in the Lower Division at Stanford University*; B. Lamar Johnson, *What About Survey Courses?*; Keith Briant, *Oxford Limited*, in *American Sociological Review*, 3, no. 4 (August): 605–6.

1939   Review of Trigant Burrow, *The Biology of Human Conflict; An Anatomy of Behavior, Individual and Society*, in *Journal of Criminal Law, Criminology and Police Science*, 29: 779–80.

1940   Edited *War in the Twentieth Century* (New York: The Dryden Press): Editor's Introduction, pp. vii–xi; "War in the Twentieth Century," pp. 3–35; "War and Social Institutions," pp. 478–532.

War and the Family (New York: The Dryden Press).

"Counseling and the Mores," *Journal of the National Association of Deans of Women*, 3 (January): pp. 51:55.

Review of Clifford R. Shaw, and others, *Brothers in Crime*, in *American Journal of Sociology*, 45, no. 4 (January): 604–5.

Review of Mandel Sherman, *Mental Conflicts and Personality*, in *American Journal of Sociology*, 45, no. 4 (January): 611.

Review of Claude C. Bowman, *The College Professor in America*:

A Study of Those Who Influence and of Those Who Are Influenced in Discussion; Willard S. Elsbree, *The American Teacher;* Goodwin Watson and others, *Redirecting Teacher Education;* Kenneth L. Heaton and Vivian Weedon, *The Failing Student;* Newton Edwards, *Equal Opportunities for Youth;* Norman Foerster, *The Failure of the Liberal College,* in *American Sociological Review,* 5, no. 6 (December) : 994–95.

"War and Women," *Barnard Quarterly,* pp. 18–22.

Review of Clifford Kirkpatrick, *New Germany: Its Women and Family,* in *American Sociological Review,* 5, no. 6 (December) : 974–75.

1941   Waller, Willard, Goldstein, Sidney E., and Frank, Lawrence K., "The Family and National Defense," *Marriage and Family Living,* 3, no. 1 (February) : pp. 1–3.

Review of James H. Barnett, *Divorce and the American Divorce Novel, 1858–1937,* in *American Sociological Review,* 6, no. 1 (February) : 151–52.

1942   Review of Ernest R. Mowrer, *Family Disorganization,* in *American Journal of Sociology,* 47, no. 5 (March) : pp. 791–92.

Review of Charlotte Buhler, *The Child and His Family,* in *American Journal of Sociology,* 47, no. 5 (March) : 790–91.

1942   "Introduction" in Edward C. Jandy, *Charles Horton Cooley, His Life and His Social Theory* (New York: The Dryden Press), pp. 1–6.

1943   "The Family and Other Institutions," *The Annals of the American Academy,* 229 (September) : 107–16.

"Revolt in the Classroom," *Saturday Review of Literature,* 26 (September 18) : 4–6.

Review of Jesse Bernard, *American Family Behavior,* in *American Journal of Sociology,* 48, no. 6 (March) : 779–80.

Review of Quincy Wright, *A Study of War,* in *American Sociological Review,* 8, no. 4 (August) : 479–80.

1944   *The Veteran Comes Back* (New York: The Dryden Press).

"Help for the Returning Veterans," *Science Digest,* 16 (October) : 79–82.

"The Road Back," *This Week,* November 12, p. 2.

1945   "What You Can Do to Help the Returning Veteran," *Ladies Home Journal,* 61 (February) : 26–27.

"The Veteran's Attitudes," *The Annals of the American Academy,* 238 (March) : 174–79.

Komarovsky, Mira and Waller, Willard, "Studies of the Family," *American Journal of Sociology*, 50, no. 6 (May) : 443–51.

"Which Veterans Should Go to College?" *Ladies Home Journal*, 62, (May) : 142–43.

"Why Veterans Are Bitter," *American Mercury*, 61 (August) : 147–54.

"A Sociologist Looks at Conscription," *The Annals of the American Academy*, 241 (September) : 95–101.

Review of Frank J. Sladen, ed., *Psychiatry and the War*, in *American Sociological Review*, 10, no. 2 (April) : 318.

Review of Ruth D. Wilson, *Jim Crow Joins Up*, in *American Journal of Sociology*, 51, no. 2 (September) : 174.

Review of L. L. Bernard, *War and Its Causes*, in *American Sociological Review*, 10, no. 6 (December) : 809.

"The Coming War on Women," *This Week Magazine*, February 18, pp. 4–5.

"What the Disabled Veterans Need," *Pic*, April 10, pp. 9–11.

"Heading for Home and a Job," *Pic*, October, pp. 12–13.

"Job for a General," *This Week*, July 21, pp. 4–5.

1951   *The Family: A Dynamic Interpretation*, Reuben Hill, rev. (New York: Holt, Rinehart and Winston).

1961   *The Sociology of Teaching*, reissue (New York: Russell and Russell).

1965   *The Sociology of Teaching*, Science Ed. (New York: John Wiley and Sons).